Daniel James Hollins

Dark Psychology Secrets

The Essential Guide to Persuasion, Emotional Manipulation, Deception, Mind Control, Human Behavior, NLP and Hypnosis, How To Stop Being Manipulated And Defend Your Mind

How to Analyze People

The Ultimate Guide for Reading the Language of Body and Mind, Learn Techniques for Speed Analyzing Behavior with Human Psychology and Instantly Read People

Empath Healing

A Survival Guide for Highly Sensitive People Can Heal Psychologically and Spiritually. Overcome Negative Mindsets and develop Self-Confidence to Gain Control over Emotions

TABLE OF CONTENTS

DARK PSYCHOLOGY SECRETS

Chapter 1
What s Dark Psychology?

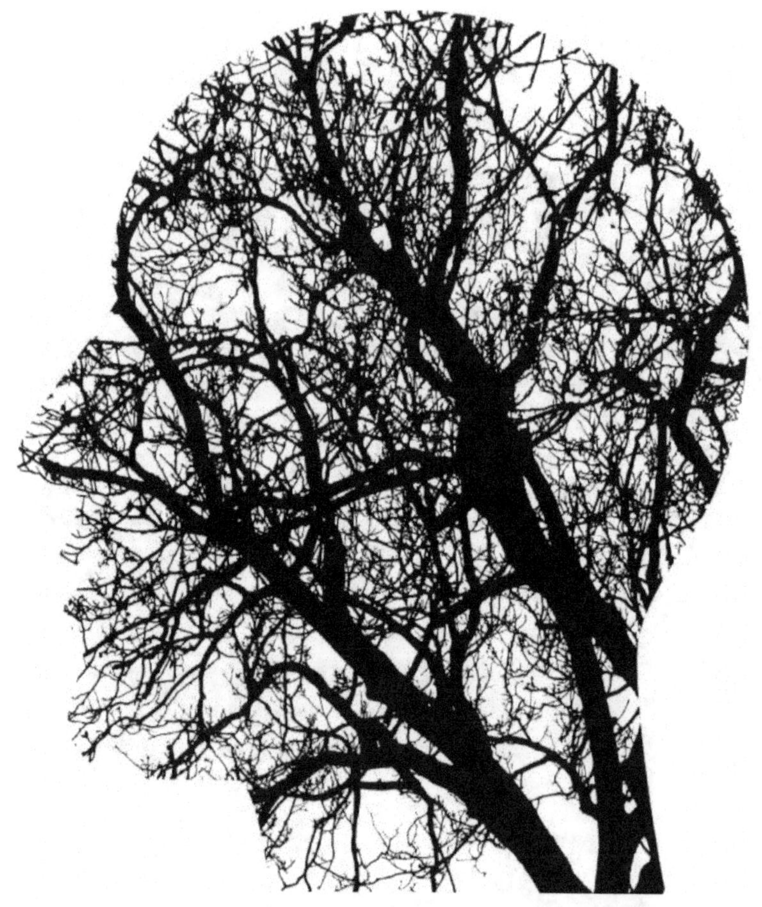

In recent years psychology has tried to uplift the human spirit with lots of popular psychology terms such as, "Positive Psychology" or the numerous books released to tell the masses how to behave to lead a fulfilled successful life from talking about parachutes, ten steps to something, the mired of "how to" titles and much more. Most are nothing but misguided pop psych or a fad of the moment. Can life be as easy as reading the right book and following some basic concepts and everything is going to be OK for you and me?

This paper is different, we shall explore the "Dark" side of the human mind - that part that sees disengagement, destruction, vile acts as part of the everyday human psyche that emerges in us all from time to time - that part that finds excitement, glee and pleasure in the dysfunctional part of our existence. How can society reconcile with its dark side? I use the word insane to refer to those in society who oppose the social norm.

Dark Psychology is both the study of criminal & deviant behavior and a conceptual framework for deciphering the potential for evil within all human beings. Dark Psychology is the study of the human condition as it relates to the psychological nature of people to prey upon other people motivated by criminal and/or deviant drives that lack purpose and general assumptions of instinctual drives and social sciences theory. All of humanity has this potential to victimize other humans and living creatures. While many restrain or sublimate this tendency, some act upon these impulses. Dark Psychology seeks to understand those thoughts, feelings, perceptions and subjective processing systems that lead to predatory behavior that is antithetical to contemporary understandings of human behavior. Dark Psychology assumes that criminal, deviant and abusive behaviors are purposive and have some rational, goal-oriented motivation99% of the time. It is the remaining1%, Dark Psychology parts from Adlerian theory and the Teleological Approach. Dark Psychology postulates there is a region within the human psyche that enables some people to commit atrocious acts without purpose. In this theory, it has been coined the Dark Singularity.

First, let's examine how we can identify the "Dark Side" of psychological thought and behavior. We need a measure, to know, what is normal and what is considered abnormal behavior. Our first measure is social norms; this means in any society of what is considered normal everyday behavior given a set of circumstances that confront our perception. For example in Western culture to strike another person violently is considered a criminal act and one that is repulsive to a peaceful society. However, we condone violence when the person is given societal permissions such as a soldier in the act of war, a policeman in the act of apprehension of a dangerous criminal, a citizen defending his family from a serious threat from another person. These double standards can be misinterpreted in many ways. The soldier who commits war crimes such as genocide, the policeman who uses violence to intimidate a witness while interviewing them or the citizen who violates another person's rights in order to further their own position in some way.

The second measure is a moral one? How do we as a society decide what is right and wrong, who has the power to decide these rights, do laws follow moral conviction or do they become protection of the weak against the strong or the rich against the poor? Most societies agree that killing another human being is against a moral code - it is simply wrong to kill and should be punished by an act of equal severity, by the society that supports the moral-legal stance imposed on the masses by its lawmakers. To most societies, this has been a religious code of conduct such as the 10 commandments of the Christian faith and other such codes from Buddhism to the Muslim Koran. Faith in divine reward and punishment are reflected in the legal language and laws seen as the bedrock of any civilized nation of people. Having accepted these rules why then do people readily deviate from these morals, laws and religious guidelines that allow us all to live in a peaceful society governed by agreed principals of behaviors that protect the individual from danger, hurt and abuse?

The third area of behavior is that not set down in law or religious concepts but those everyday sets of behavior the English would refer to as, "manners" or being "polite". The conduct or way of acting that conforms to behavior accepted as that of a superior member of a society who knows how to conduct themselves in the company of others to a set of standards that are seen as the mark of an advanced civilization. These can sometimes be seen in the etiquette of table manners or a man opening a door for a woman and allowing her to pass first, the recognition of man's duty to protect and defend women. Today in some cultures women's rights have cast doubt of manners towards woman as sexist and therefore demeaning to a woman's independence. Never-the-less manners are seen as the mark of being well-bread and in the upper echelons of a society whether they are traditional Englishness or a Japanese tea ceremony.

Having set out societies differing ways of measuring behavior either through, law, morals or social acceptable norms humans still manage a wide range of dysfunctional behavior that often impacts on and influences others to the point where the perpetrators of this behavior see themselves outside the law, moral codes and etiquette of the rest of society. Sometimes through the feeling of guilt, we all recognize when we have transgressed those rules that we see as essential to a well-ordered civilization. However, there are those other people who feel nothing when faced with dealing out violence, destruction, and death against others as merely their right to live without those rules and the freedom to live a life that is determined by nothing more than what they wish to own, possess or destroy.

The Dark-Side:

What possess the man who kicks the dog, when he is frustrated by society that pens his existence? What feelings does he release at that moment when the dog screeches and howls in pain and fright? Why does he smile and wish further harm to the dog and enjoy the sight of an animal in pain? On-lookers feel outraged by his behavior and sympathy for the defenseless dog for which this man has sought to treat cruelly and without remorse. Who is this man? Why he is all of us from time to time. We all lose our sense of psychological calm and rational thoughts as we grapple with life's unfairness or lack of opportunity. On the other hand - wait - for this man is wealthy, has all his needs fulfilled, yet still feels great delight in kicking and watching the dog suffer at his hands. A sense of power at his ability to inflict pain and the pleasure at feeling superior to other lesser humans whom he sees as incapable of taking what they want and so end up his employees and servants. This superior positional thinking leads to a lack of sympathy or empathy for others as only fools who accept the dominance of his kind as leaders and law-makers.

The above example is too give an insight into a behavior that breaks our three measures of social norms, law (hurting a defenseless animal) moral (the taboo on senseless behavior seen as wrongdoing) socially acceptable behavior, (while everyone might lose their temper and kick their dog, most will feel pangs of guilt and remorse). Here however we meet people who feel no guilt, no remorse and see themselves as exempt from laws they do not agree with. In England, fox-hunting was a cruel sport mostly carried out by intelligent, professional, wealthy men and women? Yet these same people claimed a right to hunt and destroy a defenseless animal for nothing more than a good time as seeing their hounds rip apart and devour a fox. Even though the majority of English people voted on numerous occasions to ban this sport it took several years of campaigning to get this put into law. Now fox-hunting is an illegal activity however these same people continue to flout the law and hunt under local by-laws that have yet to catch up with national lawmaking. These people know what they are doing is illegal, immoral and against social norms as defined by majority opinion. Yet they claim they are superior parts of society and therefore above the day to day moral concerns of the ordinary masses. The surprising thing is in England these people are members of parliament, police, judges and others who control aspects of society in England such as estate owners (land given often by Royal consent in the past by robbing the rightful land of the poor). In other words, the very people who should set an example to society are the same ones flaunting the law and socially acceptable behavior.

In another example, we have to look at the criminal. Criminals are often seen as the rejects of society as they have come from flawed backgrounds, disadvantaged families and poor parental upbringing. Yet in society, the largest harm done to the public is often from corporate crime such as pension fund embezzlement, stocks, and shares insider trading and theft of assets and wealth by CEO's and government officials. This so-called white-collar crime is often undetected and the hardest to bring to justice. Everyday criminals are more visual to the public as their crimes cause localized distress and make the media cry for police action and civil authority action. Therefore most laws are about visual crime that is easy to understand and comprehend. Punishment of visual crime is also straight forward and dealt with every day in our courts and media. How do we distinguish between the two types of criminal - the so-called victimless crime of white-collar criminals who see no direct victim or the murderer who during an armed robbery kills and maims those who oppose his will to steal what he wants from society and the distress they leave behind?

So what does psychology have to say about the deviants who do not see their actions as a problem to themselves and feel others who do not take control of their lives as weak and therefore deserve to be victims of those who are smarter, stronger or more powerful? The media often cries about the passive masses that accept the status quo and in the same paper would condemn the local person who took the law into their own hands perhaps to avenge some wrong-doing against them or their families? The first area that psychology expounds the reasons behind this dark behavior of others is "developmental" that upbringing is at the route of this behavior, that the dog-kicker was not loved or cared for in the correct manner. That during their formative years, they were subject to cruelty, sexual abuse or lack of social education. That the same transgressors were victims of bullying at school and therefore need to act out their own frustration on those in society that are weaker than themselves. The question we have to pose here is why some victims, in fact, most, go onto being law-abiding citizens and it is only the few that turn into the monsters who kill and maim for reasons of developmental mistakes? At this point, many scientists like to point to a genetic factor in behavior. This old chestnut has been around for some time now. There is evidence amongst violent criminals that they often possess an extra Y chromosome (men) that gives them a high amount of testosterone leading to violent outbursts towards frustrating situations in which they use terror and fear as the key to getting what they need. However, as a percentage of violent criminals, this is statistically minute even though in the general prison population this may be higher. All genetic research so far has led to speculation about genetic factors but with no firm evidence to back up the claims. The most often cited evidence is that from twin studies where twins separated at birth have high incidences of similar behavior and outcomes. Again as a percentage of twins born and studied this evidence is weak for genetic determinism and high for developmental environments being similar and twins experiencing environments that are so accord that it is more likely to be a surprise if they did turn out differently from each other. So if we remove developmental outcomes, genetic predispositions then what makes some people flaunt socially acceptable behavior and some who comply to everything society demands of them? This then is the propositional position that makes psychology hard to always see as a positive view or a deterministic way of the world and that in fact maybe it is in fact that normal behavior amongst humans is to be cruel, deceitful, violent and tendency towards criminal behavior under a variety of circumstances. Those morals are a luxury of a settled society where everyone is equal both economically and in caste or class.

The Psychology of the Survivalist:

There are those particularly in the USA that see the end of society as a real possibility whether they advocate nuclear annihilation (today more likely bio-warfare) or the breakdown of capitalism leading to social chaos and civil strife. These people are often referred to as survivalists. They store weapons against the uncontrollable hordes that would roam the country in the event of civil breakdown and food for the possibility of shortages caused by economic meltdown. (Looking at 2009 in the USA many survivalists would argue they, in fact, have a good case). The survivalists believe they have a basic right to defend themselves and their families in the case of societal breakdown and lack of protective laws. On occasions, these groups come into conflict with existing legal statutes that become enforced by federal authorities such as the FBI. Therefore the survivalist's mentality is while on the one hand in conflict with society and in the other seen as a genuine attempt at controlling one's own fate against future disasters. After all insurance companies survive just on that premise alone - and ironically would be the first not to survive an economic breakdown of capitalism as seen by the failure of many banks in 2008/9 around the world. Today the most popular movies at the box office are disaster films, those where flood, sun-flares, bio-warfare, alien invasion, and other catastrophes cause the social breakdown of society. The heroes of these movies are always the resourceful survivalists who through violence protect their kin from all-comers. Why do the public find these people as attractive, as hero's and yet the real survivalists are vilified as public enemies of the status-quo? Judging by the success of these movies ordinary people recognize that the breakdown of society is something that may happen or is in fact inevitable. So they look to these movies as a type of hope for another future that may come about by the demise of their own everyday world.

Psychology as Evolution:

In human history, all people started out as survivalists as hunter-gatherers roaming the land looking for easy accessible animals for food and warmth. As time goes by we see these societies settle into agro-cultural settlements that create rules, laws, leaders and a moral code. As they develop and grow these settled societies create art, music, and religion to compensate for a limited existence within the constrictions of the very society they have formed. From these beginnings land and property become important. The possession of goods and chattels becomes essential to growth. As time goes by these settlements become villages, towns, and cities which eventually form countries with boundaries. Survival becomes now the group and not the individual as was human's natural instincts from the beginning of time. However, eventually, all these societies fade and crumble away. Some for unknown reasons such as the Mayan and other South American civilizations. Most fail as they grow into empires who dominate the weak with a version of their own laws and religions. However, one thing history teaches us all is that societies do disappear for all sorts of reasons. (Greek, Roman, Egyptian in the ancient world and British, French, German and Japanese empires in the modern world). All of these societies had one thing in common they did not envisage their own demise. In today's world, a European and American could not imagine the fall of the EEC or the USA yet these new modern empires have their own Achilles heel, "Capitalism". Although Karl Marx saw the evils of capitalism and its eventual failure he could not have seen how it would grip the modern world to such a point that wars over oil and gas would dominate the 21st century. Marx, however, would probably laugh with glee at the failure in 2009 of the banking system based on greed and debt around the first nations of the planet. Most of the failures can be contributed to mismanagement but in fact, it was a loss of confidence in the financial system by ordinary people that caused a rush on funds and inability to service crippling debt through high-interest rates and little return on investments. When people panic they go into survival mode - they look after themselves first.

At this junction, it is time to conclude from these observations that social norms, laws, and morals are actually "not normal" for human beings and that society often forces group behavior based on what the powerful want over the powerless. That in fact, survivalist mentality is our norm and that what society tries to do in fact is control the wild beast in every human by training them from an early age to obey the laws, rules, and morals of the controlling group, usually the rich, who dominate our governments and institutions. Therefore should we condemn those that feel society is not offering them a fair deal - which in fact they should take what they need in order to survive an often hostile environment where privilege depends on your school, family or wealth? Psychology itself needs to come out of the closet and admit that normal human behavior is to oppose rigid societies and rules? That in fact, people resent society but because they are powerless against those who control law-making and morality they feel certain helplessness in trying to live amongst the sheep. Is it any wonder then occasionally a lone individual takes it into their own hands to change society or their own environment in order to live a more free self-controlled existence away from the rigors of societies that as we have seen all eventually breakdown and reinvent themselves as the new rich and powerful take control once again. In the last century we saw China go from an Empire ruled by depots to a military regime controlled by the rich and powerful, to transform itself into a communist stare of the 1950's where Marxism would determine a fair life for all and eventually to the China of today as a capitalist-socialist state based on a ruling party that determines the lives of the powerless populace, that in fact fought for the rulers to lord over them much as the Emperor of old - nothing changed except the rich and powerful.. Will another revolution occur in China in the future - at the moment it looks unlikely despite the unrest in many parts of China by minorities forced to comply with central rule. All empires cannot see their own demise! How will psychology then deal with this question of human behavior as a basic survivalist mechanism, that in fact humans are naturally violent, cruel and dominating of others who are weaker than themselves? Psychiatry in mental hospitals is often seen as the agents of social control - if you do not agree with society and its rules then you must be insane - therefore you should be committed and controlled for the safety and benefit of all. Psychology, on the other hand, is seen as the liberating aspect of mental health - where we help those out of synch with society of find their place and fit back into what is considered normal behavior for that group. Where will the answer be for those who rebel against the society they live in and want another way of existence without the interference of the powerful and the freedom to live a life they choose as suiting themselves? Or do we wait - for the movies to come true - the disaster that awaits all humans and a return to a dog eat dog existence called survivalism - the real social norm!

How Dark Psychology Is Used Today?

Training programs that teach dark, unethical psychological and persuasion tactics are typically sales or marketing programs. Many of these programs use dark tactics to create a brand or sell a product with the sole purpose of serving themselves or their company, not the customer. Many of these training programs convince people that using such tactics are okay and is for the benefit of the buyer. Because, of course, their lives will be much better when they purchase the product or service. Who uses Dark Psychology and manipulation tactics? Here's a list of people who seem to use these tactics the most.

Narcissists - People who are truly narcissistic (meeting clinical diagnosis) have an inflated sense of self-worth. They need others to validate their belief of being superior. They have dreams of being worshipped and adored. They use dark psychology tactics, manipulation, and unethical persuasion to maintain.

Sociopaths - People who are truly sociopathic (meeting clinical diagnosis), are often charming, intelligent, yet impulsive. Due to a lack of emotionality and ability to feel remorse they use dark tactics to build a superficial relationship and then take advantage of people.

Attorneys - Some attorneys focus so intently on winning their case that they resort to using dark persuasion tactics to get the outcome they want.

Politicians - Some politicians use dark psychological tactics and dark persuasion tactics to convince people they are right and to get votes.

Sales People - Many salespeople become so focused on achieving a sale that they use dark tactics to motivate and persuade someone to buy their product.

Leaders - Some leaders use dark tactics to get compliance, greater effort, or higher performance from their subordinates.

Public Speakers - Some speakers use dark tactics to heighten the emotional state of the audience knowing it leads to selling more products at the back of the room.

Selfish People - This can be anyone who has an agenda of self before others. They will use tactics to meet their own needs first, even at someone else's expense. They don't mind win-lose outcomes.

Yes, I know. I probably stepped on some toes. As a speaker and a person who is involved in selling services, I fall into this category as well. This is why I must remind myself that working, writing, speaking, and selling with character requires that I avoid manipulative and coercive tactics.

To differentiate between those motivation and persuasion tactics that are dark and those that are ethical, it's important to assess your intent. We must ask ourselves if the tactics that we are using have an intention to help the other person. It is okay for the intention to be to help you as well, but if it's solely for your benefit, you can easily fall into dark and unethical practices.

Having a mutually beneficial or a "win-win" outcome should be the goal. However, you must be honest with yourself and your belief that the other person will truly benefit. An example of this is a salesperson who believes everyone will benefit from his product and life will be much better for the customer because of the purchase. A salesperson with this mentality can easily fall into using dark tactics to move the person to buy and use an "ends justifies the means" mentality. This opens the person up to any and all tactics to get the sale.

Chapter 2
The Basics of Covert Emotional Situation and Manipulations

What is Covert Manipulation?

Some forms of covert manipulation, have likely been around for thousands of years. However, new and organized covert manipulation methods like neuro-linguistic programming and pick-up artist techniques, have risen to prominence within the last 15 years or so with the advent of the Internet. It is probable that more average people are now engaging in covert manipulation than ever before.

Covert is an adjective meaning covered, hidden, or disguised. Manipulation is the act of moving something around by hand, or, the act of controlling by artful, unfair, or insidious means, especially to your own advantage. It is important to note that not all covert manipulation techniques are essentially harmful, and not all people who use these tactics are using them with the intent to harm, dominate, or outsmart. However, the term covert manipulation is an accurate descriptor for all of the methods discussed below, regardless of the intent of the user. For better or worse, the aim is to subtly persuade or direct others without revealing a hidden agenda.

Covert emotional manipulation is the process in which one gains control over the other's mind without their knowledge just by making conversations by the listener's subconscious mind. The ultimate aim here is to change the opinion of the person in question by manipulating their thoughts and making them do things your way. In this process, the manipulator changes the thought pattern of the people, their behavior, emotions, and perception of life on a subconscious level. Unlike with conventional hypnotherapy sessions, covert manipulation does not involve closing of the eyes or any kind of moving pendulum or weird hand gestures.

Specific covert manipulation techniques include the use of propaganda, neuro-linguistic programming (NLP), pick-up artist techniques (PUA), obfuscation, subversive symbolism, etc. Covert manipulation tactics are a form of mind control, albeit more subtle than overt forms such as brainwashing.

In practice, covert manipulation tactics can include all of the following: using nonverbal cues to get someone to like or to agree with you, guiding or directing conversations in such a way as to reveal only select information, encoding subliminal commands into speech or gestures, trying to build a (sometimes false) sense of trust or rapport in a target, making assumptions about a target's worth, psychological motivations, wants, needs, or intelligence, not providing all the relevant facts and information, or even concealing the truth.

The commands or suggestions given by the person manipulating to the person being manipulated are more of a metaphor and presented in an indirect fashion, although in certain cases they are also given directly. Stories are one of the tools of covert manipulation which can be effectively used to convey your actual message across and help remember it with much more probability. The initial step in covert manipulation though is to build a rapport with the listener. It is easy to do it with friends and family but also not that difficult to do it with strangers. All you have to do is use some compliment on them or laugh at their jokes to build a comfort level with your unknown listener. It is not necessary that you go too deep into building a connection with your listener.

The next step after building a rapport with the person to be manipulate you have to try and switch off the listener's critical mind. It is nothing but diverting the listener's mind from its normal thinking state to an imaginary thinking state. You can always start by using some scenarios and asking them questions like "What if..." or "Imagine this...". This immediately shuts off their critical mind and lets their imagination dominate their thought process. After successfully taking the listener off his/her critical mindset you may now make your irresistible commands and describe the things you want him/her to do. The effectiveness of this method depends on a lot of things that you put into it. It depends on the way you transform their mind from critical thinking to imagination and the kind of statements you make to convince them well enough to perform the task you give them.

This technique can be well practiced by salesmen, businessmen, therapists and so on. It is essentially used to bring about positive outcomes out of the listener but may at times be misused by some evil-doers who have mastered this art. It is an interesting activity which can be learnt to help others as well. So why not use this powerful technique to enrich your relationships and business affairs and also help others to attain the same power.

I might as well state the conclusion that I have drawn first before we examine some of these specific techniques in more detail below. All covert manipulation tactics are unethical and here is why: we may be tempted to employ covert persuasion techniques when it benefits us, but we don't like the thought that someone is secretly manipulating us without our knowledge. You should treat others how you would like to be treated.

I personally started studying these tactics to ensure that it would be harder for anyone to use them against me. While some seem relatively benign, others seem manipulative at first glance. In fact, while I was studying these techniques, the desire to use persuasion techniques to my own advantage, especially in job interviews or adversarial situations was strong, until I stopped to consider whether it was ethical and honest to do so. Wisdom always asks, "Is it right?" Would I like it if this was done to me? Am I capable of using this knowledge without abuse or strictly for personal gain and profit?

Even if we are comfortable with the idea of someone secretly manipulating us, that still doesn't make it right for them to do so. Covert manipulation tactics, even those which are not inherently harmful to others, are still an attempt to subvert someone's free will without their knowledge, for personal gain or to suit an unstated agenda. Covert manipulation means having power over someone, and with that power comes the potential for use or abuse.

Propaganda

Propaganda is covert manipulation directed at the masses. Some techniques include the use of dialectics (presenting premeditated choices to the public in order to manipulate the preferred outcome), misdirection, social engineering, obfuscation of relevant facts to skew public opinion, and so forth.

Propaganda can also include non-verbal techniques. The use of patriotic music at sporting events and military parades is purposely used to bypass the logical faculty of the mind because music appeals to the right brain and to the emotions. Patriotic music is a useful emotional tool to promote coherence or shared identity within a specific group or nation. Like other covert manipulation tactics, propaganda is generally unethical because it is subversive; an attempt to circumvent the free will of the individual and the group by nefarious or subconscious means.

Neuro-Linguistic Programming

Neuro-Linguistic Programming or NLP is a group of techniques popularized by the New Age and self-help movements for use in conversation, self-improvement, and behavior modification. NLP ostensibly has two purposes. You can use it to train your own mind how to overcome bad habits, become more productive, and so forth. There is no ethical problem with using NLP techniques on yourself if you find them effective.

However, NLP doubles a powerful covert manipulation tool that can be used on others in the guise of persuasion techniques. NLP can include deliberate use of body language, such as mirroring (subtly imitating what the other person is doing, such a crossing your legs when they do) to get someone to like or agree with you, guiding or directing conversations to your benefit, anchoring (using specific words to direct others' thought processes), hiding subconscious suggestions within sentences or gestures, and trying to build trust or rapport with a target in order to unduly influence them.

Understanding NLP is essential in adversarial situations so that you can defend yourself and react effectively if someone uses NLP on you. Some NLP proponents are not content to use traditional debate and rhetorical skills; they must rely on subterfuge in order to make their points. Defenses against subversive NLP include assertively pointing out when someone is interrupting you, not allowing you to answer a question, changing the subject, or trying to deliberately misdirect the conversation. When you call someone out on their underhandedness, they no longer have the advantage.

Pick Up Artist Techniques

Pick up artistry, or PUA is a set of popular covert manipulation techniques which rely on elements of pop psychology, evolutionary psychology, and game theory. The general aim is to evaluate targets based on their physical attributes or sex rank and use covert manipulation to seduce them or secure them as a romantic partner. Pick Up Artist is a means to an ends. The end game is advancing your own agenda, which can be anything from finding a good mate to luring a random person into bed with you as soon as possible.

Pick Up Artist techniques can include overt displays of confidence or self-worth, getting someone to trust you through quickly building rapport, subtly putting someone down (negging) to demonstrate your own superior worth, touching someone in order to quickly escalate an encounter sexually, misdirecting to make a target think your goal is not sex when it is, and so forth. PUA can even include outright lying depending on the motives of the person using it.

A lot of the criticism of PUA comes from feminists who think that PUA is practiced by predatory men who objectify women. While some PUAs are certainly predatory, I would argue that gender issues are irrelevant to the ethical problems inherent with PUA. I realize that the majority of PUAs are men, but some are women. This isn't about so-called feminism or mens' rights. I argue that PUA can be equally unethical when used by both genders. Any belief system which advocates the dominance or superiority of one gender over the other is inherently unethical. Both genders balance and compliment one another. Egalitarianism is the natural result of neither gender trying to aggressively dominate its opposite.

The ethical problems with PUA begin with the failure of egalitarianism. Rather than approaching someone from a position of equality or human dignity, you approach them from a position of dominance and superficial judgment of their relative worth. You think only of what you can gain from them, or how you can use your superior knowledge of psychology to manipulate or influence them without tipping your hand. Even if you are not predatory in your use of PUA, the practice of the same includes hidden power over others, and for less ethical pick up artists, using that power someone at else's expense.

I realize that it can be hard to meet partners and that there are a mass of superficial and social conventions which are supposed to govern the courting processes. That does not change the fact that being straightforward and assertive about your desires is ethical and indicative of a person of character. Using dishonest and covert means to "game" others, or lull them into a false sense of security is not. The fact that PUA works is a sad commentary on the present intellectual and moral state of humanity.

Defending Against Covert Manipulation Tactics

The first defense against covert manipulation tactics is to recognize that they exist in the first place and that they are relatively widespread within society. While I don't advocate a negative or cynical worldview, I do advocate a realistic one. Not everybody is honest, assertive or straightforward, and many people, corporations, and governments have hidden agendas of their own to push.

The second line of defense against covert manipulation is to study all of the methods available in detail, with the aim of understanding and recognizing them if they are ever used on you, or if you see them used by the media. We should learn about everything, even things we don't agree with. Some types of covert manipulation, like propaganda, are more or less one directional. You aren't interacting with the source of the manipulation, but you can still recognize the forms that it takes.

Assertive communication can help defend against NLP or PUA techniques when you feel someone is misdirecting a conversation, trying persuade you, invading your personal space, or steering you into something that you don't want. It's also a good idea to have strong personal boundaries which help to protect you from predators and manipulators.

Chapter 3
Analyzing Dark Psychology

Dark Psychology posits that all humanity has a reservoir of malevolent intent towards others ranging from minimally obtrusive and fleeting thoughts to pure psychopathic deviant behaviors without any cohesive rationality. This is called the Dark Continuum. Mitigating factors acting as accelerants and/or attractants to approaching the Dark Singularity, and where a person's heinous actions falls on the Dark Continuum, is what Dark Psychology calls Dark Factor.

Dark Psychology is a concept this writer has grappled with for fifteen years. It has only been recently that he has finally conceptualized the definition, philosophy, and psychology of this aspect of the human condition. Dark Psychology encompasses all that makes us who we are in relationship to our dark side. All cultures, all faiths, and all humanity have this proverbial cancer. From the moment we are born to the time of death, there is a side lurking within us all that some have called evil and others have defined as criminal, deviant, and pathological. Dark Psychology introduces a third philosophical construct that views these behaviors different from religious dogmas and contemporary social sciences theories.

Dark Psychology assumes there are people who commit these same acts and do so not for power, money, sex, retribution or any other known purpose. They commit these horrid acts without a goal. Simplified, their ends do not justify their means. There are people who violate and injure others for the sake of doing so. Within in all of us is this potential. A potential to harm others without cause, explanation, or purpose is the area this writer explores. Dark Psychology assumes this dark potential is incredibly complex and even more difficult to define.

Dark Psychology assumes we all have the potential for predator behaviors and this potential has access to our thoughts, feelings, and perceptions. As you will read throughout this manuscript, we all have this potential, but only a few of us acts upon them. All of us have had thoughts and feelings at one time or another of wanting to behave in a brutal manner. We all have had thoughts of wanting to hurt others severely without mercy. If you are honest with yourself, you will have to agree we all have had thoughts and feeling of wanting to commit heinous acts.

Given the fact, we consider ourselves a benevolent species; one would like to believe we think these thoughts and feelings would be non-existent. Unfortunately, we all have these thoughts, and luckily, never act upon them. Dark Psychology poses there are people who have these same thoughts, feelings, and perceptions but act upon them in both premeditated and impulsive ways. The obvious difference is they act upon these thoughts while others simply have fleeting thoughts and feelings of doing so.

Dark Psychology posits that this predator style is purposive and has some rational, goal-oriented motivation. Religion, philosophy, psychology, and other dogmas have attempted cogently to define Dark Psychology. It is true most human behavior related to evil actions is purposive and goal oriented, but Dark Psychology assumes there is an area where purposive behavior and goal-oriented motivation seems to become nebulous. There is a continuum of Dark Psychology victimization ranging from thoughts to pure psychopathic deviance without any apparent rationality or purpose. This continuum, Dark Continuum, helps to conceptualize the philosophy of Dark Psychology. Dark Psychology addresses that part of the human psyche or universal human condition that allows for and may even impel predatory behavior. Some characteristics of this behavioral tendency are, in many cases, its lack of obvious rational motivation, its universality and its lack of predictability. Dark Psychology assumes this universal human condition is different or an extension of evolution. Let us look at some very basic tenets of evolution. First, consider we evolved from other animals and we presently are the paragon of all animal life. Our frontal lobe has allowed us to become the apex creature. Now let us assume that being apex creatures does not make us completely removed from our animal instincts and predatory nature.

Assuming this is true if you subscribe to evolution, then you believe that all behavior relates to three primary instincts. Sex, aggression, and the instinctual drive to self-sustain are the three primary human drives. Evolution follows the tenets of survival of the fittest and replication of the species. We and all other life forms behave in a manner to procreate and survive. Aggression occurs for the purposes of marking our territory, protecting our territory and ultimately winning the right to procreate. It sounds rational, but it is no longer part of the human condition in the purest sense.

Dark Psychology assumes this dark side is also unpredictable. Unpredictable in the understanding of who acts upon these dangerous impulses, and even more unpredictable of the lengths some will go with their sense of mercy completely negated. There are people who rape, murder, torture, and violate without cause or purpose. Dark Psychology speaks to these actions of acting as a predator seeking out human prey without clearly defined purposes. As humans, we are incredibly dangerous to ourselves and every other living creature. The reasons are many and Dark Psychology attempts to explore those dangerous elements.

The more readers can visualize Dark Psychology, the better prepared they become to reduce their chances of victimization by human predators. Before proceeding, it is important to have at least a minimal comprehension of Dark Psychology. As you proceed through future manuscripts expanding this construct, this writer will go into detail about the most important concepts. Following are six tenets necessary to fully grasp Dark Psychology and as follows:

1. Dark Psychology is a universal part of the human condition. This construct has exerted influence throughout history. All cultures, societies and the people who reside in them maintain this facet of the human condition. The most benevolent people known have this realm of evil, but never act upon it and have lower rates of violent thoughts and feelings.

2. Dark Psychology is the study of the human condition as it relates to peoples thoughts, feelings, and perceptions related to this innate potential to prey upon others devoid of clear definable reasons. Given that all behavior is purposive, goal-oriented, and conceptualized via modus operandi, Dark Psychology puts forth the notion the near era person draws to the "the black hole" of pristine evil, the less likely he/she has a purpose in motivations. Although this writer

assumes pristine evil is never reached, since it is infinite, Dark Psychology assumes there are some who come close.

3. Because of its potential for misinterpretation as aberrant psychopathy, Dark Psychology may be overlooked in its latent form. History is replete with examples of this latent tendency to reveal itself as active, destructive behaviors. Modern psychiatry and psychology define the psychopath as a predator devoid of remorse for his actions. Dark Psychology posits there is a continuum of severity ranging from thoughts and feelings of violence to severe victimization and violence without a reasonable purpose or motivation.

4. On this continuum, the severity of the Dark Psychology is not deemed less or more heinous by the behavior of victimization but plots out a range of inhumanity. A simple illustration would be comparing Ted Bundy and Jeffrey Dahmer. Both were severe psychopaths and heinous in their actions. The difference is Dahmer committed his atrocious murders for his delusional need for companionship while Ted Bundy murdered, and sadistically inflicted pain out of sheer psychopathic evil. Both would be higher on the Dark Continuum, but one, Jeffrey Dahmer, can be better understood via his psychotic desperate need to be loved.

5. Dark Psychology assumes all people have a potential for violence. This potential is innate in all humans and various internal and external factors increase the probability for this potential to manifest into volatile behaviors. These behaviors are predatory in nature and, at times, can function without reason. Dark Psychology assumes the predator-prey dynamic becomes distorted by humans and losing all motivations, thought to be innate as part of the planet's living organism. Dark Psychology is solely a human phenomenon and shared by no other living creature. Violence and mayhem may exist in other living

organisms, but humanity is the only species that has the potential to do so without purpose.

6. An understanding of the underlying causes and triggers of Dark Psychology would better enable society to recognize, diagnose and possibly reduce the dangers inherent in its influence. Learning the concepts of Dark Psychology serves a twofold beneficial function. Accepting we all have this potential for evil allow those with this knowledge to reduce the probability of its erupting. Secondly, grasping the tenets of Dark Psychology fits our original evolutionary purpose for struggling to survives.

Chapter 4
Manipulation

Renowned critic and always MIT linguist Noam Chomsky, one of the classic voices of intellectual dissent in the last decade, has compiled a list of the ten most common and effective strategies resorted to by the agendas "hidden" to establish a manipulation of the population through the media.

Historically the media have proven highly efficient to mold public opinion. Thanks to the media paraphernalia and propaganda have been created or destroyed social movements, justified wars, tempered financial crisis, spurred on some other ideological currents and even given the phenomenon of media as producers of reality within the collective psyche.

Media manipulation is part of our daily life. Each event is presented by the media in a way that is convenient for each of them. The misconception of the reality created by the media in the audience can lead to wrong assessment and behavior in humans. Media not only have a social role, but they actually are tools for controlling public temperature. Media manipulation consists of the way news is presented and depends on how people will understand a process and how they will react to it. The media have a social role to varying degrees. They can talk about certain issues and keep silent about others. This is exactly what turns them into a new type of power.

In closed and authoritarian countries, media aim at persuading the audience that we should accept unconditionally all political and social actions of the government. So they become part of the state power bodies. While in the open and democratic societies, the media are an intermediary between the authorities and people. They should provide a two-way flow of information from the institutions to society and vice versa. Media competition leads to differentiation of news and information, also called media manipulation

But how to detect the most common strategies for understanding these psychosocial tools which, surely, we participate? Fortunately, Chomsky has been given the task of synthesizing and expose these practices, some more obvious and more sophisticated, but apparently all equally effective and, from a certain point of view, demeaning. Encourage stupidity, promote a sense of guilt, promote distraction, or construct artificial problems and then magically, solve them, are just some of these tactics.

These are strategies for steering whole populations. Sylvain Timsit is named in several places. Elsewhere a search ends with the French-speaking interdisciplinary journal Les Cahiers Psychologie politique and Noam Chomsky is wrongly identified as the author.

Whether the strategies were or were not originally meant satirically is not important to me. That the strategies seem relatively plain, plausible and empirically observable - with a little everyday distance - is more important. Those persons may agree who do not only rely on mainstream media with its fragmented selection of themes and abridged information bombardment.

Whoever does this and sees the world from the perspective of a liberal pluralism according to which there is no power center, no elite and no rule in society but many different groups of actors who exert their influence in a somewhat balanced way so those ideas prevail that correspond to the fundamental interests of the majority will probably reject the list.

Steering Attention

An essential element of social control is the strategy of distraction, which is to divert public attention from problems and important changes decided by the political and economic elites. Through the technique of flooding, constant distractions and trivial information the mind becomes more docile and less critical. The strategy of distraction is also essential in preventing mass interest in science, economics, psychology, neurobiology, and cybernetics.

The keyword here is "insignificance." Attention is a very limited resource. If a democratic society should be organized so relatively few profit while most others have to watch, the majority must be occupied with such things so they do not get in the way of particular interests. Such a state of diversion was attested by Juvenal of the Roman Republic under the term "bread and circuses."

Whoever respects the choice of themes in TV, radio, newspaper and conversations of fellow persons should ask about the relevance of particular themes for one's life or the life of fellow persons by focusing on the conditions of long-term joy in existence and then examine how the relation of employment time or attention expense to relevance for life may reveal a kind of "inversion" of things.

To make certain themes sensational, there are special offers in the supermarket, tables of favorite teams, love affairs of the prominent, name curiosity of the neighbor child, advantages of medium-fat compared to normal margarine and so forth vs. dismantling civil rights, torture and threatened mass murder and secret wars through western "models," anchoring war, racism, and precariousness in normality as well as falsification of causes of war and promotion of crises through war ideologies and so forth.

The Forced Cycle Of Problem, Reaction, And Solution

This method is also called "Problem-reaction-solution." They create a problem, a "situation" to cause some reaction in the audience so that this becomes the norm of the measures you would accept. For example: 'let us intensify urban violence, or organize bloody attacks so that the public becomes more accepting of the laws and policies that are detrimental to their freedom'. Or: create an economic crisis in order for the public to accept as a necessary evil the annulment of social rights and dismantling of public services.

When social problems are concocted to provoke a specific need for orientation in the population, that makes possible a solution in the ideological direction desired from the beginning. A serious crime is committed especially when the living conditions of people deteriorate.

Neoliberal advocates are very gifted as shown in the example of state financing that was increasingly destroyed when public debts skyrocketed and the necessary fear was produced with the backing of the media and business lobbies to carry out false solutions in the form of debt brakes. Ultimately these lead to follow-up problems (financing bottlenecks, economic stagnation, further rise of state debts) which revitalize the old familiar privatization concept as a subsequent solution and strongly expand the sphere of influence for massively concentrated private capital.

This means privatization, deregulation and cutting state expenditures. Resistance against the trimming of the state on the spending side comes from the bureaucracy and subsidy recipients. Therefore the emaciation or thinning must probably start on the tax side with tax cuts to support the dictate of the empty treasury. This allows state deficits to climb as experience demonstrates. This kind of strategy can be seen in the current "Euro-crisis." Through social cuts, economic collapses are forced to drive up mass unemployment. Dismantling the collective bargaining system fuels wage cuts which lead to corollary problems.

In her book "The Shock Doctrine," Naomi Klein showed many examples of this process. Whoever sees the elites' information advantage over their diverted populations, particularly when the mass media acts as a "fourth branch" under resource scarcity and factors of capital-connection and under a unanimous mentality does not need much imagination to recognize how easily crises, catastrophes, and other problems in many areas can be intensified and exploited.

Gradation Of Changes

To make an unacceptable measure acceptable, gradually apply enough pressure, drop by drop, for a few consecutive years. It is in such a way that new, radical socioeconomic conditions were imposed during the 1980's and 1990's: the minimal state, privatization, insecurity, flexibility, mass unemployment, wages that do not ensure decent incomes, many changes that would have given rise to a revolution if they had been applied all at once.

As is obvious for light, pressure, and noise, etc., the perception of political processes of change also depends on their gradation. The economization of all areas of life cannot be introduced in the crisis from today to tomorrow. Rather it must be culturally sedimented across generations by influential institutions if the cost-benefit, market- and management-model should become the all-pervasive social principle. These techniques are also applied on a smaller scale. In the case of planned cuts in the school- and university area, an OECD publication recommends keeping state grants constant and not lowering them on account of the danger of protests of "watchful political" groups.

Postponement Of Changes

Another way to accept an unpopular decision is to present it as "painful and necessary", in order to win over public acceptance at that time. It is easier to accept a future sacrifice than an immediate sacrifice. First of all, because the measure is not used immediately; secondly, because the public, the masses, always have the tendency to expect naively that "everything will improve tomorrow" and that the sacrifice required may be avoided. This gives more time to the public to get used to the idea of change and accept it without resignation when the time comes.

If planned deteriorations of conditions for a large part of the population are on the agenda, the alleged reasons for this should be set out early. As long as the constructed problem is not yet acute, civil society will have little motivation to examine the assertions. When it is acute, the constructed problem is made to appear as a familiar fact. In Germany, demographic change and global competition were put in the limelight so wage, pension- and social cuts appear as "painful" but modern necessities in times of permanent neoliberal breakdown.

Address In Children's Language

Most ads targeted towards the general public use discourse, arguments, characters with especially childish intonation, often targeting frailty, as if the viewer were a creature of very young age or mentally impaired. The more you try to fool the viewer, the more childish the adopted tone. Why? If one goes to a person as if she had the age of 12 years or less, then, due to suggestive quality, the other person tends, with some probability, to respond or react without much thought as a person 12 years old or younger would.

To announce unpleasant subjects, vague messages are used where anything can be interpreted in what is said. No attack surfaces arise for serious criticism. On the other hand, if the population is addressed directly, the collective counterpart is forced in the children's role by a plain language that renounces relevant details in a patronizing or solicitous sympathetic tone. Early on people are accustomed to correspond to certain role models that are activated by environmental incentives. In a strongly conservative society with clear hierarchies and behavior patterns engraved, this technique may have the desired success in the form of unquestioning obedience and trustful acceptance inspiring confidence.

Replace Reflection With Emotions

The puppet-masters don't want to activate people's thoughtful sides. They want to stir up emotions and reach people's unconscious. That's why so many of these messages are full of emotional content. The point is to cause a kind of "short circuit" in rational thinking processes. They use emotions to capture the overall meaning of the message, but not the specifics. This is another way they kill people's critical thinking abilities

"Thinking" as ability is recent in evolutionary history. The basis of the human spirit is an emotional core that leads to powers of judgment at whose gates watchmen of reason simply refuse their service. Inequality and unemployment increase quickly; "competitiveness" and population rivalry become the supreme motivations of humanity and German tank deliveries to dictators for quelling rebellions become the normal case.

Promoting Ignorance

Make sure the public is incapable of understanding the technologies and methods used to control and enslave. The quality of education given to the lower social classes should be as poor and mediocre as possible so that the gap of ignorance between the lower classes and upper classes is and remains impossible to achieve for the lower classes.

Ignorance can include not-knowing and not wanting to know. Both conditions may be coupled closely together. Not-knowing can trigger shame. Different possibilities of avoiding shame could then favor not-wanting to know.

One can completely stay away from milieus and themes of political power to take the shame-filled knowledge of one's not-knowing out of the limelight or one can deny the relevance of knowledge and jump out of the way in formulas like "nothing will change anyway! " "nothing can be done!" and "the world runs that way!" which like curtains are appropriate wherever the calm ambiance would otherwise be disturbed. These are human behavior patterns used to the disadvantage of the majority of the population by the state and capitalist authority. An enormous discrepancy exists between knowledge and knowledge relevance in economic affairs. What is money? What is the function of wages and productivity within a national economy? What do the distribution conditions look like and how did they develop? Who owns what and why? Why is there mass unemployment and how does it affect the pecking order or balance of power within a society?

Strangely enough, those questions are hardly discussed in school and commercial television or only in a non-controversial or fragmentary way - although the ideas bound with them always have the last work in justifying incisive changes of macro-social range. "That costs jobs!" "We cannot afford this social state anymore!" "We need structural reforms!" and "Competitiveness must be increased!" are heard. Comprehensive knowledge would be a democratic necessity here (at least if democracy should not be restricted to a blind motor act at the ballot box). However systematic ignorance of people is promoted by private enterprise lobbyism, through media brainwashing or through increasing work concentration, income competition, and status anxieties - that narrow the focus to the near environment.

Propagating Mediocrity

Most trends and fashions don't just come out of nowhere. There is almost always someone setting them in motion and promoting them. They do it to create homogenized tastes, interests, and opinions. The media constantly promotes certain fashions and trends. Most of them have to do with frivolous, unnecessary, even ridiculous lifestyles. They convince people that acting this way is just what's in style.

Standardized reality consists in working, consuming, taking advantage of mass entertainment possibilities and being honest in small things. People accept the standardized reality and obligingly pass it on to their fellow persons.

Give Resistance A Bad Conscience

Make the individual believe that he/she is the culprit of their own misfortune and make them doubt their intelligence, their abilities, or their efforts. So, instead of rebelling against the economic system, the individual devaluates and blames himself, which generates a depressive state, the purpose of which is to stifle action, and without action, there is no revolution.

In a little book, Stephan Hessel, the renowned fighter of resistance and co-author of the human rights declaration urged: "Be outraged!" He aimed at the discriminating, antisocial and power-concentrated conditions of our time radically threatening civilization and pleaded for an engaged and informed standard of living that uses civil disobedience.

To sabotage the presuppositions of this kind of attitude, persons must be given a bad conscience paralyzing them in maintaining conditions from the perspective of the functional elites. They are told they are inadequate or even that human nature altogether is bad. The person is an egoist, greedy and lazy. The person who does not believe that is a "good person."

This implicit message can be heard in the varied TV entertainment [24], resounds in slogans like "We have lived beyond our means" or in devaluing and punishing life environments created through the social system that was accompanied by a public rabble-rousing against the socially disadvantaged.

The atmosphere produced here demoralizes large parts of the population since it steers the general aversion against those fellow persons who are bound to the social state instead of directing this aversion against the real collective causal agents of the suffering. This atmosphere breaks solidarity in that everyone is called to a bad conscience and urged to retreat in the near environment so they can be reliable and ready to achieve.

Knowing More About Persons Than They Know Themselves

Over the last few decades, science has given us access to such knowledge about human biology and psychology. But this information still isn't available to most people. Only a tiny bit of information ever reaches the public. Meanwhile, the elites have all this information and use it as they please. Once again we can see how ignorance makes it easier for the powers that be to control society. The goal of these strategies of media control is to make the world into whatever the most powerful people want it to be. They block everyone's critical thinking abilities and freedom. But it's our responsibility to stop passively letting them control us. We must put up as much of a fight as we can.

While all kinds of daily barrage and commercial attention magnets fix the population in ignorance and diversion about social conditions, those who have much to lose and extensive resources [do nothing to prevent this according to the motto "knowledge is power.

Think tanks for example function here as institutions that receive millions from powerful capital interests and produce dominant knowledge through studies suited for functional elites and decision-makers.

If one views the world as a causal network where an endless variety of causes and effects are bound together on the most different planes, institutions with huge resources produce a fabulous intervention-knowledge on the social plane through extensive documentation and statistical analyses (big data and data mining), not radical academic theories. This serves their "soft manipulation" available to the whole population for immunization.

Chapter 5
Hypnosis

Self-Hypnosis

In today's ever-changing world, we sometimes need help to get rid of habits and calm our fears. We can turn to the traditional methods: doctors, government agencies and over the counter medication. We can talk to therapists and psychologists. We can even go-it-alone. Sometimes, however, when it seems nothing we do is helping our situation, we need a little help that is outside the box. It is time to consider self-hypnosis. It can work where all other methods have let us down.

Self-hypnosis is a relative of hypnosis. It simply replaces a hypnotherapist or other qualified individual with the client. In other words, the hypnotist is also the client. Self-hypnosis, like hypnosis, is tool of self-discovery and awareness. It is a means through which anyone can access the subconscious mind. You do so deliberately with the intent to alter the current pattern of thought held by the subconscious. In doing so, you begin to lay the groundwork for change.

The purpose of Self-hypnosis varies in accordance with the individual's needs. The basic function of this technique is to help an individual reach deep down into his or her subconscious. In doing so, you can retrain it to reflect and embrace what you wish to accomplish. Some typical purposes of self-hypnosis include:

- To quit smoking

- To help with a diet

- To improve your overall self-image

- To help you overcome any fears

- To stop such things as procrastination

- To aid you in addressing phobias

- To assist you in improving your memory

Stage Hypnosis

Stage hypnosis is not hypnotherapy. Rather, stage hypnosis is the application of hypnosis for entertainment purposes. In such shows, it is the hypnotist's craft to convince the audience that hypnosis is a magical and mysterious power. The greater the magic and mystery, the better the show. It is important to know that what the audience sees is not a pure and magical display of the powers of hypnosis. Like a good magic show, there is more going on than that which you see or are told.

A major factor rarely revealed is the power of the stage subjects complying with commands due, not so much to hypnosis, but of a phenomenon called group or crowd expectation. Psychologists know that it is much easier to predict, influence and determine an individual's behavior when the individual is in a crowd or large group of people. There is a strong power called stage conformity that greatly enhances the stage hypnotist's apparent magical powers. Through stage conformity the stage subject(s) agrees to go along with the hypnotist, not because of the hypnosis, but because they don't want to let down the audience. They follow the directions of the hypnotist to incredible ends; however not because they are in hypnosis and don't have a choice. But because they want to please the audience and avoid personal embarrassment from a crowd caused by not doing what is expected of them. It does not matter if they end up doing embarrassing things, like quacking like a duck; that's not the point. The better and louder they "quack", the more bizarre they are, the more that hypnosis comes off as mind control... then the better a performer they are. The audience will like, approve, and embrace them more if they "go with show" instead of resisting the directions of the entertainer. Stage conformity can indeed be stronger than the effect of hypnosis. Having been a stage subject on two different occasions I can attest to what that experience is like.

Does hypnosis play a part in the stage show? Yes, but mostly only to a degree. In stage shows, hypnosis is serving to help focus the mind. Using hypnosis to focus and clear the mind places the multitude of conscious, oftentimes random, thoughts aside for the time. Again, a clear and focused mind is a very powerful thing. This, combined with stage conformity, makes the hypnotist's job not very difficult indeed. You will notice they are able to concentrate a lot of their own energy simply on entertaining and livening up the show. The more they can convince the audience hypnosis is mind control, the more interesting the show. And that is what gets presented; it is not what is going on.

Hypnosis is a very pleasant, relaxing and mentally refreshing experience. It's like taking a refreshing mental rest. As a stage subject, it is easy to want to go along with the show because you sense that not doing so will end the pleasant experience of hypnosis you are in. Your mind relaxes, it is not analyzing, grabbing or holding onto random thoughts. This does not mean the subject is unconscious, in a coma, or has had their mind taken over. You are aware of what's going on and aware of the sounds around you; perhaps more so than in normal waking consciousness. You know that if you really wanted to you could immediately wake yourself up. But for what purpose? If the hypnotist is respectful of your limits it is just as well to go with the experience.

When subjects are asked to do or say something that goes against their moral, ethical, or religious beliefs they either wake themselves up or simply do not comply with the hypnotist's command. A subject doesn't do anything while in hypnosis that they wouldn't normally do when they are awake; in the same context and setting. This came into question once with one stage subject that started taking off her clothes during the show, while the other subjects went only so far as that which is socially acceptable- pretending to "strip" but stopping well short of crossing the social standard. The hypnotist himself was quite surprised and realized he had to stop the woman, which he did. It wasn't until after the show that he found out that her occupation was that of a stripper.

Most hypnotherapists do not condone or endorse stage hypnosis. There is a real split between stage hypnotists and hypnotherapists. The reason is understandable for a stage hypnosis show works by portraying hypnosis as an unconscious sleep state which lends itself to mind control. This is a misrepresentation of hypnosis. It works to reinforce the false, socially held belief that hypnosis is weird, strange, and bizarre- which it isn't. You don't fall asleep, you aren't in a coma, your mind is not being controlled. Hypnotherapists choose to use hypnosis as a tool to help others live a happier, healthier, and more rewarding life. In comparison, stage hypnotists use hypnosis as the central prop in their entertainment shows. It is clear why a split exists.

Despite the obvious differences between the stage hypnotist and hypnotherapist, the stage hypnotist does, inadvertently, serve a percentage of humankind through their application of hypnosis. The stage show, along with television depictions, fuels the collective belief that hypnosis is a powerful and miraculous thing that taps the power of the mind. It doesn't take much to put the pieces together. "I have tried everything else, why not try hypnosis as a last resort? It's strange, I don't know how it works (fear of the unknown), but I don't care... it just might work". That is the line of thinking that prompts many telephone calls to the hypnotherapist listings in the yellow pages.

In a perfect world, people would be taught in school what hypnosis is and how it works. The value and benefits of hypnosis would be understood and there would be a more prominent place for it in society. However, that is not the world today. Hypnotherapists have their work cut out for them when it comes to educating the public about hypnosis. Mass education should be a long-term goal of the profession. Ironically, this hypnotherapist sees a lack of public education being enacted by hypnotherapists. Many brochures written by hypnotherapists themselves tend to lack educational value about hypnosis. I suspect that a number of hypnotherapists prefer to keep hypnosis "magical" and "mysterious" because this quality, unquestionably, can boost clientele. To flat out condemn stage hypnosis is quite premature at this point in time.

Stage hypnotists are in a unique position to literally reach thousands of people who attend their shows. Stage hypnotists are encouraged to realize the high degree of influence they have which can be used to inform and educate people on the benefits of hypnosis and hypnotherapy. Perhaps at the end of the show, they can remind the audience what has been demonstrated, "We've had a great time here tonight. I want each of you to know that what you have seen is just a glimpse at what a focused mind can do. Aside from entertainment, hypnosis is just as powerful at helping to improve peoples' lives. A hypnotherapist can use hypnosis to focus your mind on living a happier, healthier, and more rewarding life."

How does Self Hypnosis Differ from Stage Hypnosis?

Hypnosis and self-hypnosis are respected forms of therapy. These forms of hypnotherapy are used to achieve a specific purpose - one in which only the person desiring change or seeking a solution and the therapist take part. The goals the therapist and client set are individualistic and meant to address a real need. The sessions and subjects are personal, private and performed in a safe and secure environment. If you use self-hypnosis, only you need to know why you are there.

In the case of stage hypnosis, the major difference is the stage. This is a public performance. People have paid the hypnotist/magician to see what he or she can "make" someone do. The "client" or stage prop is not there to achieve any personal goal except, perhaps for their few minutes of fame. The stage hypnotist can be manipulative and even exploitative to obtain his or her goals. Moreover, the whole strategy requires more than a little of illusion and even self-delusion.

Types of Hypnosis

There are four main types of hypnosis that are used in today's society to hypnotize another person or to hypnotize one's self. The four main types of hypnosis are traditional hypnosis, Ericksonian hypnosis, NLP hypnosis, and self-hypnosis. Each type of hypnosis varies in terms of use and practice. The main common denominator between the four types of hypnosis is that they all begin with some sort of hypnotic induction, such as fixed eye induction or counting backwards, to induce a hypnotic state.

Traditional Hypnosis. Traditional hypnosis is the most basic form of hypnosis and is most widely used because of the belief that anyone can do it with very little instruction and training. Traditional hypnosis is also believed to be the easiest form of hypnosis because it relies on simple suggestions and commands. This is the form of hypnosis that is widely advertised with hypnosis CDs and MP3s, along with hypnosis tapes. Once in a hypnotic state, traditional hypnosis methods connect with the subconscious and use direct suggestions and commands to influence a person's behaviors, thoughts, feelings, and actions. Examples of these commands could be a suggestion about self-confidence, or about quitting a bad habit like alcoholism or smoking. Because traditional hypnosis relies on suggestions and commands, it is often not seen as entirely effective for people that have critical and analytic thought processes. The conscious mind has a tendency to interfere with the processing of the suggestions and commands, critiquing the messages and not allowing it to be fully absorbed by the subconscious. Traditional hypnosis is also the basis for stage hypnotism, which is popular in today's culture among partygoers and comedy club attendees.

Ericksonian Hypnosis. Ericksonian hypnosis is based off of the principles developed by Dr. Milton Erickson. This form of hypnosis is particularly excellent for those that are skeptical of hypnosis because it uses metaphors instead of just direct suggestions. Metaphors allow the brain to think creatively and arrive at conclusions that may not be reached by employing the more unilateral form of traditional hypnosis. Metaphors work by comparing and contrasting two things in a more complex way than simple commands and suggestions. They also allow the mind to wrap around an idea or a thought in a more organic way than a direct suggestion, which is why skeptics often are able to be hypnotized using this method and not the traditional method. Ericksonian hypnosis uses isomorphic and interspersal metaphors. Isomorphic metaphors tell a story that has a moral, which makes the unconscious mind draw a one-to-one comparison between the moral of the story and a problem or issue that it is already familiar with. Interspersal metaphors use embedded commands that distract the conscious mind, allowing the unconscious mind to process the message of the metaphor.

Ericksonian hypnotherapy uses more of what it is called indirect suggestions. Indirect suggestions are much harder to resist because they are often not even recognized as suggestions by the conscious mind since they usually disguise themselves as stories or metaphors. An example of an indirect suggestion is " and perhaps your eyes will grow tried as you listen to this story, and you will want to close them because people can, you know, experience a pleasant, deepening sense of comfort as they allow their eyes to close, and they relax deeply."

Think about the following scenario: A child of five years of age is carefully carrying a full glass of milk to the dinner table. The parent of the child warns in a stern voice, "don't drop that!" The child looks up at the parent, stumbles, drops the glass, and spills milk everywhere. The now angry parent shouts, "I told you not to drop that! You're so clumsy. You'll never learn!"

As unintentional as it may be, this is an example of hypnosis. The powerful authoritative voice (the parent), having created through indirect suggestion ("don't drop that!), an altered state (trance), has issued a direct post-hypnotic suggestion ("You're so clumsy. You'll never learn"). "Post-hypnotic" because, if the child accepts the suggestion (and children often do), he or she will always see themselves as clumsy. This post-hypnotic suggestion by the parent may well adhere to the directive in the future, sabotaging the child's success.

NLP Hypnosis. NLP hypnosis combines neuro-linguistic programming (NLP) with hypnosis, to achieve remarkable results. NLP is a form of psychotherapy the connects neurological processes to behavioral patterns - in essence, it connects what we do to how we feel. Hypnosis is a way by which the subconscious is communicated with directly, often bypassing the conscious mind; this means that the hypnotized person becomes highly suggestible and open to instructions and thought modification.

NLP hypnosis is used along with self-hypnosis to deal with issues such as self-confidence, self-esteem, and overall mental well-being. NLP hypnosis is also used to quell anxieties and conquer fears and phobias. This method of hypnosis is effective because it uses the same thought process as a fear or problem to reverse or get rid of the problem.

Perhaps the most common NLP technique is anchoring, and probably everyone has experienced it at some point. Is there a song which when you hear it, it triggers feelings from the past? If yes, then that song has become an anchor to those feelings. With NLP hypnosis, you can anchor whatever you want to whatever feelings or mental states that you desire. For example, you can anchor touching your ear with feelings of self-confidence. Whenever you are feeling anxious about something or experiencing stage fright, you can simply touch your ear and access those feelings of self-confidence and control. When choosing an anchor (e.g. touching the top part of your right ear), it is important to choose one that is specific, intermittent (otherwise desensitization would occur), and that it is anchored to a prompt and unique reaction (otherwise association would not occur).

A more advanced NLP hypnosis technique is the flash. It is used to dismantle a conditioned response, in other words, to remove an association between two behaviors. For example, many people tend to have a cigarette when they are feeling hungry. With time, their minds will associate being hungry with having a cigarette, and they will start craving for a cigarette whenever they are hungry. The flash can be used to remove this association.

Another NLP hypnosis technique is called the reframe, and it is used to change the behavior of a person. The outcome (what the person's goal is) is identified, and then the subconscious is accessed and made to substitute one set behavior with another, which is acceptable to the conscious but will be more beneficial towards achieving the goal than the previous behavior.

The appeal of NLP hypnosis is that you do not need to master the whole art to benefit from it. Even if you just understand one concept or technique of NLP hypnosis, you can use it in isolation to improve your life. The anchoring is the easiest technique to learn, and we suggest that you try that first. NLP hypnosis is thought to be one of the most effective forms of hypnosis when the techniques are used either separately or all together.

Self-Hypnosis. Self-hypnosis as already discussed is performed by oneself to achieve a deep state of relaxation by utilizing any one of the aforementioned types of hypnosis. Self-hypnosis allows the mind to relax and reach a hypnotic state without a hypnotist or hypnotherapist. Suggestions and commands are then made by yourself, or by a CD or MP3 that is guiding you in the hypnosis session. Many people now prefer self-hypnosis instead of guided hypnosis because they do not trust others with their fragile and influential subconscious mind.

Subliminal Message

When you're trying to make a change but don't seem to get results, there are limiting beliefs that are blocking you, and you must eliminate them and instill new ones. This process can happen only through the subconscious mind. Subliminal messages are the most powerful, easy, effective and friendly technique that deals directly with the root - the subconscious mind.

Subliminal messages have been researched extensively and time after time and are proven to be the best method to create profound changes. This method can be performed by anybody, and its effectiveness, results, and ease of use make it extremely popular and the most studied. From a little- known technique that was used by the elite, subliminal messages have become widespread among millions.

Play subliminal messages during sleep

Subliminal messages during sleep can help you create great changes and stick with them for the long term. With minimal effort, you can turn your 6-8 hours of sleep time into a personal development seminar. By exposing your brain to subliminal messages, you can easily invest 1/3 of your day in improving the issues you're dealing with and program your subconscious mind to get rid of negative thought patterns.

Subliminal messages will push you further than ever before! You can use this way of subliminal messages like the most successful people do. You will increasingly build your confidence while reading the daily news online; you can develop spectacular social skills and learn to make new friendships easily while checking out recipes of your favorite pie. You can program yourself to feel happy when checking your email box; you can create positive money paradigms while liking posts on Facebook.

With only a few moments of listening, you'll start to feel the stress leaving your mind and body. You'll find yourself immersed in a deep feeling of pure relaxation and being free of worry. Besides all the wonderful goals you can achieve by using subliminal messages, you can also improve your sleep and wake up energetic, fresh, and lively with a positive spirit. You can find life-changing subliminal messages here at Vortex Success audio library.

Watch subliminal flashes on your computer screen

As you know, subliminal messages can be transmitted by audio, but also visually. The visual subliminal messages will appear as quick flashes on your computer screen. By using this method of subliminal messages, you can invest only a few minutes a day. The subliminal messages carry positive affirmations and being exposed to them over and over will create a new neural network in your brain. The meaning of all of this is that you can be the person you want to be.

The subliminal affirmations can become your reality and you can finally let yourself become the powerful individual you've always wished to be. With those subliminal messages in forms of flashes, you can easily manifest the affirmations and make them come true. It's very simple to set the subliminal messages on your PC; watch this video, scroll down and click on the 'live demo' button, to see how it's done.

Play MP3 subliminal messages during daytime

Although it's recommended to listen to subliminal messages before or during sleep, when the mind is in a receptive state, there are other efficient ways to use subliminals during the day.

Can the subconscious mind absorb the subliminal messages and be programmed while we are awake? Absolutely! During waking time, the brain functions with beta waves, but new information can still reach the subconscious mind. New information gets to the subconscious all the time. The only difference is that we can communicate with the subconscious mind easily during alpha and theta waves production. During the day, we don't have to communicate deliberately with the subconscious; we can simply let it absorb the subliminal messages automatically.

In addition to subliminal flashes, another highly effective way to use subliminal messages during the day is to play MP3 subliminal meditations in the background. You can cook, clean the house, take a relaxing bath or watch your favorite TV show.

Chapter 6
Persuasion

What is Persuasion?

When you think about persuasion, what comes to mind? Some people might think of advertising messages that urge viewers to buy a particular product while others might think of a political candidate trying to sway voters to choose his or her name on the ballot box. Persuasion is a powerful force in daily life and has a major influence on society and a whole. Politics, legal decisions, mass media, news, and advertising are all influenced by the power of persuasion and influence us in turn.

Sometimes we like to believe that we are immune to persuasion. That we have a natural ability to see through the sales pitch, comprehend the truth in a situation and come to conclusions all on our own. This might be true in some scenarios, but persuasion isn't just a pushy salesman trying to sell you a car, or a television commercial enticing you to buy the latest and greatest product. Persuasion can be subtle, and how we respond to such influences can depend on a variety of factors.

When we think of persuasion, negative examples are often the first to come to mind, but persuasion can also be used as a positive force. Public service campaigns that urge people to recycle or quit smoking are great examples of persuasion used to improve people's lives.

So what exactly is persuasion? According to Perloff (2003), persuasion can be defined as "...a symbolic process in which communicators try to convince other people to change their attitudes or behaviors regarding an issue through the transmission of a message in an atmosphere of free choice."

The key elements of this definition of persuasion are that:

- Persuasion is symbolic, utilizing words, images, sounds, etc

- It involves a deliberate attempt to influence others.

- Self-persuasion is key. People are not coerced; they are instead free to choose.

Methods of transmitting persuasive messages can occur in a variety of ways, including verbally and nonverbally via television, radio, Internet or face-to-face communication.

How Does Persuasion Differ Today?

While the art and science of persuasion have been of interest since the time of the Ancient Greeks, there are significant differences between how persuasion occurs today and how it has occurred in the past. In his book The Dynamics of Persuasion: Communication and Attitudes in the 21st Century, Richard M. Perloff outlines the five major ways in which modern persuasion differs from the past:

The number of persuasive messages has grown tremendously. Think for a moment about how many advertisements you encounter on a daily basis. According to various sources, the number of advertisements the average U.S. adult is exposed to each day ranges from around 300 to over 3,000.

Persuasive communication travels far more rapidly. Television, Radio and the Internet all help spread persuasive messages very quickly.

Persuasion is big business. In addition to the companies that are in business purely for persuasive purposes (such as advertising agencies, marketing firms, public relations companies) and many other businesses are reliant on persuasion to sell goods and services.

Contemporary persuasion is much more subtle. Of course, there are plenty of ads that use very obvious persuasive strategies, but many messages are far more subtle. For example, businesses sometimes carefully craft very specific image designed to urge viewers to buy products or services in order to attain that projected lifestyle.

Persuasion is more complex. Consumers are more diverse and have more choices, so marketers have to be savvier when it comes to selecting their persuasive medium and message.

Modern Persuasion

Pratkanis & Aronson (1991) argue convincingly that Western societies prefer persuasion even more than other societies do. Marriages aren't arranged, they are left up to the persuasive tactics of each couple. Unlike communistic countries that control trade, the creation of consumer tastes and choices is left to the advertiser. Arguments aren't settled by clan leaders or religious authorities, but by the wrangling of attorneys. Rulers are not royally born, or chosen because of their ability, but arise through one of the largest persuasion rituals of all, the election campaign. The candidate that has both good looks and a persuasive demeanor almost always wins.

The ancient Greeks had a more grounded approach to persuasion. A Greek citizen could hire a Sophist to help him learn to argue. Sophists were itinerant lecturers and writers devoted to knowledge--you might say they were the graduate students of the ancient world. The sophists argued that persuasion was a useful tool to discover truth. They thought the process of arguing and debating would expose bad ideas and allow the good ones to be revealed. A sophist didn't particularly care which side of an issue he was arguing. In fact, Sophists would sometimes switch sides in the middle of a debate. Their stated goal was reasoned argument that exposed the truth. They believed in the free market of good ideas.

Does that sound like our world? No - we rely on the use of persuasive and compliance tactics much more than did the ancients. But does the modern approach to persuasion take the form of reasoned argument and debate? Hardly. Today's persuaders appeal to the masses "through the manipulation of symbols and of our most basic human emotions" to achieve their goals.

Since the ability to persuade and to resist persuasion is directly related to one's success in life, you'd think the topic would be taught in school. You'd think people would know their persuasion tactics as well as they know the letters of the alphabet, or the ten commandments, or how to perform CPR.

But how many of us can recite ten principles of persuasion? How many of us can evaluate a situation and choose the right persuasive tool for the job at hand? How many of us are even aware of the thousands of times each day we are influenced by someone else?

Do this: take a look in your medicine cabinet, or your pantry, or your garage. Each item you see is a war trophy, representing some company's victory over their competitors. For some reason-- or maybe for no reason at all-- they convinced you to trade your hard-earned money for their product. How did they do that, exactly?

Make no mistake. There are legions of influence agents operating in our society. They thrive - they exist at the pinnacles of power - by getting you to think things and to do things they want you to think and do.

Most people are either unaware of these influences, or when they are, vastly overestimate the amount of freedom they have to make up their own minds. But the successful influence agent knows that if he can manage the situation and choose the correct technique, your response to his technique will be as reliable as the springing of a mousetrap.

Methods of Persuasion

The ultimate goal of persuasion is to convince the target to internalize the persuasive argument and adopt this new attitude as a part of their core belief system. The following are just a few of the highly effective persuasion methods. Other methods include the use of rewards, punishments, positive or negative expertise, and many others.

Create a Need

One method of persuasion involves creating a need or an appealing a previously existing need. This type of persuasion appeals to a person's fundamental needs for shelter, love, self-esteem, and self-actualization. Marketers often use this strategy to sell their products. Consider, for example, how many advertisements suggest that people need to purchase a particular product in order to be happy, safe, loved, or admired.

Appeal to Social Needs

Another very effective persuasive method appeals to the need to be popular, prestigious or similar to others. Television commercials provide many examples of this type of persuasion, where viewers are encouraged to purchase items so they can be like everyone else or be like a well-known or well-respected person. Television advertisements are a huge source of exposure to persuasion considering that some estimates claim that the average American watches between 1,500 to 2,000 hours of television every year.

Use Loaded Words and Images

Persuasion also often makes use of loaded words and images. Advertisers are well aware of the power of positive words, which is why so many advertisers utilize phrases such as "New and Improved" or "All Natural."

Get Your Foot in the Door

Another approach that is often effective in getting people to comply with a request is known as the "foot-in-the-door" technique. This persuasion strategy involves getting a person to agree to a small request, like asking them to purchase a small item, followed by making a much larger request. By getting the person to agree to the small initial favor, the requester already has their "foot in the door," making the individual more likely to comply with the larger request. For example, a neighbor asks you to babysit her two children for an hour or two. Once you agree to the smaller request, she then asks if you can just babysit the kids for the rest of the day.

Since you have already agreed to the smaller request, you might feel a sense of obligation to also agree to the larger request. This is a great example of what psychologists refer to as the rule of commitment, and marketers often use this strategy to encourage consumers to buy products and services.

Go Big and Then Small

This approach is the opposite of the foot-in-the-door approach. A salesperson will begin by making a large, often unrealistic request. The individual responds by refusing, figuratively slamming the door on the sale. The salesperson responds by making a much smaller request, which often comes off as conciliatory. People often feel obligated to respond to these offers. Since they refused that initial request, people often feel compelled to help the salesperson by accepting the smaller request.

Utilize the Power of Reciprocity

When people do you a favor, you probably feel an almost overwhelming obligation to return the favor in kind. This is known as the norm of reciprocity, a social obligation to do something for someone else because they first did something for you. Marketers might utilize this tendency by making it seem like they are doing you a kindness, such as including "extras" or discounts, which then compels people to accept the offer and make a purchase.

Create an Anchor Point for Your Negotiations

The anchoring bias is a subtle cognitive bias that can have a powerful influence on negotiations and decisions. When trying to arrive at a decision, the first offer has the tendency to become an anchoring point for all future negotiations. So if you are trying to negotiate a pay increase, being the first person to suggest a number, especially if that number is a bit high, can help influence the future negotiations in your favor. That first number will become the starting point. While you might not get that amount, starting high might lead to a higher offer from your employer.

Limit Your Availability

Psychologist Robert Cialdini is famous for the six principles of influence that he first outlined in his best-selling 1984 book Influence: The Psychology of Persuasion. One of the key principles he identified is known as scarcity or limiting the availability of something. Cialdini suggests that things become more attractive when they are scarce or limited. People are more likely to buy something if they learn that it is the last one or that the sale will be ending soon. An artist, for example, might only make a limited run of a particular print. Since there are only a few prints available for sale, people might be more likely to make a purchase before they are gone.

Spend Time Noticing Persuasive Messages

The examples above are just a few of the many persuasion techniques described by social psychologists. Look for examples of persuasion in your daily experience. An interesting experiment is to view a half-hour of a random television program and note every instance of persuasive advertising. You might be surprised by the sheer amount of persuasive techniques used in such a brief period of time.

Chapter 7
Deception

What in Deception?

Deception refers to the act - big or small, cruel or kind - of causing someone to believe something that is untrue. Even the most honest people practice deception, with various studies showing that the average person lies several times a day. Some of those lies are big ("I've never cheated on you!") but more often, they are little white lies ("That dress looks fine,") that are deployed to avoid uncomfortable situations or spare someone's feelings.

Deception isn't always an outward-facing act. There are also the lies people tell themselves, for reasons ranging from healthy maintenance of self-esteem to serious delusions beyond their control. While lying to oneself is generally perceived as harmful, some experts argue that there are certain kinds of self-deception - like believing one can accomplish a difficult goal even if evidence exists to the contrary - that can have a positive effect on overall wellbeing.

Researchers have long searched for ways to definitively detect when someone is lying. One of the most well-known, the polygraph test, has long been controversial, and evidence suggests that those with certain psychiatric disorders like Antisocial Personality Disorder cannot be accurately measured by polygraphs or other commonly-used lie detection methods.

Do lies have a functional purpose in life? Despite what your parents told you, psychologists think that, in some situations, telling the whole truth may actually set you back. Not only that, but research shows that lying is more common than you might expect. A study led by Dr. Bella DePaulo found that people lie an average of twice per day. Over the course of a week, the average person tells a lie to roughly one out of every three people they talk to one-on-one. Like it or not, we've created a world where telling the truth does not always get you ahead. Lies can actually make it easier to get along with the people around you, evidenced by study results showing that people regularly lie for others' benefits.

DePaulo found that it's quite common for people to lie for no other reason than to make others feel comfortable. Women do this far more often than men, who were found to lie more in order to improve their own reputations. In fact, a conversation between two men typically involves eight times as many lies about themselves than about anything else.

Even people who are told little white lies benefit from the lies. A study published in the April 2012 edition of the Journal of Consumer Research demonstrated that people who were lied to were later treated with more kindness and generosity. It's not that we don't know we're lying; we know, and many times we feel badly enough to let it influence our future behavior.

The ease with which we can mislead one another and the prevalence of lying make dishonesty an element of our society that is not to be ignored and is not going away anytime soon. Do most people tell lies to succeed, however? Personal gain doesn't seem to be the motivation behind most lies, and repeated lies can certainly come back to haunt you in your professional and personal life. Instead, evidence overwhelmingly suggests that we lie more for others and for the sake of everyone getting along--instead of getting ahead.

No one likes being deceived, and when public figures are caught in a lie, it can become a major scandal. But while many people pride themselves on their scrupulous honesty and try to distance themselves from individuals who are more comfortable with falsehoods - the truth is that everyone lies, for a variety of reasons. In fact, some experts suggest that a certain amount of deception may be necessary for maintaining a healthy, functioning society. The formal study of deception was once the domain of ethicists and theologians, but more recently, psychologists have turned their attention to why people lie, and the conditions that make them more likely to do so.

Case Studies

Are meat eaters more selfish than vegetarians? Do chaotic situations promote stereotyping? Do we feel smarter when those close to us win awards? These and other intriguing questions have been recently addressed by the research of prominent Dutch psychologist Diederik Stapel. Just 15 years after receiving his Ph.D. with honors in 1997, Stapel had published over 130 scientific papers, received a career trajectory award from the Society of Experimental Social Psychology, and risen to become dean of the faculty at his university. In 2011, however, it began to dawn on his students that there was just one problem with his research: he was making up the data.

An investigation by his university has so far revealed that Stapel fabricated the data for no fewer than 55 of his papers. This has led many prominent scientific journals, including Science, to issue retractions. Stapel has since publically apologized to his colleagues and students. He also published a memoir, Derailed, in which he recounted his personal descent into scientific misconduct. Fellow psychologists have characterized it as "priceless and revealing," especially its "unexpectedly beautiful" final chapter, though they also note that it is rife with plagiarized lines from the writings of Raymond Carver and James Joyce.

How did such an internationally recognized psychologist, a man whose work was featured in The New York Times and Time, become entangled in such a web of deception? Most of us would like to suppose that the appearance of deception in a scientific field such as psychology is a fluke, the work of a rogue researcher on the fringes of the discipline. Yet the real roots of the problem are deep and widely spread. The problem goes to the core of contemporary psychology: Deception has been accepted by many psychological researchers as a necessary evil in the pursuit of truth.

Consider the following account.

Beth is a sophomore psychology major at a large urban research university. As a requirement for her introductory psychology course, she volunteered as a subject for a study examining the difference between communication that takes place online and in person. A pair of graduate students dressed in white lab coats led her to a small cubicle, where she read a short article about the history of medicine and discussed it in a chat room with someone she was told was another student. She was surprised when her chat partner expressed disbelief about the accomplishments of an African American researcher, but she brushed off the remark and finished her assignment. Afterwards, a third graduate student took her into a different room and informed her that this was, in fact, a study on contemporary racism. Beth then remembered the other graduate students casually making derogatory remarks about another student, who was also African American. The debriefing graduate student gave her some paperwork to read about the study's procedures and aims and sent her on her way. Reflecting on her experience,

Beth felt regret and disappointment. Why had she been deceived?

There is something deeply problematic about employing deception in the search for truth. Yet deception has played a prominent - and many would say integral -- role is psychological research for well over a century. A participant who enrolls in a research study is often misled about its real purpose, the responses researchers are actually monitoring, and the true identity of fellow "subjects." In some cases, participants are not even informed that they are involved in a research study. How did the tradition of deception develop in psychological research, where does it stand today, and what are the problems with its ongoing use?

Numerous rationales may be offered for deception. One is that deception is all around us, permeating fields such as advertising and politics. Proponents suggest there is no reason to hold psychological researchers to a higher standard. Another is the argument that subjects are not really harmed. Feelings may be hurt, but no one is being asked to donate blood or sacrifice a limb under false pretenses. The most frequent argument is that much research would be impossible without deception. Just as physicians check respiratory rates without calling attention to a patient's breathing, psychologists need to observe behavior when subjects are unaware. Deception is rationalized as the only way to reproduce natural behavior in the laboratory setting.

Over the first two-thirds of the 20th century, deception became a staple of psychological research. According to a recent history of deception in social psychology, before 1950 only about 10 percent of articles in social psychology journals involved deceptive methods. By the 1970s, the use of deception had reached over 50 percent, and in some journals, the figure reached two-thirds of studies. This means that subjects in social psychology experiments -- at least those that survived the peer-review process and made it to publication -- had a better than 50-50 chance of having the truth withheld from them, being told things that were not true, or being manipulated in covert ways.

Proponents of deception argue that they are using little lies in order to uncover large truths. Many subjects voice no objection, and sophisticated ethical defenses of the practice are readily provided. In a perfect world, perhaps, deception would be scrupulously avoided, but ours is not perfect, so proponents argue that compromises must be made. Of course, they admit, researchers should do their best to avoid deception wherever possible, employing it only as a last resort. In some cases, it may be possible to develop alternative methodologies that do not require it. In the end, however, deception is an indispensable tool in the pursuit of knowledge.

The American Psychological Association gives explicit support to the argument that dishonesty is necessary for scientific progress. The view that the ends justify the means in apparent in the APA's Ethical Principles of Psychologists and Code of Conduct, which reads as follows: "Psychologists do not conduct a study involving deception unless they have determined that the use of deceptive techniques is justified by the study's significant prospective scientific, educational or applied value and that effective non-deceptive alternatives are not feasible." Moreover, the APA code explicitly forbids the use of deception in research that is reasonably expected to cause "physical pain or severe emotional distress." The implication seems to be that deception by itself is not harmful or objectionable.

Psychology is the nation's second most common undergraduate major, numbering around 90,000 students since the mid-2000s. Permissive attitudes toward deception permeate many introductory psychology courses. To receive a passing grade, students are often required to serve as subjects in several psychological studies, like the one described above. In the beginning, many students have no idea that they may be deceived by researchers, teachers, and fellow students. As the course progresses, they learn that many of the best-known psychological experiments of the 20th century were founded on deceptions of one kind or another. By the end of the semester, students may be convinced that deception is a legitimate technique.

Suppose an undergraduate psychology student goes home to visit her family during a school break. During the visit a friend poses a question that the student would prefer, for one reason or another, not to answer truthfully. Having been told by textbook authors and professors that deception is often justified for the sake of higher ends, might such a student be more likely to withhold information, provide false information, or distort the truth? After all, if deception is permitted in scientific experiments in the pursuit of knowledge, why should it be impermissible in the context of everyday relationships? Where is the harm in a white lie?

Consider the interaction between a used car salesman and a customer. Should the buyer blindly trust everything the salesman says? Of course not. But should this same principle apply in the domains of research and higher learning? "Buyer beware" may be the motto of the marketplace, but "Let research subjects beware" is hardly the sign we want to see hanging above the laboratory door. The practice of deception in research damages the relationship between science and the community it studies. The more suspiciously subjects regard research, the less scientifically valuable their participation becomes. The more we expect to be deceived, the less authentically our responses represent what we really think and feel.

Yet the effect of deception on research is not even the most important thing at stake. The fundamental concern is ultimately the ethos of our entire culture. Scientists are highly trusted. As such trusted figures repeatedly turn out to be engaging in deception, trust in them and perhaps in everyone else -- inevitably declines. Deception in psychological research undermines the notion that we can expect honesty from those entrusted with the pursuit of truth.

Deception, like truth-telling, can be habit-forming. The more frequently we engage in dishonesty, the easier and more natural it becomes. Do we really believe that the practice of deception can be safely contained in the lab? Are we ready to sacrifice the standard of truthfulness and the habit of honesty for the sake of a seriously misguided conception of scientific progress? Scientifically sanctioned deception, we must accept, is inherently incompatible with the pursuit of truth.

Chapter 8
Ways To Protect Yourself From Emotional Manipulation

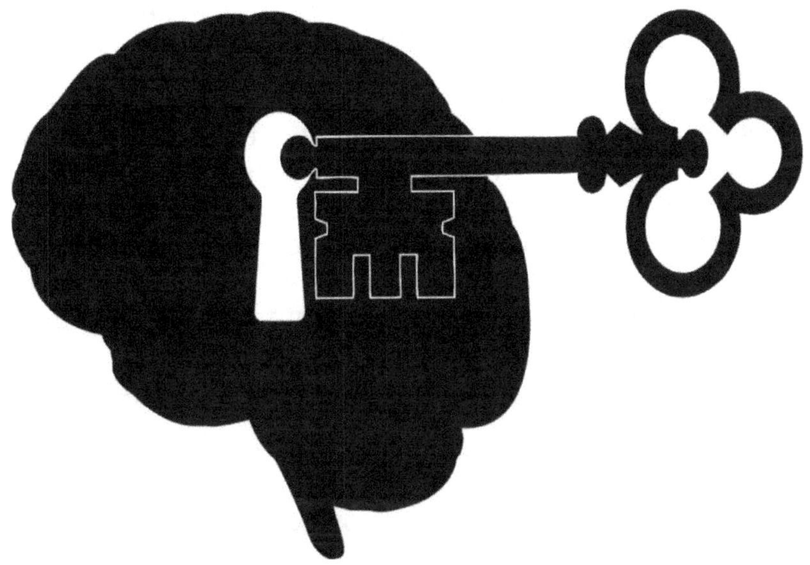

We all enjoy chasing the other sex once in a while - men as well as women. It's fun and a good sport, as long as we are honest about it and keep in mind that it has nothing to do with love. Why? Because pursuing is manipulation and love can't be manipulated – we don't find love, love finds us. Accordingly, we should treat a love relationship as sacred ground.

Unfortunately, too many people believe in manipulation – in relationships as well as in business. I read something in my early twenties that got stuck in my subconsciousness for good: if you can align yourself with the cosmos, success comes easy. What does that mean for this subject? It means that at the end of the day manipulations are futile. Manipulations may help bring about a short-term advantage, but on the long run will inevitably lead to repercussions, because the cosmos opposes manipulations. But if we go with the cosmic flow instead, we will gravitate towards our goal – more or less effortlessly. Too good to be true? Each one of us plays a part in the cosmic game. We just have to know our role in the scheme of things and let it play out. That's why Jesus said that his cross is as light as a feather. Of course, this means to surrender a lot of wishes and desires that are not part of our cameo; however, our cosmic purpose usually turns out to be much more grandiose than our puny, egoistic objectives.

Having said that, we still need to protect ourselves from childish manipulations of other people, even those close to us. Don't take this lightly, emotional manipulation is painful and can leave deep scars on people's psyche and soul. And once you're in a manipulative situation it's very hard to get out. But don't take this affair too seriously either, we do many things subconsciously and your partner may not even be aware that she's manipulating you.

There's always going to be people trying to shake your confidence - people trying to instill seeds of self-doubt within you. These people will do their best to manipulate you into believing that their opinions are objective facts. They'll tell you that everyone in the entire world thinks you're arrogant, crazy, or not good enough. Then they'll tell you how concerned they are about you - about how you're living your life, spending your money, raising your kids, on and on.

If you don't change in exactly the way they want you to change, your life will be ruined. That's what they want you to believe. The truth is these people don't want to help you. They want to control you. They want to change you, not to better your life, but to validate their lives and to keep you from outgrowing them.

Don't be confused. Manipulative people are not worried about your interests. They're worried about their interests. Once you let manipulative people in your life, they can be extremely hard to get rid of. The key is having enough confidence in yourself to give manipulative people the boot as soon as you spot them. Here are some strategies for eliminating manipulative people from your life:

Don't Fall Into Their Trap

Most of us come across situations when the others try to control our emotions, perception or behavior and take an advantage for their own benefit. In one such situation, you fail to realize the real motive. The person controls you psychologically and you get into the trap. This emotional manipulation sometimes costs you a lot when you make some important decisions under the influence of other person and realize it later when it is too late.

When a relationships sounds too good to be true you must be aware. They shower love, praise, appreciation, compliments, and affection on you. You feel as if you are living your dream where everything seems perfect. They give you no reasons to complain. You simply find no faults in them. Even if something goes wrong, they may start crying or feeling sorry. You may even become the victim of intense sex and get the feeling of a fairy tale love.

It is the result when the relationship actually started off with love bombing and all of a sudden you start feeling neglected. You get appreciation, gifts, and praise, but only rarely. You feel as if you are losing your grip or they have someone else in their life. The moment you make up your mind to move on, you get another gift from them. You find it difficult to make up your mind. In one such situation, they try to get control over you. To your amazement in most cases, it works. You get even closer to them.

After sporadic reinforcement, people mostly succeed in controlling their victims. When you fight back or demand an explanation, they may stop behaving in the same manner. The reason is that they actually get full control over you now, so they say goodbye to the sporadic reinforcement. They do not need it anymore. Manipulators have many different faces and in the same manner, they may use many different ways to get things done. The person may make a commitment and later deny in a way that you start doubting your own perception. When you try hard to make them aware of their promise, they make you feel guilty. They may use superficial sympathy and burst into crocodile tears. You end up trusting them eventually and even doubt whether you heard right.

You cannot trust smiling faces that appear confident and powerful. Manipulative people always have self-serving bias and they hardly care for the feelings of the other person. They have a motive to seek out people who validate them and make them feel even superior.

Steer Clear Whenever Possible

The behavior of a manipulator usually varies depending on the situation they are in. For instance, a manipulator could speak rudely to one person, and act politely towards another the next moment. When you notice such extremes frequently in an individual, it would be advisable to stay away from them. Don't interact with this individual unless you really have to. This will protect you from being a victim of manipulation.

One way to detect a manipulator is to see if a person acts with different faces in front of different people and in different situations. While all of us have a degree of this type of social differentiation, some psychological manipulators tend to habitually dwell in extremes, being highly polite to one individual and completely rude to another - or totally helpless one moment and fiercely aggressive the next. When you observe this type of behavior from an individual on a regular basis, keep a healthy distance, and avoid engaging with the person unless you absolutely have to. As mentioned earlier, reasons for chronic psychological manipulation are complex and deep-seated. It is not your job to change or save them.

There are certain situations where you can't exit a relationship completely - most commonly if this person is a parent or a member of your extended family. Unless the person is causing significant harm or psychological damage, you probably can't go cold turkey. First, you need to fully recognize this person for who they are and alter your expectations of the relationship accordingly. If they were previously someone you wanted validation from, then you'll have to stop seeking their validation. If they were someone you got advice from, recognize that their advice isn't something you need in your life. If they continue to offer it, you can thank them for it and then silently discard it.

Be as subtle as you can when setting these boundaries, and don't tell the other person that you are setting them. Creating this change on your end is going to require some energy, and when you anger the other person in the process you'll have to handle their reaction on top of that.

Knowing that this will drain your energy a bit, set boundaries around the time you spend with this person. If you have been hanging out with your controlling mother-in-law every Saturday, cut it down to once a month and schedule something later that day so that your hangout has a definite end time.

Call Them Out On Their Behavior

Manipulators are always hard to confront, but covert manipulators are the worst. When confronted, they will remain cool as cucumber, and yet rigid and unbending. When you begin to spot their flawed logic, you might start to get frustrated. If you continue to argue with them, it'll be hard for you not to raise your voice a bit. You'll start to look like the irrational one and they'll try to take back control based on their "maturity" in remaining calm.

It's tempting to defend yourself and try to get the other person to see what's really going on. But a true manipulator is not going to change their tune, and the more you give in to that temptation to defend yourself, the more they will continue twisting your words. It won't be long before you find yourself trapped in that distorted web of lies and false perceptions. If you're in a situation with a true manipulator, your two goals for any confrontation that occurs should be to diffuse and exit, whether that means exiting the current conversation or exiting the friendship. Avoid insults, arguments, losing your temper, accusing the other person of manipulation, or getting overly emotional. When you speak, stick to statements that are truthful, objective, and peaceful.

There are aspects of dealing with a manipulative person that require a high level of maturity, patience, or self-discipline. You may not have the self-control to respond without losing your temper and making the situation worse. If that is the case, accept this about yourself and take extra steps to avoid a nasty confrontation (for example, invite a mediator into the discussion or send an email rather than talk in person so you have time to think through what you are saying).

For me, dealing with anyone who loses their temper can produce a bit of anxiety. I've had to bring a friend with me in order to feel comfortable in situations that had a lot of potential for blow-ups. As much as I wished I was able to handle the confrontation on my own, I knew I wasn't quite in a place to do that. If I had refused to accept this about myself, I would've experienced a lot of unnecessary anxiety because of my decision to act tougher than I was. Don't wish you were better at dealing with the situation than you are. There will be people who criticize your weak areas and try to make it look like the situation should be easier for you to handle than it is. Don't compare your reaction in a situation to someone else's reaction.

Ignore Everything They Do And Say

Manipulative people are meant to be ignored. These people flip flop on issues, they're slippery when you try to hold them accountable, they promise help that never comes, they make you feel guilty constantly - everything you don't want in person.

When dealing with a manipulative person, the biggest mistake you can make is trying to correct them. By correcting them, you sink deeper into their trap. Manipulative people will use frustration and confusion to bait you into conflict. They want to get you emotional so they can see how you tick. Once they know the things that trigger you, they'll use them to influence your actions. A better strategy is to ignore them completely.

Simply delete them from your life. If you can't delete them right away - like if they're a boss, coworker, or family member - agree with what they say and then go do your own thing anyway.

Hit Their Center Of Gravity

Manipulative people are constantly using their own strategies against you. They'll become friends with your friends and turn them against you. They'll dangle some small reward in front of you and make you chase it continuously - every time you get close to it, they'll pull it away. They'll hold past actions over your head forever. On and on.

Stop letting manipulative people use their strategies against you. Instead, turn the tables. Create a strategy of your own and hit them where it hurts. If you're forced to deal with a manipulative person who keeps making your life hell no matter how hard you try to ignore them, you only have one option, find their center of gravity and attack it. This center might be the manipulative person's friends, followers, or subordinates. It might be a high-level skill or an advanced understanding of a particular field. It might be a particular resource that they control.

Either way, find out what their center of gravity is and make it yours. Create allies with people close to them, recruit people with their skillsets and knowledgebase to replace them, or siphon away their prized resource. This will throw them off balance and force them to focus on controlling their life, not yours.

Trust Your Judgment

You know what's best for your life better than anyone else. Too many people go around asking for other people's opinions about everything. What should I do with my life? What am I good at? Who am I?

Stop looking for other people to define you. Define yourself. Trust yourself. What separates winners from losers is not the ability to listen to other people's beliefs, it's the ability to listen to one's own beliefs. By setting your own beliefs and holding onto them strongly, you prevent manipulative people from affecting your life. In this way, your beliefs will act as a blockade, keeping manipulators ostracized and out of your way.

Try Not To Fit In

Keep reinventing yourself. The idea that consistency is somehow virtuous or tied to success is a misconception. Manipulative people want you to be consistent so they can count on you to push their agendas forward. They want you to show up every day at 9 am and work for them for minimum wage. They want you to get home on time and clean the house and make them feel good about themselves.

Assembly lines are consistent. Prison is consistent. Consistency is how manipulators keep you in a box. It's how they control you. The only way to keep from being manipulated is to actively push against all the boundaries that others try to set for you.

Stop trying to fit in. Instead, work to stand out. Work to be different in every possible way and to never stay the same for too long. Personal growth, by definition, requires a lack of consistency. It requires constant change - constant reinvention.

Stop Compromising

Guilt is a useless emotion. But it's a powerful tool. Guilt is one of the weapons that manipulative people will use against you. They'll make you feel guilty for past failures and small mistakes, or they'll make you feel guilty for being prideful and overconfident. Any time you spend feeling happy or sure of yourself, they'll use against you. No one should ever feel too good about themselves, they'll say.

Another weapon that manipulators will use against you is doubt. They'll work to instill a sense of self-doubt within you

- doubt about your abilities and your worth. Their overall goal is to knock you off balance and make you second guess yourself. Manipulators gain power in this state of uncertainty. Their influence becomes stronger and they are twice as likely to convince you to compromise on your values, your goals, and yourself.

The solution is simple - stop feeling guilty. Stop doubting yourself. When it comes to your own life, you don't owe anyone anything. You deserve to feel good about yourself and to be proud of your accomplishments. You deserve to feel a strong sense of confidence and self-belief in what you're doing. Compromising on any of these things is not moral or enlightened. Rather, it's the road to self-destruction.

Never Ask For Permission

It's easier to ask for forgiveness than permission. The problem is that we've been trained to constantly ask for permission. As a child, we had to beg for everything we wanted—to be fed, changed, and burped. Throughout school we had to ask permission to go to the bathroom, we had to wait to eat lunch at a designated time, and wait our turn to play with toys. As a result, most people never stop waiting for permission.

Employees around the world wait to be promoted and wait for their turn to talk. Most are so used to being picked that they sit silently in meetings, afraid to speak out of turn or to even raise their hands. There is a different way to live.

What if you did whatever you wanted to do whenever you wanted to do it? What if you stopped being overly concerned with politeness and making others feel comfortable? What if, instead, you live your life exactly the way you want to? These are all things you can do at any time.

Manipulative people want you to feel beholden to some imaginary rule or ideal that says you cannot freely take action without consulting either an authoritative figure or some group. The truth is you can disregard this sense of confinement at any time. You can start living your life today radically different that you lived it yesterday. The choice is yours to make.

Create A Greater Sense Of Purpose

People driven by destiny are not easily fooled. The reason manipulators continue to thrive in this world is because so many people are living purposeless lives. When your life lacks purpose, you'll believe anything. You'll do anything. Because nothing really matters.

People who lack purpose are just killing time. There's no rhyme or reason behind how they're living their lives. They don't know where they're going or why they're here. So, to keep from going crazy, they work at pointless jobs and stuff their brains full of celebrity gossip, reality TV, and other forms of useless information. They stay busy to avoid the feeling of desperate emptiness growing inside of them. This busyness and emptiness empowers manipulative people.

There's a sucker born every minute. If you're constantly distracted, constantly consuming useless content, constantly trying to stay busy - you're the sucker. Manipulators control purposeless people by peddling useless information and activities to them. The only way to escape this fate is to develop a sense of destiny. Destiny destroys distraction. When you know you're going, manipulators can't hurt you. They can't distract you or misguide you.

Keep Taking New Opportunities

The world wants you to put your eggs in one basket. Everyone and everything around you is telling you to lock yourself into a mortgage, a car payment, a stable relationship, a single office job, on and on. They want you to stay staked down to a single opportunity for the rest of your life.

Nowadays, being ambitious is often looked down upon. Staying hungry is often seen a sign of weakness. Why can't you be content with what you have? Why are you so greedy? This is what manipulative people will ask you when you express a desire for more. They will call you selfish, arrogant, and prideful. They will make you feel cold and awkward like you are inhumane and heartless. The truth is they want to keep you in your place. They want you to stay at the same job and live in the same place for the rest of your life. They want you to stay dependent on them and the systems they control.

The only way to stay independent is to constantly seek out and create new opportunities. Keep applying to new jobs, keep starting new businesses, keep building new relationships, and keep chasing new experiences.

Quit Being A Baby

If someone fools you once, shame on them. If someone fools you 10 times, you're an idiot. Stop letting manipulators walk all over you. Stop being a punching bag. No one feels bad for you and you're only embarrassing yourself. Have enough self-awareness and self-respect to say no to manipulative people.

You can't just walk through life blaming other people for your problems. You can't just walk through life oblivious to the people trying to manipulate you either. Yes, negative and manipulative people exist. And yes, these people will try to use you. But that doesn't mean you get a free pass to make mistakes and be used.

No one can manipulate you without your permission. You're responsible for your own successes and failures. If others outthink or out-strategize you - it's your fault, not theirs. Be accountable. Learn from your mistakes. Don't keep trusting the same slippery person over and over again. Cut them loose. Delete them from your life. Commit to surrounding yourself with likeminded people who aren't going to use you.

Bet On Yourself

Take a chance on the one thing you can control in life - yourself. When it comes to making tough decisions, too many people limit themselves to considering just external factors. They consider the financial and relationship consequences of a situation. But they fail to consider the effects their decision will have on their personal happiness and sense of self-worth. As a result, they take chances on other people when they should be taking chances on themselves. Then they wonder why they're miserable.

When you only take chances on external people and things, you place yourself at the mercy of those people and things. This makes you vulnerable and ripe for manipulation. Instead, you should be taking chances on yourself. In any difficult situation you're faced with, don't ask questions like, "Who is the better person to side with?" or "Which option is more likely to be successful?" Instead, ask, "What do I want to do most?" and then go out and do it.

If, for example, you're faced with an opportunity to start your own business or stay working at the same dead-end job, don't stay at the job just because the pay is only slightly pathetic. Don't stay just because the relationships are only slightly miserable. When you do this, you're betting on external factors. This is always a mistake. A better strategy is to bet on yourself.

You'll never regret betting on yourself. Sure, you'll have to take full responsibility for any mistakes you commit. Sure, you'll have to hold yourself to a higher standard. But you'll also be fully responsible for your own victories too. You'll continue to grow and achieve greater and greater levels of success.

Avoid Emotional Attachment With Them

With a manipulator, everything you do is wrong. Every fight you've had is your fault. Being manipulated will wreak havoc on your emotions. You go from crying to being angry to feeling guilty and unworthy in short order. Then you're regretful you didn't stick up for yourself. You're embarrassed that you let them get over on you yet again. When you've left a manipulator your emotions are more stable.

Life is an adventurous journey. Along the way, many people come to give us company for the certain period of time at different stages and go after playing their part in our lives. There is no problem with coming and going of the persons in itself, but the difficulties arise when you become emotionally attached to the persons and feel helpless, tensed and worried when the relationship ends especially with an emotional manipulator. Hence, if you want to remain happy and make progress in life, then you need to overcome emotional attachment as early as possible.

There is no doubt that some persons become the driving force for you to move towards the chosen path. But you should be careful not to get distracted when you separated from them. You need to make use of relationships judiciously. Be attached to the persons with detached approach and take care of them to create a trustworthy atmosphere. However, you should not be dependent on that persons for your growth and halt your life when you let them go out of your life for being a manipulator because some other relationship is waiting on your path towards your journey. You need to re-focus on your journey leaving behind the memories of the past.

Handling emotional attachment tests one's level of maturity and seriousness of their journey toward the chosen path. Enjoy the moment you spend with people. Learn from them, love them and take care of them but do not make them walking sticks. Most of time, people generally fear of losing someone due to their incapability to move ahead in life alone. So, if you dare to walk on the chosen path alone, you no longer need to overcome emotional attachment anymore.

Meditate Often

Are you interested in feeling calmer? More centered? More in control of your emotions? If so, meditation can provide emotional stability, something many people long for in today's fast-paced, high-tech busy world. If you struggle with depression, mood swings, stress or other related issues, meditation can help provide the calm and clarity that you seek in just a few minutes a day.

Whether the issues you face are linked to depression and stress, a past trauma, or a chemical change in brain function, everyone can benefit from daily meditation. In fact, there is no better time to start meditating than today! The effects of meditation build over time, but you may notice a sense of calm, quiet and peace almost immediately.

Meditation brings the body into a state of deep relaxation and provides the tools and resources needed to deal with stress. As the body and mind learn to relax through deep breathing exercises and techniques, the mind calms and the body experiences a state of tranquility.

Meditation can actually neutralize the negative consequences of stress hormones that overtax your body and your emotional state. As hormone levels return to normal, emotions settle and stabilize. And the next time you feel upset or anxious, you will be better equipped to deal with intense emotions and situations, using your breath to calm down and relax. Emotions can truly hold you captive, making you feel as though you're living your life on a roller coaster of uncontrollable ups and downs, twists and turns. Meditation, on the other hand, involves a great deal of visualization – a powerful tool which can help you reshape your current way of thinking and create a more positive, stable emotional environment.

Meditation can help you build self-esteem, heal from past traumas, and experience more joy in the present moment. Visualization during meditation not only gives you the tools to deal with emotional upset by providing stability, but it can also help you map out a course of change for your future. Meditation can change your life from the inside out and help you deal with the emotional manipulators.

Inspire Them

Use all the knowledge you have gained about becoming your best self to help them become their best self, too. Work with a counselor if you're having trouble changing their behavior. Changing their behavior can be very difficult, and you might not be able to do it on your own. A counselor or therapist can help him identify behaviors they need to change and address the thoughts behind them. They'll also help him learn new behaviors that are healthier for him.

Tell Them "You're Right"

This starts with no longer responding to their techniques the way you used to. You say "no" if you don't want to, or speak your mind even if they don't like it. Work on feeling okay with how they might respond negatively. If it's not yours, don't pick it up.

You can only control your actions. That is important because you will not be able to change the behavior of a manipulator, but you can stop being their victim. That happens when you start saying "no." We are manipulated because we allow it and refusing to be manipulated is the first step in breaking the cycle. Manipulators are good at what they do, so pay attention to their response. They are likely to say or do things that pull at the heartstrings. We should stand firm in our "no," knowing that we are taking the first step towards freeing ourselves from their influence.

Let Go Of Harmful Relationships

Toxic relationships can be difficult to let go of. Many people get caught in a cycle of going back to relationships that are not good for them. This only creates a cycle of grief and hurt. There are ways to let go of toxic relationships. Psychologists have worked with people who have had this problem enough to be able to write an entire handbook on the subject. \

The very first step to freeing yourself from a toxic relationship is to admit to yourself that the relationship isn't okay. You may notice the signs of a toxic relationship and try to justify them to yourself. If you notice that uncomfortable feeling in the back of your mind, it's called 'cognitive dissonance', and it's your brain trying to protect you from what you know is true. Take note of the things in the relationship that make you feel this way. Accepting that your relationship is toxic is the first step. Before you can really be free, you have to be aware of all the things that are harming you.

Relationships are a two-way street. Two people are participating in the relationship, which means that two people are participating in all of the disagreements, arguments, and behavior. You can't take the blame fully on yourself. If you blame yourself for all of the problems in the relationship, you will find yourself going back to try and fix them. Recognize that sometimes, both parties are at fault for a toxic relationship. Acknowledge your responsibilities – but only your responsibilities. You don't need to be putting up with anyone else's problems in a toxic relationship. When you're not to blame, there's no reason to hoist it on yourself.

Cutting off contact is one of the best things that you can do when trying to let go of a manipulative partner. Keeping in contact is only going to make letting go harder. This includes checking up on toxic people who are no longer in your life. Resist scrolling through their social media or asking your mutual friends how they're doing. According to Sarah Newman, M.A, you should always follow your gut when it comes to cutting people out of your life. Even though it may sound extreme, Newman advises loosening the ties when it comes to a toxic relationship. In order to move on, you need to be in a place where you're able to feel neutral about the lack of contact, rather than pain.

Mariana Bockarova, Ph.D., says that closure is one of the best things for moving on from a broken and manipulative relationship. Bockarova acknowledges that closure can help people reconstruct their entire lives in a healthy and productive manner. Finding closure is one way to help you let go of a toxic relationship. For a lot of people, closure comes from within and recognizing all the ways that the relationship went wrong in the first place. For others, writing one final letter or having the other person acknowledge their toxicity can bring closure. Whatever it is, closure is important for moving on.

The most important thing in leaving any toxic relationship and letting it go is having someone there to catch you if you fall. Letting go can be jarring, especially if they're long-term. Get together with friends and family who can help support you during the more difficult times. They can also help keep you accountable when it comes to not checking up people that you have already cut off. Support systems are invaluable when it comes to letting go of toxic relationships. Don't be afraid to reach out to the people who love you most.

Develop A Strong Mentality

While one toxic person may use manipulation and lies, another may resort to intimidation and incivility. And if you're not careful, people like that can take a serious toll on your well-being. Mentally strong people, however, deal with manipulative people in a skilled manner. They refuse to give away their power, and they continue being their best selves no matter who surrounds them.

Putting a name to your feelings decreases their intensity. So whether you're feeling sad, anxious, angry, or scared, acknowledge it--at least to yourself. Also, pay attention to the way those emotions can affect your choices. When you're feeling anxious you may be less inclined to take risks. When you're excited you may be more impulsive. Increasing your awareness of your emotions can decrease the chances that you'll make irrational decisions based on emotions only.

Naming your emotions is only part of the battle--you also need skills to regulate your emotions. Think about your current coping skills. Do you eat when you're nervous? Do you drink to calm down? Do you vent to your friends when you're angry?

Do you stay home when you're anxious? Those common strategies may make you feel better in the moment but they will make you feel worse over the long-term.

Look for coping skills that are good for you over the long-term. Keep in mind that what works for one person won't necessarily work for you so you need to find what helps you deal with your emotions best. Experiment with various coping skills to find out what works for you; deep breathing, exercising, meditating, reading, coloring, and spending time in nature are just a few of the strategies that could help.

The way you think affects how you feel and how you behave. Thinking things like, "I can't stand this," or "I'm such an idiot," robs you of mental strength. Pay attention to your thoughts. You'll likely notice common themes and patterns. Perhaps you talk yourself out of doing things that feel scary. Or maybe you convince yourself that you have no control over your life.

Respond to unproductive and irrational thoughts with something more helpful. So instead of saying, "I'm going to mess this up," remind yourself, "This is my chance to shine and I'm going to do my best." Changing those conversations you have with yourself can be the most instrumental thing you could do to change your life.

The best way to train your brain to think differently is by changing your behavior. Do hard things--and keep doing them even when you think you can't. You'll prove to yourself that you're stronger than you think. Establish healthy daily habits as well. Practice gratitude, exercise, get plenty of sleep and eat a healthy diet so your brain and your body can be at their best. Seek out people who inspire you to be your best. And create an environment that supports your efforts to build a healthy lifestyle.

All the good habits in the world won't be effective if you're performing them right alongside your unhealthy habits. It's like eating donuts while you're running on a treadmill. Pay attention to your bad habits that rob you of mental strength (we all have them). Whether you feel sorry for yourself or you resent other people's success, it only takes one or two to keep you stuck in life. Once you become aware of your bad habits, devote energy into replacing them with healthier alternatives. Then, you'll be able to step out of the hamster wheel and actually move forward toward your goals.

Just like it takes time and practice to become physically strong, building mental strength takes dedication as well. But building mental muscle is the key to feeling your best and reaching your greatest potential.

Give Yourself Positive Self-Talk Throughout The Day

An emotional manipulator can completely tarnish your mood, so make sure you restore yourself with uplifting self-talks during the day. Each of us has a set of messages that play over and over in our minds. This internal dialogue, or personal commentary, frames our reactions to life and its circumstances. One of the ways to recognize, promote, and sustain optimism, hope, and joy is to intentionally fill our thoughts with positive self-talk.

Too often, the pattern of self-talk we've developed is negative because of our manipulative partner. We remember the negative things we were told as children by our partners, parents, siblings, or teachers. We remember the negative reactions from other children that diminished how we felt about ourselves. Throughout the years, these messages have played over and over in our minds, fueling our feelings of anger, fear, guilt, and hopelessness.

One of the most critical avenues used in therapy with those suffering from depression is to identify the source of these messages and then work with the person to intentionally "overwrite" them. If a person learned as a child he was worthless, we show him how truly special he is. If while growing up a person learned to expect crises and destructive events, we show her a better way to anticipate the future.

Try the following exercise. Write down some of the negative messages inside your mind that undermine your ability to overcome your circumstance. Be specific, whenever possible, and include anyone you remember who contributed to that message. Now, take a moment to intentionally counteract those negative messages with positive truths in your life. Don't give up if you don't find them quickly. For every negative message, there is a positive truth that will override the weight of despair. These truths always exist; keep looking until you find them.

You may have a negative message that replays in your head every time you make a mistake. As a child you have been told, "You'll never amount to anything" or "You can't do anything right." When you make a mistake - and you will because we all do - you can choose to overwrite that message with a positive one, such as "I choose to accept and grow from my mistake" or "As I learn from my mistakes, I am becoming a better person." During this exercise, mistakes become opportunities to replace negative views of who you are with positive options for personal enhancement.

Positive self-talk is not self-deception. It is not mentally looking at circumstances with eyes that see only what you want to see. Rather, positive self-talk is about recognizing the truth, in situations and in yourself. One of the fundamental truths is that you will make mistakes. To expect perfection in yourself or anyone else is unrealistic. To expect no difficulties in life, whether through your own actions or sheer circumstances, is also unrealistic.

When negative events or mistakes happen, positive self-talk seeks to bring the positive out of the negative to help you do better, go further, or just keep moving forward. The practice of positive self-talk is often the process that allows you to discover the obscured optimism, hope, and joy in any given situation.

HOW TO ANALYZE PEOPLE

Introduction

Whether in the office or out with friends, the body language of the people around you speaks volumes. It is often suggested that body language constitutes more than 60% of everything we communicate, so learning how to see the nonverbal cues people send is a valuable skill. From eye behavior towards the direction by which a person points his or her feet, body gestures reveals what you are really thinking.

When talking about reading the language of the body, these are not skills you are born with but can be learned. When communicating with someone, pay attention to them to see if they make direct eye contact or look away. Inability to create direct eye contact can indicate boredom, disinterest, and even deceit. Especially if an individual looks away and or gives a sideways glance. If somebody looks down, however, it often indicates nervousness or submissiveness.

Search for dilated pupils to determine if someone is responding favorably toward you. Pupils dilate when effort that is cognitive, therefore if someone is focused on someone or something they like, their pupils will automatically dilate. Pupil dilation can be tough to detect, but under the right conditions, you should be able to spot it. A person's blink rate can speak volumes about what is going on inside them. Blink rates increase when individuals are usually thinking more or are stressed. In some cases, increased blinking rate indicates lying – particularly when combined with touching the face (particularly the mouth and eyes).

Glancing at something can suggest a desire for that thing. For example, if someone glances at the door during your conversation, this could indicate a desire to leave. Glancing at a person can indicate a desire to speak with her or him. When it comes to eye behavior, additionally, it is suggested that looking upwards or to the right during a conversation indicates a lie is probably being told, while looking upwards and or to the left indicates the individual is telling the turth. The reason behind this really is that folks look up or to the right when utilizing their imagination to concoct a story, and look up and to the left when they're recalling an actual memory.

Chapter 1
Body Language in Relation to Emotions

It is very easy to make a blunder when considering body gestures one, as we have a tendency is to glance at one action or gesture at the same time. When the body that is interpreting, essential to have a look at clusters of gestures or actions, the congruence, and context of the message. A gesture of an individual has numerous meanings when put into a cluster of gestures as does a person word put into a unique sentence. For example, the crossing of hands over the body may mean cold or could imply a defensive barrier according to the words spoken together with tone behind the text.

Another aspect of interpreting body language is always to go through the congruence for the message. Is the body displaying the message as same the language spoke? Nonverbal signals are said to influence the message more than the language significantly and often then the verbal message is ignored if they are contrasting. An individual might be telling another person that they really take care of them, but the body gestures is rigid in accordance with no eye contact.

Context is yet another influencing factor when reading body gestures, as tightly crossed legs and arms while waiting for a bus may be interpreted as cold or defensive. On the other hand, rubbing your forehead may imply you have got a headache or even hiding your tears. Environmental surroundings have to be taken into account before an interpretation is finally made. Furthermore, it is really worthy to consider the physical restrictions or disabilities of the people may suffer while looking at body gestures as a weak hand shake may mean an arthritic hand or an occupation of a surgeon whose hands are his income and clothing may impact on body gestures by hiding body parts or restricting movements. Additionally, the status, power, or prestige has been related to a communication ability of person. An individual in an increased socio economic group or occupation is able to communicate greater impact to his actions with words and gestures than someone who is less educated or unskilled who relies more about gestures than words. Some individuals are thought to be more perceptive or intuitive in reading and understanding the non verbal cues of body or communication language and women are generally more perceptive than men. The perception or intuitive nature can be learned through studying people, but others are believed to simply have a all natural tendency to feel and understand people's emotions, through observant examination, emotions could be distinguished from non-verbal signs. Remember that these are indicators and never exact confirmation. In addition, related clues may be used; in particular congruence, context, back ground information, believed towards the person, the tones, and pronunciation in the voice. You will find 80 muscles in the face, 36 of which are involved with facial expression, which combine to create numerous of facial expressions, and seven are regarded as universal.

A powerful tool that is expressing and recognising emotions happens to be posture while the body gestures portrayed through the posture can work as a wealthy resource of data that can expose goals, intentions, and emotions. A body that is sunken will be suggestive of depression while an intensifying posture indicates authority and strength. Strong and swift movements are pertaining to aggression. Horizontal movement patterns of the arms imply communication whereas vertical movement patterns relate to giving a presentation.

Inner characteristics of an individual can be interpreted through the way in which a person stands or moves; the thinker that is creative move about the area to greatly help thought processes and keep ideas flowing. The person which stands securely on the ground and conveys strength and determination in walking, may be seen as a pragmatic individual. The person who is inflexible in arguments, may sit and stand in a position will permanent make few variations in posture. A modification of posture may indicates a change in point of view. "The movement model of dominant individuals are often characterized by relaxation in the torso, and easy, asymmetrical posture such as for example leaning and hip shifting".

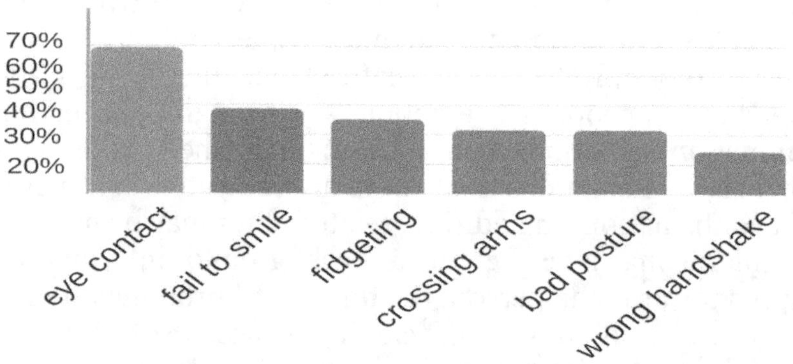

A lot of studies have been developed and tested on facial and verbal emotion expression along perception, but there is limited research on body movement. Facial expressions are a really useful supply of information into understanding emotions, which might sometimes require a proximity that is close as reading body gestures may be observed from a distance and provide an overall view for the situation. A couple of methods have been developed to raised understand body gestures including the bodily expressive action stimulus test and Laban Movement Analysis, but these methods are time consuming, use researchers own perception, and intuition of characteristics without any concrete data analysis. They assess the body movements by using electromyography or accelerometers, motion tracking systems to measure gait, and emotional arm movements. These all become limiting in showing true behavioural movements and restricted to laboratory settings due to equipment set and expensive specialised equipment.

From all of these, one research methods has been developed and it has now the name of Body Action and Posture (BAP) coding system that has been made to study emotions, which are multiple, the BAP categorizes actions and postures in 2 kinds of units called the physical body posture units and action units. The body posture units which "represent the general alignment of 1 or a couple of articulators (head, truck, and arms) to a particular resting configuration, which will show periodic changes known as posture shifts (e.g. a person leaning backwards, arms crossed)". "Action unit which can be a nearby excursion of just one or a collection of articulators (mostly arms) outside a configuration that is resting a very discrete onset (start point), a relatively short duration, and distinct offset (end point) where in fact the articulators returns to a resting configuration (e.g. head shaking, pointing arm gesture)". Utilizing the two units researchers were able to categorize emotions. A study was able to distinguish the difference between this emotions through behavioral patterns or body language and generate meaningful ambiguity between similar emotions such as pride and elated joy or sadness and relief as individuals, we all show similar emotions.

Why Women Are More Intuitive Than Men

Are women truly more intuitive than men or could it have to do aided by the real way women can be socialized to empathize with other people? What are the physiological reasons that exist there? Based on some recent research findings, women are possess a lot more of the biological functions essential for being more attuned into the subtle cues of intuition.

An ability that is vital needed when you're developing intuitively will be in a position to observe subtle alterations in just how things look or appear. Women pick up on these changes that are subtle more often than males. A woman could possibly tell from registering these subtle changes in a person's face, what emotions the individual is experiencing. This can be a practical and necessary skill when gathering information that is intuitive.

Findings shows that ladies are better at facial recognition than men. Research has revealed that this will be because of the known undeniable fact that women can be more interested in emotional bonding based upon their need certainly to recognize, bond and nurture their offspring. To put this in perspective, just how long achieved it take for the spouse to notice that you'd changed something regarding the appearance? Your wife is probably noticed the full minute she saw you. Your husband probably needed hints that are few, "Does something look different about me?"

Due to their more hearing, they are more aware of subtle changes in tone than men that is accurate. Research reports have proven that ladies have slightly better hearing than men. They cull "more" meaning from the text they hear than males for their capacity to hear at a wider range. They sense alterations in tone more easily and from that, derive the signals that are emotionally encoded when you look at the words they're hearing. This can explain why ladies are more likely to know someone emotionally upset, even prior to the person has told them so?

Another reason women appear to be more tuned in to the needs of others intuitively may be due to their higher estrogen levels, this hormone may cause them to deeply experience emotions more, especially during peak times of these menstrual cycle. The capacity to feel another person's emotional pain and share their emotions is named empathy. Scientific studies show that women exhibit more of an empathic response than men do as they are more attuned to emotions than males.

Comparative Brain Studies: Recent comparative brain studies unearthed that there are physiological variations in men and women's brains as well as in just how info is processed due to those differences. These physiological differences point to why gents and ladies respond to the same input so differently. Women show more emotion and tend to be more sensitive to feelings when communicating while men tend to be solution oriented and logical.

Even though much of this information supports the theory for ladies possessing the factors that are physiologically being more intuitive. A 2006 study conducted by Dr. Richard Wiseman asking men and women to identify "fake smiles" versus "sincere smiles" had more men guessing correctly on the women respondents.

Guys are also better at making "snap" decisions than women. These decisions are snap intuitive responses predicated on information pulled from various stored files within the subconscious. Since men lean toward being more logical and solution oriented if this stored information comes to the surface they truly are more apt to leave "emotions out" of your decision making process. This leads to less guessing that is second of decision, which will be often the reason their "business like approach" yields positive results.

Most errors in judgment can be linked back to "thinking too much" which fosters second-guessing and allows emotions to get into the equation. For example, when you're too emotional over a choice you be concerned about the way the decision will affect others or you to alter your decision from the right one to the wrong one if it might hurt someone's feelings.

What exactly can we conclude using this? Men are better at guessing whose smile is genuine over women and better at snap intuitive decision-making? Maybe making snap decisions well and knowing who is sincerely enthusiastic about them versus disingenuous is a vital factor in propagating our species?

My very own "hunch" is that while women do involve some physiological advantages toward being intuitive men are equally as intuitive as females, but in a way that is different.

Women can be socialized to be much more expressing that is comfortable discussing emotions and also this allows them to stay in touch due to their intuition more easily. Outward displays of emotion haven't been encouraged for males, which may be changing, when it comes to the men part that is mostly still refrain in larger numbers than women from doing things that are classified as "touchy feely" such as for instance actively using or developing their intuition.

At run on Intuition, I focus on intuition development as a success skill, which can be used to help make the right life and business decisions. In my opinion intuition, development can benefit both women and men. Perhaps if more men were aware of most of the practical uses for their intuition they wouldn't be so fast to shy far from developing the greater amount of empathetic side of their intuition.

Universal Gestures

After examining a variety of gestures is to identified and performed by representatives of those cultures, Dr. Matsumoto and Dr. Hwang was able to derive a series of loose categories with which to conceptualize cultural similarities and differences.

One of these categories were evaluative gestures, like the Western "thumbs up", but other categories conveyed more nuanced social norms. Perhaps it is unsurprisingly, gestures fitting to the category of insults seemed to be quite common across many cultures. Other categories included the act of indicating something or of articulating inner physical or mental states, such as being in pain.

Overall, even though many gestures were the same across cultures, some similar gestures had radically different meanings based on where they were used. Moreover, certain gestures appeared to be culturally unique together with no correlates various other cultures, such as South Asian gestures for apology or East Asian messages hunger that is concerning.

The absolute most consistently universal among these gestures sought to convey very basic messages that tied to universal physical forms. As an example, this manifested in common insults that referred to gross components of the body that is human. Most cultures are associated excrement that is human disgust, so tying this to obscene gestures seems intuitive. Moreover, it could connect profoundly with evidence that ties basic emotions to facial expressions.

Some Universal Gestures

Body gestures is an essential factor when you want to rise above words to hear somebody. No matter what the personality type, culture, education, sex, or body language can, and certainly it will tell even more than just words, to those happy to hear. There are universal gestures, such as smiling, blushing, or the wide-eyed expression of fear that come from the human biological makeup and they've got exactly the same significance in the main globe, in every culture. As a result, they are called gestures that are universal.

Smiling

Regardless of culture or location, all humans are born with all the great capacity to smile. There's no doubt that all person has a unique method of smiling, but on the whole, any person with working facial muscles smiles when he/she desires to convey a message that is positive. People smile for various reasons, either embarrassment or pleasure, give reassurance or smile in complicity. You will find the fake smiles together with genuine ones. You can consider that genuine smile, showing pleasure or affection when you see a smile that does not involve just a movement of the mouth in a smile-like shape, but also the eyes crinkling at their outer edges.

Blushing

Needless to say, embarrassment signals shows its presence through blushing. What happens when a person blushes? The blood flows to your chest and cheeks, giving that reddish look of embarrassment. Again, regardless of the location or culture, you will discover this gesture each time embarrassment gets control of you. To manage it then take several slow, deep breaths in order to take control of your nerves, and blood flow. However, don't confuse embarrassment blushing with that blush from the cold within the winter, it is excessive heat during summer or that natural blush some men and women have always.

Shrugging

When individuals are shrug they involuntarily make use of this gesture to protect themselves somehow. A shrug is full because the head is dipped into the shoulders, the sides for the mouth turned down, the palms turned upwards as well as the eyebrows raised, such a shrug can indicate indifference, either or disdain, uncertainty, and embarrassment.

Crying

All across the entire world, everybody recognizes crying as a universal sign of sadness. Crying is an all-natural instinct it comes down from the human make-up that is biological. For instance, the first action of an infant is crying just after birth because it happens to be torn from the comfort and safety regarding the womb. The newborn cries with not been taught how to cry, it absolutely born with this ability.

In addition, there are various universal gestures and hundreds of other small and unique gestures are for an individual particularly. However, despite having universal gestures, you have to consider the whole body and see just what one other body parts are doing to be able to know which attitude will be expressed.

Body language is an element that is essential for human behavior and plays an unique role in intercommunication. It could betray you or support your words, provide you with insight about a person's thoughts or personality, or simply just reassure you through a warm smile. It may manipulate public perception if used properly or makes it possible for you to get to know better the person close to you. Sometimes, body gestures are reveals far more than words, you simply have to pay attention.

Roles of Nonverbal Communication

Nonverbal communication plays many important roles in intercultural situations. As messages are delivered inside the verbal channel convey the literal and content meanings of words, the nonverbal channel is relied upon to carry the undercurrent of identity ties and relational meaning. Occurring with or without verbal communication, nonverbal cues offer the context for interpreting and understanding how the verbal message should be understood, such as they can create either confusion or clarity. Usually, they could create friction that is intercultural misunderstandings for three major causes. First, just one cue that is nonverbal have different meanings and interpretations in different cultures; second, multiple nonverbal cues are sent simultaneously; and third, a higher degree of rules should be considered, such as for instance variations in gender, personality, relational distance, and socioeconomic status together with situation.

Nonverbal messages are often the principal way of conveying emotions, attitudes, and our relationships with others, so we rely on nonverbal cues to "say" things that are tough to vocalize. A quick look away when one tries to make eye contact with you can be interpreted in myriad ways, from "I'm too busy" to "I don't wish to speak to you" or "I'm embarrassed."

Nonverbal cues are defined as those messages embedded in nonlinguistic and paralinguistic cues, which can be expressed through multiple communication channels in a specific social setting. Nonlinguistic cues could be eye contact, smiles, touch, hand gestures, or silence.

Paralinguistic is based on your voice, and that can be speed, volume, tone or pitch. Multiple channels ensures that nonverbal cues are sent through multiple channels at once, e.g. eye contact, facial expressions, and body movement. Sociocultural setting reflects the necessity of our cultural norms and expectations in evaluating appropriateness and inappropriateness of a message that is nonverbal.

Kinds of Nonverbal Communication

Researchers have identified numerous types of nonverbal communications: physical appearance, paralanguage (vocal cues), facial expressions, kinesics (body movements), haptics (touch), eye contact, and proxemics (space).

Physical appearance includes body type, height, weight, hair, and skin tone. These characteristics affect our communications that are daily. We also wear clothing, so we display artifacts, which are ornaments or adornments that themselves communicate. Our clothing and artifacts mark our unique or co-cultural identity, or the many smaller cultural groups to which we belong within a more substantial culture. Whatever you wear or don't wear, this says something in regards to you.

Paralanguage or vocal cues can also mark our cultural, ethnic, and gender identity. This is one way we say something is not what we way. This includes the next areas: accent (how words are pronounced together); pitch range (high or tone that is low); pitch intensity (high or low carrying of your voice); volume (loud or soft); articulation (precision or slurring); and rate (speed). We tend to evaluate others' speech according to our standards that are own. If you shout out during a discussion, chances are that will soon be interpreted while you being angry or irritated. However, raising your voice is frequent among many cultural groups are as an indication of sincerity or authenticity.

For example, some African Americans have a tendency to have expressive voices and are passionate about their speaking points, which is often seen erroneously as anger. Also, putting the accent on an alternate element of a word or a word that is different a sentence can send completely different meanings, as can shift in tone at the end of the phrase (rising or falling). Decoding nonverbal cues are only at that level requires a sophisticated understanding of the language.

Facial expressions are falls under a more substantial category of nonverbal communication, kinesics, or body movement. The face area can perform producing 250,000 different expressions. Many of these vary cross-culturally, but some may be recognized across cultures. These are the facial expressions accompanying emotions represented by SADFISH: Sadness, Anger, Disgust, Fear, Interest, Surprise, and Happiness. Folks of some cultures are taught from a very age that is young to demonstrate certain emotions, making it more challenging for folks because of these cultures to identify these emotional expressions when they see them.

Probably the most expressive part of the face may be the eyes, as well as for this reason, many scholars categorize gazes separately from facial expressions. Eye contact is a rather communication tool that is powerful. Holding eye contact can be an indication of respect, truthfulness, attraction, attention, or domination and power. Failure to create eye contact can be an indication similarly of respect, fear, intimidation, lack of interest, and much more. Several of this is determined by the culture. For example, in many Western cultures, it's considered appropriate behavior to look someone, when you look at the eye during a discussion and also to comfortably hold that gaze because of the other individual. Infact, neglecting to make eye contact often raises suspicion about ulterior motives. In several Eastern cultures, however, making an eye contact that is maintaining can indicate disrespect when it involves individuals of different positions over the social hierarchy; it really is considered impolite to appear a teacher in the eye.

Gestures are another kind of kinesics and these are culturally specific. Researchers have sub-divided gestures into four areas: emblems, or gestures shat substitute for words and phrases, such as for instance raising your shoulders for "I do not know'"; illustrators help illustrate that which we are making an effort to say, perhaps by indicating "this big"; regulators are accustomed to control, maintain, or "regulate" the pace and flow of conversation. For example, setting up your forefinger to indicate you are not finished speaking; and adaptors are habits or gestures that fulfill some style of psychological need, such as picking lint off your shirt or having fun with your own hair. Some cultures rely far more heavily on gestures as accompaniments to their verbal communication than others. For example, the language that is italian such a high degree of emblems that entire conversations can almost be held using emblems alone. Adaptors are often employed when someone is nervous or perhaps being dishonest, yet not always because gestures are culturally specific, their meaning that is intended can very confusing when communicating across cultures.

Haptics could be the scholarly study of touch and its own rules vary considerably across cultures. Arabic men often hold hands while most U.S. men would not dare. Into the U.S. we often hug hello and good-bye while in many other nations kisses in the cheeks would be the salutations that are standard. There are different places regarding the body where touch is acceptable that give person to your relationship. It really is generally considered fine world wide to pat buttocks on sports teams, but try out this with your employer and also you're probably asking for trouble.

The analysis of space is proxemics and it is too culturally regulated. We each live within our"bubble" that is personal space all around us reserved for intimate others and feel offended or at the very least awakened, when someone violates the boundary of the space bubble without the permission that accompanies greater intimacy. Some cultures are comfortable speaking at a distance of 12-18 inches with non-intimate while other cultures need at the very least 2 feet, and others still require just as much as 5-6 feet of distance when talking to a conversation partner that is nonintimate. These differences can be create discomfort and confusion once you accidentally violate a person's space bubble.

Regulating Boundaries

As human beings, we have been definitely somewhat territorial and have a tendency to mark our spaces as a real way of claiming our territory. Our boundaries exist in space and time. We can feel attached with and develop a feeling of ownership over a particular spot. An individual are invades our territory, we start to feel sensitive, vulnerable, and threatened. If our territory is a precious commodity, we have a tendency to react without first thinking through our reactions and actions are because we feel violated. This is certainly psychological ownership, it is not ownership that is physical. As an example, in cities where parking spaces are extremely limited, people complain when others "park within their spot", despite the fact that all spots are publically owned. Research suggests that there are three main aspects of boundaries: interpersonal boundaries, environmental boundaries, and psychological boundaries.

Within the consideration of interpersonal boundaries are what exactly is a distance that is comfortable people in one cultural group can feel like crowding to those of another. In the US, research shows that we have four zones that are spatial intimate, personal, social, and public. The intimate zone is reserved for all those closest to us for instance family, close friends, and a situation that is emotional. Its distance is 0 to 18 inches. The zone that is personal reserved for closer friends, some acquaintances, and colleagues, its distance is eighteen to forty-eight inches. The social zone is that which we typically find at a more substantial event, such as a celebration as well as its distance is forty-eight inches to twelve feet. Finally, the length of twelve feet is or even more may be the public zone, when some of these zones is violated, discomfort, or anxiety might result.

For European Americans, the average conversational distance is approximately twenty inches. In lots of Latin American and Caribbean cultures, the distance reduces to fourteen to fifteen inches. In Saudi Arabia, among same-sex speakers, the perfect conversational distance reduces even more like nine to ten inches. The concept of personal space is unseen, yet can result in a good deal of intercultural discomfort and misunderstanding. Look at the colleague from a location with an inferior comfortable speaking distance, who enters your intimate zone unwittingly, engendering some discomfort for your requirements. You cool off slightly to regain your space that is comfortable bubble yet your colleague matches your step with one of his/her own, again closing the room. This will probably lead is to a rather awkward conversation, no matter what the topic. Unconsciously, we deem our personal space is our protective territory with us; it is sacred, inviolable, and nonnegotiable that we carry around. Different cultures have different space requirements for every regarding the above zones, nevertheless, the experience of space and space violation carries across cultures and gender groups.

Environmental boundaries would be the space we claim also to which we become emotionally are attached along with other members of our communities. Territory and identities are interconnected concepts because of the period of time, effort, emotion and self-worth. This is certainly invested in that which we claim as our territories that are primary. Our home territory or environment immediately surrounding put us strongly influences on our everyday lives. Furthermore, our behavior is defined by the social people we connect to and the environment in which the communication occurs.

The Middle East, Asia, and those varied environments strongly influence the behaviors of their inhabitants, for example, middle-class neighborhoods in Canada or the U.S. are very different from those of Latin America. When you look at the U.S. are physically separated from neighbors with a fence, gate, yard, or some combination consider as middle income house. Within the home and environmental boundaries are exercised through separate bedrooms and bathrooms, and many locks.

Furthermore, in Mexico, we are come across a very different approach to the area structure. Homes are designed and arranged around a central plaza, perhaps with a residential area are center and church. Members of the family share bedrooms and bathrooms, and there are very few interior locks. Thus, U.S. homes have a tendency to reflect individualistic values while Mexican homes tend to reflect values that are collectivistic.

Psychological boundaries can be defined is as the expectation of space around you in an empty elevator or movie theatre. How can you feel when someone sits right next to you on a park bench, whenever there are a number of other parks benches free? Crowded conditions in cities, such as Hong Kong, Mumbai and Bangkok ensure it is extremely hard for people to experience privacy even as we know it in the U.S. Privacy itself can be deemed offensive in a few cultures who value a far more communal-collectivistic way of living. Some languages have nonexistent or at minimum completely different terms for the expression of privacy, indicating the minimal or different importance. This concept plays within the lives of the people sharing this language.

Together, these three forms of spatial boundaries are invisible, yet we feel violated and uncomfortable when our boundaries are not respected. Cross-culturally this can lead to some confusion and discomfort – it is hard to respect a boundary which you can not see consequently they aren't aware is there.

Baseline Behaviors

The word baseline measurement can refer to a measurement of every problem be it a child's behavior problems or an ill that is social one's community. When it is comes to a child who is acting out, however, a baseline measurement relates to the start measurement of a behavior.

Say, as an example that child with Attention Deficit Hyperactivity Disorder (ADHD) repeatedly blurts out answers in class. The baseline measurement would often assess how the kid participates in this behavior. An educator is who observes the child determines, which he has these outbursts at the least 11 times each day.

How Baseline of Behavior Works

This baseline of behavior is measured before an intervention is begun. The kid's teacher or another faculty member would measure the baseline rate of this student's off-task behavior before implementing a behavior modification system designed is to increase the student's on-task behavior. The baseline measurement, when compared with later measurements after the intervention, gives a starting point to measure how effective the intervention is.

The teacher might give the child some strategies to stop screaming out answers in class in the case of the child with ADHD. The teacher might try behavior reinforcement that is positive. For example, each and every time the child raises his hand before giving the teacher an answer, she could reward the little one in some manner, such as for instance allowing him to be her helper when she passes out papers towards the students in class or giving him extra minutes of free reading time.

After using these strategies to cut down in the student's negative behaviors, the teacher would yet again measure how often the child blurts out answers instead of waiting to be called on in class. After using behavior modification strategies, the teacher finds that the little one now only blurts out answers in class about five times a day. This lets the educator realize that her intervention plan is working.

If the child continued to blurt out answers 11 times per day, the same amount he did when she took the baseline measurement of his behavior, the teacher would realize that she has to show up with an unusual intervention approach to correct the little one's behavior.

How to Proceed When a Behavior Modification Plan Fails

Teachers and parents are should think about alternatives when a behavior modification plan goes awry. In the place of using reinforcement that is positive to cut back the sheer number of outbursts the little one with ADHD has in class, possibly the child also needs to face negative consequences for his outbursts. The teacher may determine that other modifications might need to be manufactured to assist the student's behavior problems.

Moving the little one away from a particular student may help if it is determined that the classmate is egging the child on. Or simply the little one is seated at the back of the classroom and feels that shouting may be the best way for him to be heard. A school psychologist or counselor are could probably provide more insight into the basis of the child's behavior problems.

Changing Attitudes by Changing Behavior

That we can often predict people's behaviors if we know their thoughts and their feelings about the attitude object. You might be surprised to find that our actions also have an influence on our thoughts and feelings. Although, it might not have surprised you to hear. It makes sense that if I love strawberry jam, I'll buy it because my thoughts and feelings about a product influence my behavior, but it will my attitudes toward orange marmalade be more positive it instead of jam if I decide for whatever reason to buy?

As it happens that when we participate in a behavior and the one that we had not expected that people might have, our thoughts and feelings toward that behavior will likely change particularly. This may not seem intuitive, however, it represents another illustration of the way the principles of social psychology in this full case, the principle of attitude consistency lead us in order to make predictions that wouldn't otherwise be that obvious.

Self-Perception Involves Inferring Our Beliefs from Our Behaviors

Men and women have an interest that is avid understanding the factors that cause behavior, both theirs as well as others, and performing this allows us to meet the important goals of other-concern and self-concern. If we can better understand how and exactly why one other people all around us act how they do, then we're going to have a much better potential for avoiding harm from others and a significantly better potential for getting that other individuals to cooperate with and like us. And we can better work to keep that behavior in line with our preferred plans and goals if we have a better idea of understanding the causes of our own behavior.

In some cases, people may be unsure about their attitudes toward different attitude objects.

Perhaps the effects have been experienced by you of self-perception. Have you ever found yourself becoming more convinced about an argument you were making as you heard yourself making it? Or do you ever realize how thirsty you really need to have been as you quickly drank a glass that is big of? Research has shown that self-perception occurs regularly plus in many different domains. For instance, Gary Wells and Richard Petty (1980) found that those who were asked to shake their heads up and down rather than sideways while reading arguments favoring or opposing tuition increases at their school ended up agreeing with all the arguments more. Daryl Bem (1965) found that when people were told through the experimenter to say that one cartoons were funny, they ended up actually finding those cartoons funnier. It appears in such cases that individuals looked at their very own behavior: that they must agree with the arguments and like the cartoon if they moved their head up and down or said that the cartoons were funny, they figured.

The Experience of Cognitive Dissonance can Attitude that is Create Change

There were in the beginning relatively small discrepancies between self-concept and behavior are beginning to snowball, plus they are needs to have more affective consequences. Joachim is realizing that he's in big trouble—the inconsistencies between his attitudes that are prior the importance of schoolwork along with his behavior are creating some significant threats to his positive self-esteem. That we see as inconsistent, such as when we fail to live up to our own expectations, is called cognitive dissonance (Cooper, 2007; Festinger, 1957; Harmon-Jones & Mills, 1999), as we saw in our discussion of self-awareness theory, this discomfort that occurs when we behave in ways. The discomfort of cognitive dissonance is experience as pain and showing up in an integral part of the mind that is particularly sensitive to pain—the cingulate that is anterior (van Veen, Krug, Schooler, & Carter, 2009).

Leon Festinger and J. Merrill Carlsmith (1959) conducted an important study designed to demonstrate the extent to which behaviors that are discrepant from our initial beliefs can create cognitive dissonance and that can influence attitudes. University students took part in an experiment for which they certainly were asked to focus on an activity which was incredibly boring (such as turning pegs on a peg board) and lasted for an hour that is full. That he could use some help persuading the next person that the task was going to be interesting and enjoyable after they had finished the task, the experimenter explained that the assistant who normally helped convince people to participate in the study was unavailable. The experimenter explained so it would be far more convincing if a fellow student as opposed to the experimenter delivered this message and asked the participant if he will be willing to do in order to it. Thus, together with his request the experimenter induced the participants to lie in regards to the task to a different student and all sorts of the participants consented to do this.

The manipulation that is experimental the amount of money, the students were paid to tell the lie. Half of the students were offered a payment that is large $20 for telling the lie, whereas the other half were offered only a tiny payment ($1) for telling the lie. After the participants had told the lie, an interviewer asked every one of them just how much they had enjoyed the job they had performed earlier into the experiment., "Employment of Task," Festinger and Carlsmith found that the students who had been paid $20 for saying the tasks had been enjoyable rated the task as very boring, which indeed. On the other hand, the students who had been paid only $1 for telling the lie changed their attitude toward the task and rated it as a lot more interesting.

Festinger explained the linkage between this study when it is comes to consistency and inconsistency among cognitions. He hypothesized that some thoughts may be dissonant, when you look at the sense that they made us feel good that they made us feel uncomfortable, while other thoughts were more consonant, in the sense. He argued that people may feel a distressing state (which he called cognitive dissonance) once they have many dissonant thoughts—for instance, involving the indisputable fact that (a) they are smart and decent people and (b) they nevertheless told a lie to a different student just for a payment that is small.

Festinger argued that the people in the experiment who had been induced to lie for only $1 experienced more cognitive dissonance than the folks who were paid $20 due to the fact latter group had a strong external justification for having done it whereas the former failed to. The folks within the $1 condition, Festinger argued, needed to convince themselves that that the job was actually interesting to cut back the dissonance they certainly were experiencing.

Tricks to be a Better Body Language reader

Body language provides an amazing level of information on which other individuals are planning once you know what things to seek out, and that hasn't desired to read people's minds sooner or later?

You already pick up on more body gestures cues than you're consciously aware of. Research has shown that only 7% of communication is based on the actual words we say. As for the rest, 38% arises from tone of voice plus the remaining 55% originates from body language. Learning how to be alert to also to interpret that 55% will give you a leg up with other people.

When you're working hard and doing anything you can to achieve your goals, anything that can give you a benefit is powerful and will streamline the journey to success.

TalentSmart has tested significantly more than a million people and found that the upper echelons of top performance are filled up with folks who are high in emotional intelligence (90% of top performers, to be exact). These people understand the power that unspoken signals have in communication, plus they monitor body gestures accordingly.

The next occasion you're in a gathering (as well as on a romantic date or playing with your kids), watch out for these cues:

1. Crossed arms and legs signal resistance to your thinking. Crossed arms and legs are physical barriers that suggest the other person just isn't available to what you're saying. Even if they're smiling and involved with a conversation that is pleasant their body gestures tells the storyline. Gerard I. Nierenberg and Henry H. Calero videotaped are more than 2,000 negotiations for a book they wrote on reading body gestures, and not just a single one ended in an agreement when one of the parties had their legs crossed while negotiating. Psychologically, crossed legs or arms signal that any particular one is mentally, emotionally, and physically blocked removed from what's in the front of them. It's not intentional, but it is explain why it is so revealing.

2. Real smiles crinkle the eyes. With regards to smiling, the mouth can lie however the optical eyes can't. Genuine smiles reach the eyes, crinkling the skin to create crow's feet around them. People often smile to full cover up what they're really thinking and feeling, so that the time that is next want to know if someone's smile is genuine, search for crinkles at the corners of the eyes. If they aren't there, that smile is hiding something.

3. Copying the body language is a good thing. Perhaps you have been in a meeting with someone, and noticed that every right time you cross or uncross your legs, they do exactly the same? Or maybe they lean their head exactly the same way you're talking as yours when?

That's actually a sign that is good. Mirroring body gestures are one thing we do unconsciously when a bond is felt by us with the other individual. It's a sign that is the conversation certainly going well and that the other party is receptive to your message. This knowledge could be especially useful when you're negotiating, as it teaches you what each other is actually taking into consideration the deal.

4. Posture tells the whole story. Have you ever seen a person walk into a room, and immediately, you've got known that they were the one in control? That effect is basically about body language, and often includes a posture that is erect gestures made out of the palms facing down and open and expansive gestures as a whole. The mind is hardwired to equate power utilizing the number of space people take up. Standing up straight together is with your shoulders back show a power position; it appears to maximize the quantity of space you fill. Slouching, on the other hand, it is the outcome of collapsing your form; it appears to use up less space and projects less power. Maintaining good posture commands respect and promotes engagement, whether you're a leader or perhaps not.

5. Eyes that lie.Most of us probably grew up hearing, "Look me in the eye when you speak to me!" Our parents were operating under the assumption you're lying to them, and they were right to an extent that it's tough to hold someone's gaze when, but that is such common knowledge that folks will frequently deliberately hold eye contact so as to cover the fact up that they're lying. The issue is that most of them overcompensate and hold eye contact towards the true point that it feels uncomfortable. An average of, Americans hold eye contact for seven to ten seconds, longer when we're listening than when we're talking. If you're talking with someone whose stare is making you squirm especially if they're very still and

unblinkingsomething is up and additionally they may be lying you.

6. Raised eyebrows signal discomfort. There are three main emotions that create your eyebrows go up: surprise, worry, and fear. Try raising your eyebrows when you're having a relaxed conversation that is casual a friend. It is hard to complete, isn't it? If an individual who is conversing with you raises their eyebrows therefore the topic is one that would logically cause surprise, worry, or fear, there is something else taking place.

7. Exaggerated signals that are nodding about approval. They nod excessively, this means that they are worried about what you think of them or that you doubt their ability to follow your instructions when you're telling someone something and.

8. A clenched jaw signals stress.A clenched jaw, a tightened neck, or a furrowed brow are all signs and symptoms of stress. Regardless of what the person is saying, they are signs and symptoms of considerable discomfort. The conversation might be delving into something they're anxious about, or their mind could be elsewhere and they're centering on the plain thing that's stressing them out. The important thing is always to watch out for that mismatch between what the individual says and what their body that is tense language telling you.

Chapter 2
The Limbic Brain

What is a limbic system? Well, it is a collection of structures when you look at the brain, lots of of these structures play an important role in regulating emotion. Now, something that gets type of confusing whenever you talk about the limbic system is the fact that experts can not actually agree with what structures make within the entire limbic system. So for the purposes, I will address a few of the most important structures and ones that everybody more or less agrees are part of the system that is limbic. Now, I want to give you a quick overview of what are structures that we're going to talk about before I get going into the nitty-gritty so to speak. In addition to way from these structures are through this little cartoon here. This will be a hippopotamus in which he's wearing a hat. Now, why is this really hippopotamus wearing this stylish hat? Well, this really is my way of remembering in the four most crucial the different parts of the limbic system when it comes down to emotion. So we see a hippopotamus here. I'll write "hippo." And he is seen by us wearing a hat. I'll write "hat." Now, with this is to be a mnemonic, this has to be something helpful. Therefore the reason I think for this is they are the four main structures of this system that is limbic it comes down to emotion. So "HAT" stands for Hypothalamus, "A" for Amygdala, "T" for Thalamus, and "hippo," short for hippocampus.

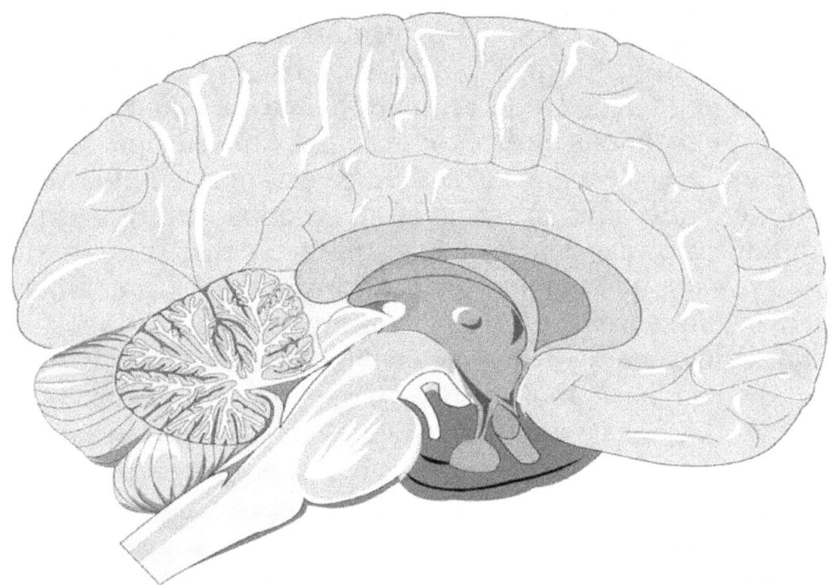

And these are actually the four structures that I'd like to speak about. And everything you see here is my attempt that is best at drawing the limbic system. Now, limbic system structures are sit on the surface of the brain stem. And also this may be the brain stem.

And you will imagine this while the bottom that is very of the brain, and listed here is the spinal cord coming from it. And the cord that is spinal most of the way down the back to regarding your tailbone. Now, the limbic system is these structures up here, which can be drawn in bright colors. Now to orient you to this diagram, this is just what you would see in the event that you pulled off such as the top section of your brain, to create the cortex. And it's facing in this direction. Quite simply, while this is not anatomically correct, let's say your eyes are here, your nose is here, and your mouth is here now. Again, it is not anatomically correct. But this you can observe may be the front, and also this is the back. Therefore I style of drew it at an angle so that you style of get a idea that is 3D. So let's remove this and return to speaking is about the anatomical structures. This thing is a blue is called a thalamus. You are also actually have two of those, one here and something on its reverse side. So your thalamus functions as like a sensory relay station, meaning what exactly that you see, hear, taste, touch, all of these senses you've got come through your nerves and ultimately land in your thalamus. While the thalamus directs these senses into the appropriate areas in the cortex, and also other aspects of the mind. And I also mentioned this in terms of an emotion lecture because emotions are very contingent on the items that you see, the things that you touch and hear. And you might have noticed there is one sense that I didn't mention. And that is a sense of smell. Additionally the feeling of smell really is the sense that is only you have that truly bypasses this thalamus. And instead, this has its very own private relay station that, when considering from the nose, it goes to a certain area within the brain. And therefore area of the brain actually happens to be very close to the areas that regulate emotion, which explains why sometimes certain scents can evoke extremely effective memories and provide you with back once again to a certain moment in time. But in terms of emotion, I mentioned thalamus because of how the senses play an role that is important your emotions. Now, you notice here there are these two structures that are purple. And also this is called an amygdala. Now, the amygdala might be called the aggression center. And experiments have actually shown that if you stimulate the amygdala, you can produce feelings of anger and violence, as well as fear and anxiety. I will put "stimulate" and represent it as dark green plus sign, and that means you stimulate the amygdala. It is evokes feelings of anger, violence, fear, and anxiety. Having said that, if you've destroyed your amygdala and I also'll represent destruction as a bad sign-- in the event that you destroy the amygdala, it may cause an extremely mellowing effect. I'll write "mellow." And also this mellowing effect in the context of a destroyed amygdala was actually noted by a psychologist named Dr. Kluver and a neurosurgeon because of the true name of Dr. Bucy. And I mention Kluver and Bucy because in medicine there's actually a syndrome referred to as Kluver-Bucy syndrome. And that is when there is a destruction that is bilateral of amygdale, and "bilateral" means both. And you put things in their mouth a lot; also hypersexuality; as well as disinhibited behavior if you have bilateral destruction of the amygdalas, that can result in certain symptoms that are often seen, like hyperorality, which means. And disinhibited behavior is when you ignore social conventions. You are able to act very impulsively, that is you do not consider the risks of one's behavior. So you do dangerous, reckless things. So that's Kluver-Bucy syndrome. And that is again whenever you destroy both sides of one's amygdalas. Therefore the real way I remember this is I think if you stimulate the amygdalas, that will cause fear and anxiety. And people who possess anxiety disorders or experiencing an anxiety attack sometimes are given a medication known as a benzodiazepine. Generally, they are called "benzos", and these benzodiazepines medications function pharmacologically nearly the same as alcohol. And think about what the results are when anyone consumes too alcohol that is much. Sometimes the truth is these types of behaviors. This thing is hyperorality, you might be eating a lot. You may have hypersexuality, and needless to say, you obtain disinhibited behavior. Think of the person with a lamp shade to their head. They are ignoring certain conventions that are social regarding the aftereffect of alcohol. To make certain that's how I recall the result of stimulating versus destroying the amygdala. And this structure that is green that you curving round the thalamus is known as the hippocampus. Therefore the hippocampus plays a key role in forming new memories. What it can is it helps to convert your short-term memory. I'll abbreviate it as "STM" it helps convert that short-term memory into your long-term memory. And I also mention that in this conversation since when you think back on the memories, be it short-term memory or memory that is long-term these memories can evoke emotions as well. So that is the hippocampus, which is an important structure in forming long-term memories. And people with injury to this area, they usually have difficulty forming memories that are new. So everything is that they experience just basically fades away. So what now's interesting about this is if your hippocampus is destroyed, you still have your old memories intact while you can't form new memories. So your long-term memory functions just fine.

Now lastly, this structure that is orange, this orange structure could be the hypothalamus, and "hypo" means below. So hypothalamus is underneath the thalamus, and here's the thalamus, it is below it, so that is where it gets its name from. Plus the hypothalamus is truly an extremely structure that is tiny. And also this diagram here really exaggerates the dimensions of the hypothalamus. The hypothalamus is really so small so it actually accocunts for lower than 1% of the total level of your brain. It is in regards to the size of kidney bean. And the hypothalamus plays a role that is incredible regulating so many functions within your body. But also for our purposes, we are dealing with the limbic system structures when it comes to emotion. So when it is comes down to emotion, the hypothalamus you are able to think about as regulating the autonomic nervous system. I'll abbreviate it as "ANS". In addition to autonomic system that is nervous can think of as fight or flight versus rest and digest. Now, I will discuss this further in a different video, but right now, it is just think of it as regulating the autonomic nervous system. It is performing this by controlling the urinary tract, by triggering the production of hormones into your bloodstream, plus some of these hormones which are triggered to release are plain things such as epinephrine or norepinephrine. Epinephrine is clearly very popularly as it is known as adrenaline, if you ever think about the phrase like "a lot of adrenaline pumping through your veins," that's actually being regulated because of the hypothalamus. Your hypothalamus is also involved with regulating other basic drives, like hunger, thirst, sleep, sex. However, in terms of emotion, I believe it is most crucial to note that it can regulates the autonomic system that is nervous that fight or flight or rest and digest response. It is the system that is limbic. These are the four basic structures, the thalamus, the amygdala, the hippocampus, as well as the hypothalamus. Therefore, it is essential structures that associated with limbic system.

Functions of the Limbic System

The system that is limbic as a control center for conscious and unconscious functions, regulating most of what your body does. In some ways, it is connect with your brain to body, bridging the gap between psychological and physiological experiences. The limbic system triggers a physical response to emotional experiences such as fear for example, by activating the fight or flight response. The limbic system acts as a control center for conscious and unconscious functions, regulating much of what the human body does.

1. Reward, Motivation, and Addiction

Research implies that feelings of motivation and reward originate into the ventral tegmental area (VTA), a group of neurons that connects towards the nucleus accumbens within the basal ganglia. Those neurons are release dopamine, a neurotransmitter that supports feelings of enjoyment.

In a healthy brain, dopamine helps people feel motivated to learn, meet new people, or try new experiences. Drug and alcohol abuse, however, can transform the functioning regarding the system that is limbic. Drugs act are on dopamine, and in the long run, the release of dopamine can be addictive. With the passage of time the addiction can be deplete the brain's dopamine stores, which makes it tough to feel pleasure without drugs. This is why many people with addictions find slight relief from activities that were once pleasurable.

2. Emotional Responses

The amygdala and hippocampus work together to modify emotions, especially that is evolutionarily"old that play a task in survival love for one's children, aggression, fear, and anxiety.

Together, those two organs also assist the brain to interpret the content that is emotional of. The amygdala assigns emotional meaning to memories and helps mental performance form fear-based memories. The hippocampus helps form memories that are sensory that are memories connected with sensory input. Once the smell of an apple that is crisp warm beach air brings back memories of a long-ago summer, the hippocampus is responsible.

3. Fight or Flight

The limbic systems can help the body react to intense emotions of fear and anger by activating the battle or flight response. This response can be sometimes called the fight, flight, or freeze response, and it is thanks to evidence that is new the role of freezing in reaction to danger.

When the amygdala perceives a threat, it activates the system that is limbic prepare to handle the threat. The adrenal glands release hormones are such as for instance epinephrine that raise blood pressure levels and heart rate, improve blood circulation to muscles and organs, and breathing rate that is elevate.

When you look at the short-term, the fight or flight response may be life-saving. As time passes, however, chronic stress can activate the limbic system in a fashion that damages your body. Long-term release of epinephrine as well as other hormones may damage blood vessels, cause blood that is high, and alter appetite.

4. Memory

Both the amygdala and hippocampus help the brain form memories that are new store those memories, retrieve them, and also make sense of their emotional content. The hippocampus is very essential in long-term memory formation. In addition, supports spatial memory and reasoning that is spatial.

5. Hormones Affecting Automatic Functions

Hormones are the body's chemical messengers, sending an indication from a single area to the body as a result to environmental input and other information.

The hypothalamus releases hormones that play a role in a wide range of emotions, including pain, hunger, thirst, pleasure, sexual feelings, anger, and aggression. It can also help the human body maintain a situation of homeostasis by regulating the autonomic system that is nervous. A few examples of the function include:

Getting information from the vagus nerve about blood pressure and exactly how full the stomach is. By using this information, it releases chemicals that regulate appetite and blood circulation pressure.

Gathering information through the reticular formation associated with brain stem about temperature and then using that to manage the body's response to heat or cold.

Regulating the body's internal clock, the circadian rhythm, based on light, darkness, along with other input that is sensory.

6. Attention and Learning

The limbic system helps the body learn and remember information by helping the brain form new memories. It also plays a role in regulating attention that is cognitive. Research suggests, for example, that the cingulate gyrus focuses the brain's attention on emotionally significant events. The anterior cingulate may also help with conscious tries to control emotions.

A bit of research suggests people who have attention-deficit hyperactivity (ADHD) have enlarged hippocampi. This can be the body's attempt to pay for problems with the hippocampus's ability to manage attention.

The brain makes new neurons from stem cells when you look at the hippocampus, suggesting the hippocampus in addition to feelings and memories it supports can change with new experiences. This ability of the hippocampus to improve with time supports the ability to learn things that are new. Research from the brains of men and women with Alzheimer's along with other dementias has found the hippocampus is attacked by the disease. This could explain why dementia so quickly compromises the capability to learn new things, even as long-ago memories remain intact.

The limbic system is dynamic, changing with input from a person's environment. Experience changes this brain that is important, and therefore may help explain why people's psychological and physiological experiences change as time passes. Therapy, too, may change the limbic system by training the brain to process information differently, assigning new emotions to old memories or supporting a customer in managing chronic stress.

Many disorders can harm the system that is limbic. Memories and experiences matter, too. Therapy might help people add up among these experiences, ameliorate some outcomes of chronic stress, help a person better manage their emotions, and potentially even reduce the chance of stress-related disorders such as for example heart problems.

Chapter 3:
Arm Crossing:

Arms, while they connect with non-verbal meaning, are like shields. They can block and shank ideas from entering as well as they possibly can drive back swords and arrows. Using the arms over the physical body in a fold is much like cutting off use of our core where our heart and lungs are present.

Arm Crossing With Clenched Fists: Happens by crossing the arms and clenching the fists underneath them. This posture indicates defensive hostility and anger nearing outright aggression.

Arm behaviour that is freezing A fear driven response that reduces or eliminates movements by the arms. In kids, it could indicate the current presence of abusive parents or relatives, as well as in adults indicates that a stressful or stimuli that are emotional present.

Arm gripping or gripped crossed arms: Happens since the person grabs each arm with all the opposite hand as they cross their arms. It symbolizes tension and it is common for folks waiting around for bad news or looking forward to a dentist appointment. It really is similar to other types of self-hugging as it protects the physical body from exposure and provides comfort. This posture shows both negativity and restraint, and therefore you were ready and expecting to face a negative outcome and isn't going to relax until that news comes.

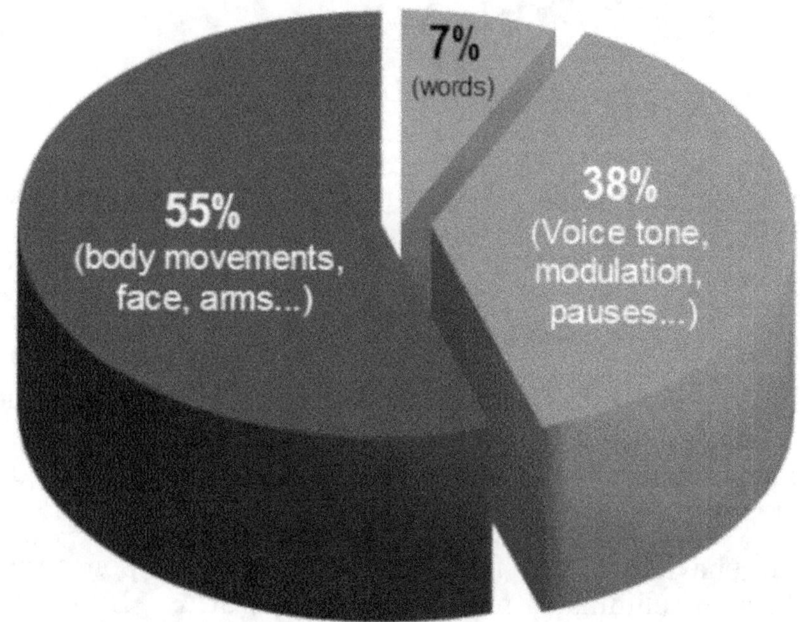

Arm Over Shoulder: a style of hug gesture done by tossing the arm over the back of another. It is a friendly type gesture signifying camaraderie.

Arms Forward: a sign which has a context-specific message. Having the arms forward can mean that any particular one wishes to hug, to battle if fists are clenched, to repel in the event that palms are facing vertical toward a begging or opponent if palms are turned upward.

Arms up posture: A gravity-defying cue that is nonverbal in triumph or victory such as for instance winning a match or scoring a goal. It really is done usually quickly and short in duration where in actuality the arms are thrust stiffly upward into the sky to be able to draw as attention that is much the victor as you can.

Arm Twister that is handshakeArm: in the middle of an ordinary handshake the hand is twisted underneath in to the submissive palm up position. A person who does this is totally committed to being on top and dominating.

Arm withdrawal: once the arms are pulled inward toward the body as opposed to away. A lack is indicated by it of agreement or a big change of opinion.

Self Hugging

Self-hugging can be achieved by grabbing both arms across the body, in extreme situations every single shoulder, or by clasping one arm onto the arm, elbow or shoulder in the opposite side (Partial Arm Cross or Incomplete Arm Cross). On occasion, the hands will pacify by rubbing the shoulders.

Self hugging is a cue signaling the need to be comforted.

How exactly to Use it: Self hugging replaces the necessity for the coziness of another. Thus, it really is to be properly used when one does not need to rely on the proper care of others, but when one still wishes to get a caring touch. The cue is typically perceived in a negative light so must be used only in occasions when one is not concerned with appearing vulnerable. Self-hugging in a business meeting, for instance, is ill advised. However, hugging the self is perfectly acceptable into the privacy of your own home, or when enclosed by close friends or family where our company is generally permitted to exhibit our softer side.

Verbal Translation: "I'm awkward and self conscious so I'm wrapping myself up in a self embrace to give care and comfort as my parents provided in my opinion in my youth."

Cue In Action: it had been the very first time away from her parents at camp and a lot of regarding the other girls were getting along fine and did actually know one another from last year. Autumn was left in a self hug by herself in line and looked awkwardly at the others while wrapping her arms around herself. She was reminded associated with care she got from her parents.

Meaning and/or Motivation: Hugging one's self is actually defensive and a body position that is closed. Individuals who hold this posture exclaim that they're cold, but in reality, the sensation that is cold from feeling awkward, timid, self conscious, or distress. Self-hugs, done in this real way, remind us of this care and comfort we received from dad and mom, so when found in adulthood, indicate a necessity for reassurance.

In adulthood, self-hugging is located when we're insecure, self-conscious, defensive or afraid, generally. As it's generally not appropriate to show vulnerability to others and seek support from other's we instead hug ourselves discreetly. The body that is astute reader will notice this signal and step up to really make the carrier regarding the signal feel much better.

How to Spot Insecurity in The Rich and Famous

The Brookes study provides some clues, then, into what makes up the personality that is narcissistic. It may offer insight into the real methods for you to interpret those things of narcissistic friends, coworkers, or partners through examining their insecurities:

The Person that is Insecure to Make you Feel Insecure Yourself

It typically around a specific person or type of person when you start to question your own self-worth, is? Is the fact that individual always broadcasting his or her strengths? In the event, that you don't feel insecure in general, but only around certain people, it's likely they're projecting their insecurities onto you.

The Person that is Insecure to Showcase his or her Accomplishments

You don't necessarily have to feel insecure around anyone to conclude that inferiority has reached the heart of the behavior. Those who are constantly bragging about their lifestyle that is great elite education, or their fantastic children might be doing this to convince themselves that they really do have worth.

The Person that is Insecure the "Humblebrag" much too often

The humblebrag is a brag disguised as a self-derogatory statement. You've all seen these on Facebook, as when an acquaintance complains about most of the travel she's got to take (as a result of the need for her job), or all the time he has got to spend watching his kids play (and, because of the way, win) hockey games. (The "Facebook gloat" is a bold-faced brag which is much easier to spot but might easily have the same roots.)

The Insecure Person Frequently Complains that Things aren't Good Enough

People full of inferiority want to show what high standards they have. You might label them as snobs, but as much that they really are better than you as you realize they're putting on a act, it may be hard to shake the feeling. What they're attempting to do, you could rightly suspect, is to proclaim their high standards as a means of asserting that not only are they much better than everyone else, but that they hold themselves to a far more rigorous set of self-assessment criteria.

Returning to the Brookes study, there might be aspects of overt narcissism that actually do work with helping the feel that is insecure confident in their abilities. However, this comes in the price of making everyone else feel less confident. I wouldn't recommend bolstering your sense of self-efficacy by putting down everyone else.

Being able to detect insecurity into the people near you will allow you to shake the self-doubts off that many people appear to enjoy fostering inside you. Taking the high road, rather than giving into this self-doubts, may also help you foster feelings of fulfillment both you know and care about in yourself and in the insecure people.

Chapter 4

We quite often can get much more info from seated variations of leg positions than from standing ones mainly because when we sit our legs can be useless we don't possess anything specific to accomplish with them, and these are the exact moments when we can quickly identify all kinds of temperaments, as soon as the legs have nothing else to accomplish but to leak nonverbal information.

Indications of Interest

The first selection of sitting leg gestures I wish to mention are the Indicators of great interest. I already talked about pointing with feet when you look at the articles that are previous I only mention it again to see that it relates to sitting positions as well.

In sitting scenarios, it's actually a lot more obvious, as anybody who ever got stuck at the final end associated with the sofa alone can tell.

Another as a type of orienting when seated will come in the design regarding the knee point - when one leg is folded underneath the other additionally the direction is marked by the knee of attention.

Whenever we talk about sexual interest, expressive man has the "crotch display" - sitting with all the legs wide apart to signal virility and availability. These men usually signal which they feel dominant, strong and also a little smug - this position takes a lot of space and exposes their groin for the whole world to see. Of course, it can easily offend others (or on the contrary - entice them) So while it's good to show confidence if you do not like to annoy anyone - mind the exact distance betwixt your knees.

Women - Shoe play

Females have something a little more sophisticated - the shoe play: Although the shoe dangling off their foot, they remove and enter their foot to and fro into it. Such display can drive men crazy, given that it reminds them for the repeated action during sex.

Leg over Leg

Crossing one leg over the other is a very popular way of sitting and it has many variations. Women, as an example, like the leg that is tight to emphasize their legs features. Men often use the 4 figure sitting cross leg positions.

The leg over leg "standard position" is generally through with the dominant leg at the top. While crossing the legs may indicate a closed and reserved attitude, it's not always so. It offers a lot to do with habit and comfort. In an uncomfortable chair with no armrests, it may be far more convenient to sit in crossed position and also to lay the hands on the thighs.

For completely another reason, we adopt the crossed position that is sitting we're cold.

Women have more trouble than man sitting in uncrossed positions mainly because their clothing often doesn't allow that (mini-skirts) or because it's an established habit.

Leg Stretch

A rather display that is sexual the legs females utilize extremely effectively may be the leg stretch. Sitting with one leg crossed over the other stretches the muscles and reveal smooth sexy legs.

Women can very quickly use this flirting gesture to draw attention, particularly if she actually is crossing and uncrossing them frequently (like within the famous scene of Sharon Stone in" Basic Instinct" as an example)

Crossing legs in sexy fashion

4 Figure Leg Cross

The 4 figure sitting position involves resting one foot over the thigh regarding the other, and it's really usually much more comfortable for men as compared to tight leg cross. It's a popular male leg cross, though it can be seen in some assertive and extrovert women too.

In an unconscious manner, it exposes the genitals and takes more space a confident, self assured and posture that is even cocky. Additionally it is a way to show competitive and challenging attitude towards the others, as though to express "I'm not impressed, try harder"

Both Feet on the floor

Placing both feet on the ground with a "standard" gap between them is the most basic, normal position it is possible to think about. The same as with hands-to-the-sides posture it functions as a neutral but powerful kick off point. It's stable, focused and lacks any other nonverbal "noise" - so it's very effective for formal and focused conversations.

I must add that placing both feet on the floor is a lot less common for females, who prefer the crossed leg position, either because they wear skirts or since they socially taught to sit like that.

Tension and Readiness to Action

Tension can wear many forms in body gestures, and it's easily exposed once we sit. Whenever we're sit we're idle get lost in our thoughts after which our thoughts that are negative through unconscious motions. Some examples that are notable

Locking Ankles

Entwining the ankles is generally a signal of self restraint; It's much like biting the lip, holding oneself from slipping another word. It can hide emotions of anger, frustration, fear or other emotion that is negative.

Men will usually lock their ankles underneath the chair and their hands will clamp into fists or grab tightly the armchairs. Females will usually close both legs and turn them to your relative side while their hands rest on their knees or even their side.

The Clasp

The guarded person will not only cross his legs but will also clasp his hands around them to reinforce his position. Like a clamp there's no way he's likely to open up easily. It's a really common posture to observe in subways where strangers sit in front of each other.

Keeping the Knees Together

This one is a tricky one, because whilst it can show a reserved and timid mindset, many females taught to stay this way for obvious reasons (skirts) and adhere to this habit throughout their lives. But men have no excuse of employing such display - also it's quite rare to observe such an obvious display of insecurity.

Covering Gentiles

Within the crotch can be carried out by holding the legs tight and\or crossing the hands on it.

Exactly like spreading the legs yells "Look at me! I am here! I'm fertile and powerful" so within the same area sends the contrary message "I am unsure, tiny and timid, please don't hurt me."

Exactly like Adam and Eve had leaves to pay for their gentiles once they felt ashamed - we mimic such behavior even when we're fully clothed. Again, this gesture applies more to men, because females in general avoid resting or touching their hands around their crotch.

Feeling at Home

In informal relaxed circumstances the variations of different leg positions is huge, most likely it really is informal - everyone can sit however s\he wants. Most informal positions have the tendency to be spread out and take strange forms.

Placing your feet on a table is the"feel that is ultimate" posture - What's more relaxed than spreading the legs up, putting the hands behind the pinnacle and enjoy life, right?

Sitting on to the floor

I won't go into detail for each form, because their meanings can be the exact same - they all are generally as relaxed and comfortable as you can.

I do want to mention the leg spread forward given that it but could really affront certain people due to its idle image. Serious and situation that is sensitive attention and readiness, which means this lazy posture is a sign that whatever happening isn't important or interesting enough for the person who adopts it. The eastern posture that is sitting even more suited for such cases.

Instead, adopt the "eastern sitting" - sitting on folded legs. It's still informal but shows more involvement than previous one.

Legs and Emotions

Our feet and legs, often neglected into the scholarly study of body language, transmit plenty of valuable information about that which we are sensing, thinking, and feeling. We pay so much awareness of the face along with other parts of the body, that we forget the significance of this vital appendages. The feet and legs are the most accurate part of our body it's a mistake most of us make and we shouldn't because in many ways. They reflect our true emotions and intentions, in real time, unlike our face along with other areas of the body, and so they can be instrumental into the detection of deception. Over an incredible number of years, our system that is limbic made that our feet and legs reacted instantly to any threat or concern; their reliability has assured, to some extent, our survival.

Someone walks as much as us late during the night while we are at the ATM machine and our legs tighten up, and our feet orient towards a getaway route, preparing us to flee if required. Within the in an identical way our limbic brain tells our feet to not walk too close to the edge of the canyon, so we don't. We crosses our legs whenever we are comfortable when you look at the elevator, yet when a combined group of dodgy strangers enter, we immediately uncross our legs so we are able to flee if required. We are speaking with a good friend and suddenly we notice one of many feet is pointed across the street. You should not ask, they have to go, they've been running late for an appointment. Wish to know if a couple talking in the hallway you to join them like you or want? If their feet don't relocate to welcome both you and they only rotate during the hips, keep on walking just by. When a relationship is turning sour, there will be less and less foot contact. They may hold hands in public places but their feet simply avoid one another. These are illustration of limbic reactions, reflected in the feet and legs, to situations, feelings, and intentions. They've been very timely and accurate.

Similarly, a kid can be sitting yourself down to eat, but they stretch to reach the floor from a high chair even when he has not yet finished with his meal if he wants to go out and play, notice how his feet sway, how. You can test to keep him set up but he will wiggle along with his feet will turn to the nearest desired exit—an accurate reflection of where his feet in which he really wants to go. This will be an intention cue therefore we have several that individuals use to reflect our needs to make a move.

Because our feet and legs are so honest, I place special emphasis in what they communicate while assessing for deception. Most people focus on the face, but unfortunately, our faces have become proficient at deceit. From an early on age we are told, "don't make that face," even though we hate what we are increasingly being fed. As we get older it continues, we put on a "party face" during the request of our significant other or we smile since the culture we come from requires it. And we feel or think with our faces for social harmony so we fake what. We also do it to guard ourselves from being discovered whenever we are being dishonest. Our feet and legs, since they're necessary for survival, make no such concessions.

What Every Body is Saying," "Nervousness, stress, fear, anxiety, caution, boredom, restlessness, happiness, joy, hurt, shyness, coyness, humility, awkwardness, confidence, subservience, depression, lethargy, playfulness, sensuality, and anger can all manifest through your own feet and legs." I focused on the feet and legs precisely because they do reveal so much information about what is in the mind and liars think about their facial displays but not their legs and feet, doing interviews in the FBI.

In 25 years observing and cataloging behavior for the FBI, I pointed out that when people commence to lie, they often times distance themselves by standing further away with their torso from you or they point their feet away from you but turn towards you. It looks ok on first inspection however these are distancing behaviors which reveal quite a lot in what is going on inside their brain.

Liars will not emphasize, they know what to state, not the emotions that go using what they've been saying, therefore we see fewer gravity-defying behaviors if they speak. Truthful people have a tendency to defy gravity by rising from the balls of their feet when they are emphasizing a true point or arching their eyebrows. Liars don't do that, because gravity behaviors that are defying limbically derived emotional exclamations we express through our body language which they lack.

When the truth is being told by us our feet tend to take a wider, sturdier stance. The minute we feel insecure in what our company is saying or if perhaps we have been lying, our feet tend to come together. Again, that is a limbic response tethered to the way we feel (insecure) in what is being said. It is reflected in our legs and feet when we aren't mentally sure.

When lying, the deceiver is worried about being detected and that which you may observe is that concern sometimes drives the things I have come to call the "Ankle Quiver." Here the ankle starts to twitch inducing the person to rock the foot sideways backwards and forwards (bottom side to edge of foot). A truthful person has no such have to pacify themselves by this repetitive rocking behavior, but a liar might find such "under the table" behaviors helpful to soothe themselves.

And they are obviously only a few the leg and foot behaviors to notice, look for the one who makes a statement and then does a leg cleanse. By rubbing his hands (sometimes multiple times) at the top of his legs while seated, this pacifies the patient that is deceptive or harboring knowledge that is guilty. This often occurs when very direct, poignant questions are asked, causing a degree that is high of.

Happy Feet

Happy feet are the ones that bounce down and up with joy, point upwards when standing, or seem to have a spring in their step when walking. Other times happy feet are feet that point or move in the direction of something they like.

Just how to Use it: use feet that are happy show others that you're healthy, confident and that good things are happening to you. Happy feet is going to be viewed by others as an indicator of your good fortune. Positive attitudes are transferred through body gestures and keeping your feet in motion shows others that you are prepared for action.

Bluff in poker by bouncing your feet. If folks are attuned, they're going to read your bouncing feet as a genuine indicator of a great hand (even though you don't have one).

Verbal Translation: "I'm happy with joy so my feet that are honest gravity by bouncing, toes rising and pointing."

Cue doing his thing: We always knew it absolutely was time for you to fold. When Kevin had a great poker hand, his feet started bouncing. These people were nearly vibrating the table that is entire.

Meaning and/or Motivation: Throughout our evolution, your own feet carried out more traditional tasks like escaping predators, avoiding hot sand or coals from fire, leaping from slithering snakes or poisonous spiders, or navigating rough rocky river bottoms. Your feet were therefore connected more to the reptilian brain which reacts to stimuli directly instead of contemplating higher order tasks that require planning. This makes your feet that is"honest reliable as clues to fear along with happiness.

Bouncing feet are called "happy feet" and is a high confidence 'tell', indicating that a person is approximately to gain something important. It is very reliable and happens as a direct outcome of having heard or seen something significant this is certainly positive to your person displaying the signal. While high affect happy feet result in the entire body bounce, happy feet may be display in a more subdued way by simply wiggling your feet. Watching for these cues in poker can be a very important tell and save a pile of cash, so be cautious to view because of it.

Legs and feet can become jittery and also fidget when one is bored and wants to go out of. Jittery feet, though, can also be due to energy that is nervous even the results of happiness such as for instance "happy feet." It's the context that will help decide what feet and legs are telling in this kind of body language.

Happy feet are feet that "defy gravity" are an honest indication of joy. When feet are happy they are going to bounce up and down and move the body in several playful ways. Your toes in many cases are extended toward things they like and true point out them. Often the toes will point confidence that is upward demonstrating. This is done by bearing the weight on a single foot and putting the heel down and lifting the toes up.

As we begin to go into detail about various nonverbal communication, beginning with the feet because they're actually the absolute most "honest" area of the body, and also the easiest to read. He attributes this to the proven fact that your feet are often the very first body part to be engaged by the freeze, flight, or fight response that is limbic. This is in direct contrast to the way we are widely used to people that are reading which is from the face down. By understanding how to reverse the method, you shall find it to be much simpler to learn people.

Another reason that the feet will be the most part that is honest of body is that since childhood, many people's efforts to disguise their emotions or intentions have always centered on the face area. Think about some typically common reprimands that are parental "Fix that person," or "At least look happy as soon as your cousins drop by." Many people have given comparatively little attention from their neocortexes with their feet.

1. "Happy feet". Bouncing or wiggling your feet often indicates satisfaction or excitement. Be careful, though; this behavior also can communicate impatience. Like the majority of nonverbal signals, you have to comprehend the behavior in its context. They are sitting while you can't always see someone's feet, this movement will show in their torso or shoulders even when.

2. Feet direction that is shifting. You will often find yourself turning the feet far from things you do not want or like. People will generally control the direction of their head and torso, however their feet will point away from you should they don't want to be speaking with you. This is certainly useful once you approach someone and aren't sure if they genuinely wish to be talking to you. That they dislike something you said, or that they simply need to leave in order to make their next appointment if you are already talking to someone and their foot turns away, it might indicate. Again, calibrate based on context.

3. The knee clasp. When an individual who is places that are sitting on the job his knees (often also shifting his weight forward), he could be prepared to leave.

4. Gravity-defying behaviors. These behaviors indicate happiness or excitement, and include pointing one-foot up

when standing, or just sitting or standing a little taller. The "starter's position," where someone lifts his heel, may indicate interest, increased engagement, or a readiness to go.

5. The leg splay. This is certainly a territorial display, where you spread your feet in an attempt to establish control over a situation. If you want to diffuse a scenario and notice you are standing in this way, bring the feet just a little closer together.

6. Standing leg cross. The direct contrast to the leg splay is crossing your ankles when standing. This indicates that you're very comfortable, anticipating need not freeze or run, which would require the balance of two feet on the floor. Crossing your legs when standing is a great way to put somebody else at ease. Interestingly, individuals will usually cross their legs so that they tilt in direction of the one who they just like the most, or who means they are probably the most comfortable.

7. Seated foot movement. This is actually the opposite of the flight response, and basically communicates, "notice me." The example the author uses is of a woman dangling or perhaps having fun with her shoe.

8. Seated leg cross. The direction of this leg cross often indicates if somebody likes you or what you're saying. In the event, that within the knee is facing you, it is probable they like you or what you are saying; if the inside of the knee is facing away, they might not.

9. Proximity. Also, falling underneath the group of nonverbal foot and leg communication is the distance that folks keep between one another. We have all his or her own level that is comfortable of space, however, when someone steps closer or further away, it provides you a clue about their feelings.

10. Walking style. Based on the author, there are about 40 different varieties of walking. Again, it really is a noticeable change in this behavior that gives you a clue in regards to what someone is feeling.

11. The foot freeze. If somebody happens to be constantly wiggling or moving their foot or leg and then stops (or vice

versa), they could be experiencing stress or any other emotional change.

12. The foot lock. When a person suddenly interlocks his feet when sitting, it really is an indication of discomfort. The case that is extreme of behavior is when someone interlocks both feet with all the legs for the chair.

Chapter 5
Palm

Palm-up and palm-down hand gestures often accompany words spoken in face-to-face conversations, and generally are used widely throughout the world. The former (supinated) cues are glossed as deferential, in Goffman's sense of the term, while the latter (pronated) cues are more assertive and dominant in tone. Analysis of socio-emotional and semantic dimensions of palm-up-and-down gestures also reveals contrast that is bipolar. Palm-up associates well with emotional uncertainty and indefiniteness--while that is semantic associates with feelings of certainty and semantic.

Neurologically, both hand gestures are pectoral-area bodily signs that link to vocalization that is laryngeal an old chordate, upper-spinal-cord and caudal-hindbrain compartment. Controlled by cord circuits for tactile-withdrawal, palm-up cues are fundamentally deferential and submissive-like. Mediated by basal-ganglia brain circuits, palm-down cues, by comparison, are more assertive and dominant-like.

Palm-up

Into the palm-up speaking gesture, a hand or both hands rotate to an upward, or supinated, position using the fingers partially or fully extended. The arm may straight be held or flexed at the elbow; the wrist may be flexed or extended. Palm-up most often associates with speaking, but in addition may be used while listening.

Palm-up cues have diverse linguistic labels, including "raised open hands" (Darwin 1872); "cupped" and "extended hands" (Birdwhistell 1952, 1970); "hand shrugs" (Ekman and Friesen 1968); "baring the palms" (Hass 1970); "bowl-like gestures," "palms oriented upward" (Scheflen 1972); "palm-rotations," "palm-shows," and that is"palm-up (Givens 1982, 2005);

"hands up" gestures (Engel 1978); "holding out a hand" (Waal 1982); "hand cradle," "hands shrug," and "palms up" cues (Morris1994); "palm-addressed" cues and "palm presentations" (Kendon 2004); "palm up open hand" ("PUOH") cues (Muller 2004); "cup," "lid," and "tray" cues, and "flat open hand with palm turned upwards" (Mittelberg 2008); "open-handed supine" gestures (Streeck 2009); "holding" cues and "palm-up cyclic" gestures (Ladewig 2011); "hand flips," "open-palm" gestures (Ferre 2012); and "conduit" gestures (McNeill 2012).

Palm-up cues have diverse interpretations as well. Darwin (1872) interpreted them as expressions of helplessness and apology. Birdwhistell (1970) characterized palm-up linguistically, as getting the structure that is grammatical of. Ekman and Friesen (1968) viewed are hand-shrugs as signs and symptoms of helpless uncertainty and confusion. Ferre (2012) pictured palm-up as a marker of speaker intonation and prosody. Mittelberg (2008) viewed cupped hands as vessels to transport ideas. Muller (2004) saw palm-up as a way through which speakers "hold" and ideas that are present listeners. Streeck (2009) viewed palm-up as a computer device to coordinate turns that are speaking.

I stated that by themselves or perhaps in combination along with other hand movements--such as reaching, showing, and pointing--palm-up cues are acclimatized to begin speaking turns, ask questions, request favors, and share personal opinions, feelings, and moods. The hand that is palm-up is a possibly universal signal of deference, in Goffman's (1956) sense of the expression, not unlike other deferential body-motion cues like the anjai mudra, bow, curtsy, genuflection, kowtow, namaste, poussi-poussi, pranama, sampeah, and wai.

Palm-Down

A hand or both hands rotate to a downward, or pronated, position with the fingers partially or fully extended in the palm-down gesture. The arm may straight be held or flexed at the elbow; the wrist can be flexed or extended. Palm-down cues may or is almost certainly not reached off to listeners. In spoken conversations, palm-down gestures are most regularly utilized by speakers, yet in certain cases by listeners as well.

Palm-down is an insistent gesture in which the hands and forearms assume the prone position found in a floor pushup. Palm-down cues have diverse linguistic labels, including "push away",); "flat" gesture (Grant 1969); "push" gesture (Brannigan and Humphries 1972); "batons"; "palm-down cues" (Givens 1982, 2015); "palm-down signs" (Norton 1983; diagnostic of a dramatic or dominant nonverbal style); "palms down" (Morris 1994; an internationally speaking gesture used to "hold down" a notion or "calm down" the feeling of a gathering "open hand prone gestures" (Kendon 2004; ". . . all share the semantic theme of stopping or interrupting. . ." [p. 248]); and "beat gestures" (Ferre 2012).

Like palm-up, palm-down cues have diverse interpretations. Darwin (1872) interpreted them as gestures of disgust, annoyance, and self protection (defensiveness, to "guard oneself against" attack) Ekman and Friesen (1969) saw them as gestures used to emphasize speech. Blum (1988) analyzed "palms turned toward a floor" as dominance signals. Morris (1994, p. 195) glossed palms front (fashioned with hyperextended wrists and palms that are pronated as showing "I disagree." Kendon (2004, p. 248) saw hand that is open gestures as expressive of stopping, interrupting, and denial. Givens (1982) analyzed palm-down as an assertive gesture that is speaking in arguments.

On their own or perhaps in combination along with other hand movements--again, such as reaching, showing, and pointing--palm-down cues are used to emphasize speaking points, give directions, express disagreement, and dictate commands. The palm-down hand is a possibly universal gesture of assertion, not unlike other commanding body-motion cues such as the raised fist, triumph display, forefinger point, ground-slap, hands scissor, overhand beat, chest beat, palm thrust, military goose-step, and sumo wrestler's stomp into the ring. All are pronated limb positions used to show assertiveness, dominance, and strength. As will undoubtedly be shown, in form, function, and significance, palm-down assertion cues complement palm-up cues precisely of politeness, deference, and tact.

Hand Shake

Handshakes are essential tools of judging an individual. And an extremely, very part that is prominent of body language. As well as in the corporate jungle it's one of the most important ways to know who's your friend and your enemy, also, everyone that's in between that we have made our habitat in.

Experts say there are certain forms of handshakes and each of them reveals a little something about an individual's personality.

Here are a few of them and what type of person they're said to be representing.

1. The main one utilizing the sweaty palms

What it means: Experts say that a person with sweaty palms is a sign of a person that is slightly nervous. This type of person generally very self-conscious and tend to over analyze everything.

2. The one like a fish that is dead

What it indicates: People who just cave in a limp turn in a handshake which feels a lot like holding a dead fish, are said to be non-committal, uninterested and frequently scared or perhaps the lack thereof, in many things. They might mostly be reserved sorts of people.

3. One that crushes your hand

What it means: this 1 is extremely cringe-worthy, and people that do the pain sensation inflicting, seem to be testing the effectiveness of one other. These folks might run into since the intimidating type.

4. The one that allows you to feel like a queen

What it indicates: Those who offer their hand in this manner, are said to be somewhat dominating in the near order of considering themselves greater than the other.

5. One that feels like a hug

What this means: It's a comfy, or a care-giving kind of handshake when you look at the most professional way possible. They are employed by politicians or those who work n a circuit that is social job is to be diplomatic.

6. The one which makes you feel strength-less

What it indicates: they are characteristically the part of the body language of a dominating person.

7. The one that allows you to feel just like being pushed

What it means: These handshakes indicate a person who is afraid of any type or sort of intimacy or closeness and prefers to keep their distance whenever you can.

8. The one like a lobster claw

What it indicates? These social people show anxiety and commitment issues. They keep all of their fingers close together and reach for minimum contact. These folks may avoid deep connections that are rooted relationships.

9. The one that's like a finger vice

What it means: These people attack simply the fingers instead of the palm that is whole may be just a tad bit insecure and through this handshake, assert the energy they think they deserve to have over others.

10. One which can be so strong about abruptly that it shakes you

What this means: this will be an indication of a stronger and a personality that is gregarious. They have a tendency to be a little too available to you and quite loud. But at the time that is same no hidden agendas.

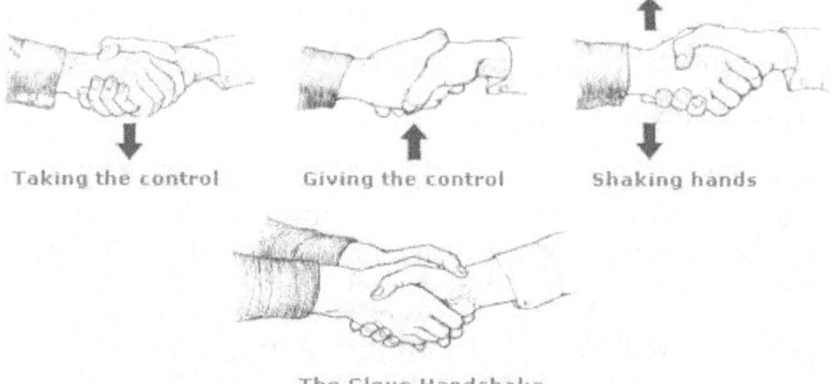

A Quick Way To Break A Dominating Handshake

The vibe amongst the two of you have been completely established with this first handshake and whatever you say using this moment forward will always have the "lower-hand" with their "upper-hand," especially with this handshake if they were trying to intimidate you.

"[It] is the most aggressive of all of the handshakes since it gives the receiver little chance of establishing an equal relationship," in accordance with Westside Toastmasters, a non-profit organization targeted at helping people boost their public speaking and leadership skills.

Toastmasters shared three techniques on getting out of these handshakes that are overbearing

1. The Step-to-the-Right Technique

Basically, if you are right-footed ("The natural position for 90 percent of men and women when shaking using the right hand), you should have a lot more of an edge when you step into the handshake along with your left foot, and the other way around.

An individual extends their hand for a dominant handshake, you are able to prevent this interaction from happening by first stepping forward with your left foot.

 Next, step forward along with your leg that is right and each other's personal space. Then you can cross your left leg across your right leg (Although, we have tried this and it's really just a little awkward).

"this plan allows you to straighten the handshake and sometimes even change it over into the submissive position. It feels as if you're walking across in front of him and is the same as winning an arm-wrestling bout. It also allows you to take close control by invading his space this is certainly personal.

2. The Technique that is Hand-On-Top

As you're going in for the dominating handshake, respond with your palms up at first; then, place your other hand the left one over your companion's hand to create a "Double-Hander" and simply straighten the handshake to a more equal position.

This technique is a very easy for females to use

3. The Last Resort Technique

If all else fails, and you also feel as though your companion is trying to intimidate you, grab their hand from the utmost effective and shake it. But only do that as a final resort as it can shock each other and is an extremely obvious maneuver.

Insecure Hand Displays

Hands in PocketsEven while you speak to someone, you can accidentally send them a mixed signal of nervousness or a lack of confidence though it may be your natural inclination to put your hands in your pockets. Try clasping your hands behind the back in the attention stance in the place of digging into those pants or jacket pockets.

Folded Arms or Self HuggingnNervous, uncomfortable, angry are all expressed words that get ascribed to people who stand making use of their arms crossed. Science has proven that crossed arms is perfect for problem solving (it raises analytical thinking) but horrible for open communication. Uncross those arms, widen your stance, and start to become viewed as more confident.

Chapter 6
Facial Expression

E ric Goldfarb knows that tuning into body language and facial expressions can indicate the thoughts and feelings that remain unspoken. He also knows how difficult those nonverbal cues can be to interpret. During a budget meeting with a direct report while doing work for Global Knowledge, Goldfarb noticed that his vice president kept toying with her necklace. He thought this mannerism was a sign of her discomfort using the financial target he was proposing. He also noticed her eyes and thought they expressed worry within the budget target. He repeatedly asked her through the meeting if she thought she could meet up with the budget, and although she consistently answered yes, Goldfarb didn't believe her. So he scheduled a meeting that is follow-up her to dig deeper. She finished up meeting the target without a problem, and Goldfarb realized her precious time by scheduling the follow-up meeting and by dragging out the first one with repetitive questions that he wasted his and. What could Goldfarb have inked differently to more accurately size up his vice president?

Goldfarb, now the CIO of auditing firm PRG-Schultz International, was astute to tune into her body gestures and expressions that are facial. However, because body gestures may be misleading and because facial expressions could be difficult to read if you're not practiced at it, Goldfarb needed to more pointedly probe his direct report. In the place of continually asking her, "Are you comfortable?" he may have said, "It's really necessary for us to have your buy-in with this target. I don't mean to pry but I simply need to know in the event that discomfort you be seemingly showing is a total result of the budget target or something like that else. If it is the goal, we are able to work something out." Had Goldfarb taken this tack, he wouldn't have experienced to worry that his incessant questioning sent a note to this individual—one of his key lieutenants that he didn't trust her, or which he temporarily lost some credibility in her eyes.

Accurately interpreting the meanings of nonverbal communications, especially facial expressions, could make CIOs more effective leaders and managers, says Paul Ekman, noted psychologist and composer of Emotions Revealed: Recognizing Faces and Feelings to Improve Communication and Emotional Life. Reading facial expressions is a particularly useful skill for business executives because, so often in operation settings, people do not say whatever they really think. If CIOs could recognize how different emotions manifest themselves from the face, they would have the ability to discern much more quickly, for instance, when an individual is needs to get angry. They would additionally be in a position to identify when people are trying to conceal their emotions—such as fear, contempt, disgust or surprise. This knowledge and ability will make CIOs more aware of unspoken political tensions in board or executive committee meetings. In addition better equips them to carry out sensitive staffing situations such as performance reviews. Ekman points to research indicating that managers who seem tuned in to the unspoken emotions of the staffs are more successful at work than managers who don't.

The Facts in Facial Expressions

While facial expressions may be difficult to decipher simply because they're fleeting (lasting anywhere from lower than one-half of an additional to three seconds) and because individuals often make an effort to conceal them, they are in fact the clearest indicator of what someone is feeling, says Ekman.

"the face area is the only system that will inform us the precise emotion that is occurring," he says. That is because each emotion has unique, identifiable signals into the face. Emotions manifest themselves in facial expressions because, says Ekman, it became useful during the period of human evolution to let others know once we sense danger. Facial expressions have since become automatic. Because each emotion has unique signals in the facial skin, facial expressions are far more reliable indicators of a person's emotional state than body gestures.

Ekman says it is possible to learn the fundamentals of reading facial expressions in about an hour. It is possible to learn how to read expressions that are facial others by getting to understand how emotions show up on your very own face. Ekman advises people to look in a mirror and remember a personal experience that made them angry, sad, fearful or disgusted in order to observe how their expression changes once the emotion washes over them. This exercise can help you recognize muscle movements which can be the clearest indicators of a emotion that is particular.

The eyes are generally referred to as the "windows towards the soul" since they are capable of revealing a deal that is great what you were feeling or thinking. As you participate in conversation with someone else, taking note of eye movements is a natural and important the main communication process. Some typically common things you may notice include whether individuals are making direct eye contact or averting their gaze, just how much these are typically blinking, or if perhaps their pupils are dilated.

When body that is evaluating, look closely at the following eye signals:

Eye Gaze: When a person looks directly into your eyes while having a conversation, this implies that they're interested and attention that is paying. However, prolonged eye contact can feel threatening. Having said that, breaking eye contact and frequently looking away might indicate that the person is distracted, uncomfortable, or wanting to conceal his / her real feelings.

Blinking: Blinking is natural, however you also needs to focus on whether a person is blinking too much or too little. People often blink more rapidly when they're feeling uncomfortable or distressed. Infrequent blinking might indicate that any particular one is intentionally wanting to control his or her eye movements. For example, a poker player might blink less frequently because he could be purposely wanting to appear unexcited in regards to the hand he was dealt.

Pupil Size: Pupil size can be a very subtle nonverbal communication signal. While light levels in the environment control pupil dilation, sometimes emotions can also cause small changes in pupil size. For instance, you might have heard the phrase "bedroom eyes" used to spell it out the design someone gives when they're attracted to another person. Highly dilated eyes, for example, can indicate that any particular one is interested if not aroused.

Glasses

Know that old impressions that are"first saying? If you see a wearer of the glasses head into an area, superficial judgments begin formulating. Will they be fashionable? Will they be conservative or flamboyant? Will they be clean, or do they let grease smudge their lenses? Whatever communication takes place is filtered through these impressions. And even though those gut-checks are surface level, there are additionally more deep-seated evaluations occurring. As an example: Will they be trustworthy?

That is where things get complex. If you believe people with glasses are far more intelligent—numerous studies back up that folks believe in this stereotype—you may also think that person is more trustworthy. But, if the frames are obstructing their eyes in a way that is overt that may morph into distrust. "Glasses cover not merely the eyes themselves, however the surrounding tissues, the cheekbones, the frown lines," Handley says. "These are all indicators of that which you mean and tend to be wanting to say." Hide them, and that's a hurdle that lens-free faces don't have to jump over.

The main point is, you don't see glasses and think nothing. Full-rim glasses give off less attractive, yet more intelligent, vibes when comparing to rimless glasses or faces that are non-spectacled. In light of this latter impression, job interviewees have already been demonstrated to perform better when wearing glasses. Plus in the realm of amateur, non-peer-reviewed studies, one 17-year-old ended his suffering during the hand of bullies by firmly taking cues from Corey Hart and donning his sunglasses at night. But while everyone thinks something about those wearing glasses, what that is has shifted.

When constant-use glasses were first introduced in the very beginning of the 18th century—before, eye assistance was relegated to occasional-use monocles and, presumably, power-squinting—spectacle wearers were folk that is mysterious. "What were these weapons that are secret had on their face?" Handley asks. "What is this person doing with this particular device on? Will they be wanting to capture my something or soul?" ("There was a suspicion which was just like Google Glasses today," he says. I don't know if you have yet had the pleasure of attending a party with a Google Glasses wearer, but that feeling of suspicion certainly jives.)

That was the start of other feelings glasses that are surrounding well. Early spectacles were made especially for reading purposes, generally, there was a better likelihood that the person wearing them was educated. Hence: People wearing them are far more intelligent. But, as is commonly the situation when someone's disabilities are prominently displayed, negative feelings begun to emerge as well. Enter: the bullies.

"No matter how clever you think you will be, reading all those books has made you weak-eyed," Handley says. "That was the perception. People thought you might damage your eyes when you're too bookish."

(In 2012, Handley analyzed the changing norms that are social glasses wearers throughout history. One revelation was that while Hitler wore reading glasses, images of him performing this were censored because of the Nazi Party for concern about his authority being weakened.)

Then again, something happened: Glasses became cool.

 Handley traces it to "10 to 15 years ago," which not-so-coincidentally aligns because of the world being introduced to a magician-in-training that is certain "Now the youngsters when you look at the school yard desire to look like Harry Potter," he says. Which, drawing a line that is straight leads us to the sickening reality associated with genetically blessed wearing lens-free frames. Exactly what happens if/when the style goes out of style?

My buddy, Meiyee Apple, recently underwent LASIK surgery after decades of wearing glasses. "I felt I became losing part of my identity as a cool glasses person," Apple says since I identified myself.

(One somewhat hilarious reason she hesitated on the decision: Her phobia of disgusting showers. Such as, glasses gave her the capacity to intentionally blur her vision and keep her from having to see shower that is gross. "Now in my decision," she says that I don't frequent gross showers, it aided me. Which, I guess, may be the positive of wearing glasses: You do have an option in your eyes' effectiveness.)

Apple's choice to ditch the frames has shifted how people perceive her. "once I see people that wear glasses on a regular basis after which they don't really, I think something is missing," she says. "I feel people genuinely believe that about me." It's also changed the amount of time she spends at the mirror. "i did not wear make-up as much as I do now because now you are seeing most of my face," she says.

Handley backed this glasses-as-make-up reading by analyzing my own hipster glasses, which have bold, black frames on the top and clear rims in the bottom, giving me the appearance of someone with quite dominant brows. "The same manner a female might pluck her real eyebrows and draw them in with make-up, you are doing the same together with your glasses," Handley says. "You have make-up on without realizing it."

Ironically, Apple's decision has affected her work as an actor. "The large hip frames allowed me to either get noticed or give myself a certain 'look,'" she says. So I can wear them to auditions"So I had an eye doctor turn a pair to clear plastic. It's a look that is in at this time."

How To Differentiate Between Real and Fake Smiles

Smiling happens to be recognized or identified as a manifestation of merry making, joy and happiness by each and every culture throughout the world. All of humankind are able to smile which reflects pleasure, gladness, gratification, inner fulfillment and so forth. In all the lexis that are facial smiling can be used most often than not.

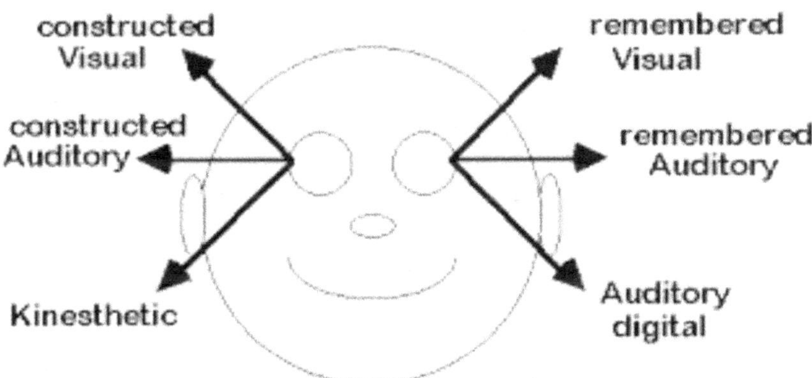

You can find basically two forms or kinds of smiles; an authentic smile and a fake smile. It often proves to be a genuine challenge to identify or pinpoint the essential difference between a real smile and a fake smile. Only few individuals have the capability or pinpoint the actual difference between those two types of smiles.

This dissimilarity between the two types of smiles happens to be of concern to researchers for quite a long while now. An authentic smile has been named after a nineteenth century physician who studied physiology of facial expressions called Guillaume Duchenne, which is therefore called the

"Duchenne smile". Guillaume is used electrical currents to excite the facial muscles.

Both forms of smiles involve the contraction of facial muscles. Contractions of a fake smile is requires the utilization of just one around, the face known as zygomatic major, whereas contractions of a real or Duchenne smile involves the usage muscles namely; the zygomatic major additionally the orbicularis oculi.

Research has revealed that the reason why a fake smile only involves zygomatic major is as it impossible to voluntarily contract the orbicularis oculi muscle, it has been discovered that both of these forms of smiles genuine smile and fake smile are essentially managed by two entirely different parts of our mind.

For example, an smile that is uneven be as a result of a damaged cortex motor regarding the left side of the brain's hemisphere. The application of the exact same group of muscles namely the zygomatic muscle is a kind of similarity between those two kinds of smiles other them is a fake smile than they are both intended to imply joy and happiness even if one of.

However, when that patient that is same laughs or smiles, the smile is typical without any irregularities. This really is evident that the actual or smile, it is duchenne controlled by some other section of the mind. On the other hand, there's absolutely no asymmetry in a smile that has been attempted by an individual with a damaged limbic system (Durayappah n.p.). The smile is authentic or normal in person, if the person that is same genuine the asymmetry is clear.

Consequently, fake smiles or as they are mostly called "cheese smile" look comparable to Duchenne smiles, but there are numerous critical dissimilarities. Unlike genuine smiles that are contributed by our inner emotions of joy and happiness, our cognizant mind tells or directs the cheek muscles to contract hence a Cheese or smile that is fake. A fake smile can be executed at one's will in other words.

These conscious directions engage the mouth only and certainly will be held on faces for as long as it is needed. Mental faculties is remarkably proficient at telling apart genuine smile from cheese or fake smiles, it can so from a subconscious level.

Studies clearly show that in circumstances where trust is important, when a sales man is trying to score a sale on video or perhaps in person a closer awareness of such person's smile ought to be keenly paid. Conclusion from such observations and their results may help decide whether or perhaps not we can trust the person or even the goods they would like to sell.

Unlike fake or cheese smile that could easily be controlled and will not engage the entire muscles that are facial genuine smiles form crinkled up muscles across the eyes. In addition to across the mouth, and it's also therefore impossible to voluntarily control muscles round the eyes and mouth, neither have control of the smile's duration on the face. Aided by the above illustrated study it really is quite possible to detect a smile that is fake a genuine one.

Another feature mostly used to differentiate both of these kinds of smiles could be the laugh lines. They are tiny wrinkles mostly present at the corners associated with the optical eye while a person is smiling. These wrinkles are formed by the orbicularis oculi muscle, one which rings the eye and contracts when one has a real smile as opposed to a fake smile.

Even though differentiating between your two can be difficult; there have been scientific developments to assist while trying to different the 2 kinds of smiles. A coding system was created by professor of UC bay area Dr. Paul Ekman.

This Facial Action Coding System is intended to aid physicians and scientists to differentiate the actual smile through the smile that is fake. Dr. Ekman continues to illustrate by saying that, you ought to be keen while attempting to point out a type of smile. Dr.Ekna illustrates a continuing state which may define both smiles and therefore might confuse an observer.

He says that corners for the lip being intensely pulled up by a large smile could pass for either genuine or fake smile. Dr. Ekna explains that the sole part that will disclose the real difference in a big concentrated smile is the skin amid the eyebrows therefore the upper eyelid. The skin amid the eyebrows and the upper eyelid will definitely move slightly down as compared to a force smile where no such movement will be present in a genuine smile.

SMILE-LENIENCY EFFECT

Research confirms the social significance of the smile like in situations where there was a wrongdoer, there was a phenomenon called the "smile-leniency effect". If the smiles that are wrongdoer others perceive the offender as more trustworthy and likable. Statistically, judges actually give shorter sentences to people who smile. Simply smiling if you're with someone else can make them greatly predisposed to like you and tune in to your message.

People just feel warmer towards those who smile, if you had a choice, would you want to approach someone who is frowning or smiling? The effects of a smile are so powerful that even a smile from the telephone produces results that are positive. Added bonus, smiling also raises your confidence.

5 Most Common Types of Smiles

Everyone smiles for several different reasons. There was a certain something about a smile rendering it flexible and usable for all different situations and expressions. Check out of the very type that is common of that we usually use, the distinctions inside their meaning and their use on different occasions.

The very first form of smile could be the happy smile. It is pretty simple to identify, if somebody is happy with something they experienced or if they're enjoying something; they're going to typically give a smile to display their joy. This can have minor differences as a smile that is happy convey love, sweetness, acceptance, kindness, and so forth.

The second types of smile could be the embarrassed smile. This usually takes place when we make a move unintentionally that could have an impact on someone else. The smile that is embarrassed the impact of the mistake or oversight and attempts to elicit a kinder response through the person affected by the incident.

Another kind of smile is the attentive smile. This will be a grin that is small the face area of a person who's listening intently and it is in a position to absorb and take in everything that's being said. This will be a kind of pleasure response but not completely obvious. This might be also the smile that is flirty. Women and men wear this smile to show their interest in some other person.

The fourth kind of smile is may be the devious smile. This smile is employed to hide someone's thoughts that are real emotions from the public. This really is also known as the smile that is fake's meant to mislead other individuals.

Finally, there is the smile that is social that is meant to show respect, openness, and trustworthiness. People usually wear this smile if they are meeting new people or in a large social event. People typically smile to show appreciation to your people who organized the function and their guests.

Everyday we have many uses for the smiles. For this reason you will need to not just express ourselves freely through our smiles, but to take care of our dental health. Atrium Family Dental offers you personalized dental care services that can help you enhance your smile and ensure that it is healthy and strong.

What To Do When There Are Mixed Signals

The next time you will end up in an identical situation, try to remember some of the following:

1. Don't jump to conclusions or assume anything. You're lured to read into everything, you can't know for certain what's

going on inside another person's head. Try not to waste a lot of energy on wondering what is happening on the other end, time will reveal all.

2. Take off your blinders. Love has a real way of clouding towards our thinking, make sure you're making the partnership accurately. What would your advice be to a close friend should they were going right on through this experience?

3. Don't go on it personally. Mixed signals could have nothing to do if you have done something wrong with you, so resist the urge to feel as.

4. Back away. Allow for plenty of breathing room.

5. Believe what you're told (until convinced you need don't). Give your partner the advantage of the show and doubt trust—until trust is broken.

6. Realize the other individual might have issues going on. The confusing behavior can lie along with your partner's life circumstances, fears, or past hurts.

7. Don't be demanding. One of several worst responses is to become huffy: "Why didn't you call? What took you such a long time?"

8. Recognize the tug-of-war that is emotional can happen. There clearly was a phenomenon that is push-pull to relationships: the more you push, the greater amount of your partner will pull away.

9. Make sure you're not contributing into the confusion. Feeling insecure may prompt you to send your very own signals that are mixed but this can only make matters worse.

10. Get a opinion that is second. A trusted friend may see things more clearly than you can.

11. Beware of overanalyzing. When we are strongly drew to someone, it is an easy task to dissect every word, action, and tone of voice.

12. Ask questions that are direct. Without getting push, a couple of well-chosen questions can clear things up in a hurry.

13. Realize you're only responsible for you. You can't control what signals your spouse conveys, but you can control how you react to them.

14. Bolster your self-confidence. A sense of self-assurance will assist you to endure the ups and downs—and will add to your attractiveness.

15. Know when to walk away. If mixed signals persist, decide what you might be prepared to live with. You deserve better than to be with a manipulator, or in the very someone that is least who is simply not readily available for a relationship.

Chapter 7
How To Determine If Someone Is Lying

Signs to look out for when you want to detect a lie

People who are lying tend to change their head position quickly

- Their breathing may also change

- They tend to stand very still

- They may repeat words or phrases

- They may provide too much information

- They may touch or cover their mouth

- They tend to instinctively cover vulnerable body parts

- They tend to shuffle their feet

- It may become difficult for them to speak

- They may stare at you without blinking much

- They tend to point a lot

How To Detect Deception

I would like to believe salespeople when they say the product they truly are selling, truly does what they say it can perform. I would like to think that the social people I work with are telling the truth. I wish to believe kids when I am told by them what they did or whom these people were with, but sometimes I suspect a few of the people I cope with are not being completely honest.

Directly confronting the people who, I suspect are lying is frequently awkward because of the sensitive nature of our relationships. The process is to identify behaviors that are disingenuous damaging relationships. To resolve this dilemma, I compiled several approaches to my book, the like change to detect deception without getting detected. The beauty of these techniques is the fact that folks are not aware they are being tested by you.

Yes-or-No questions deserve a yes or no answer. When people cannot or do not want to answer yes or no, they typically go directly to the Land of Is. This idea was produced by President Clinton's now statement that is infamous "this will depend upon what this is associated with the word 'is'. If 'is' means 'is', and not has been changed that is a very important factor. If it means there is certainly none, which was a totally true statement." The Land of Is occupies the area between truth and deception. The Land of Is comes with half-truths, innuendos, suppositions, assumptions, and verbal judo. A lot of people want to tell the reality, it entirely so they go to great lengths to contort the English language to maintain the illusion of truth without telling. People often end up into the Land of Is without ever being conscious of it.

To check people when it comes to truth, simply yes ask them yes or no question. When they are not able to answer yes or no, a red flag should pop up. After someone provides a answer that is convoluted a direct question, ask exactly the same question again. If they once again fails to answer with a yes or no, the likelihood of deception increases significantly.

In the event that you ask someone an immediate yes or no question, and also the response you receive begins with the word "Well", there was a top possibility of deception. When a person answering a primary question starts with "Well", it indicates that he or she knows the questioner is not expecting that he or she is about to give an answer.

Why should I believe you?

When truthful folks are asked why others should believe them, they typically answer, "Because I am telling the truth", or some variation thereof. Liars have a time that is difficult, "Because I'm telling the reality", because they're not telling the reality. Instead, liars offer various responses such as "I'm a genuine person", "there is no need to trust me I have no reason to lie, if you don't want to", or The question, "Why should you are believed by me?" could be asked in much ways with respect to the sensitivity regarding the relationship.

These procedures do not detect deception with 100 percent certainty, but they do provide a indicator that is strong determine if someone will be truthful or perhaps not. If somebody answers questions directly, you'll have confidence that the answer is truthful and that the person shall never be conscious that you've got tested their veracity, thus preserving the integrity of ongoing relationships. If the person will not directly answer questions, it does not necessarily mean you might be being deceived, you should examine the individual's answers in more detail.

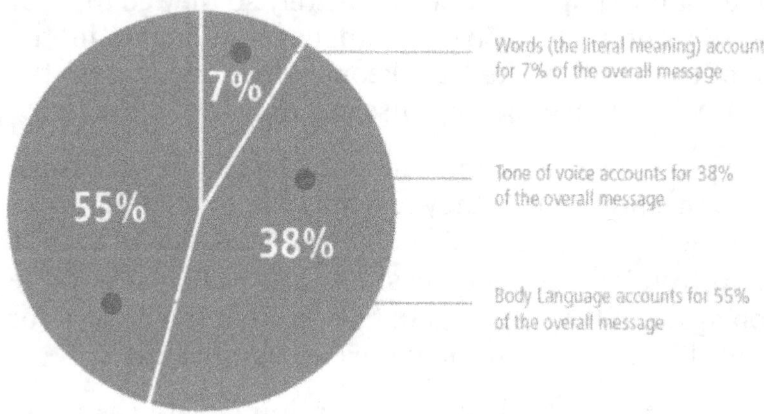

Chapter 8
Common Female Dating Signals and Gestures

Women use the majority of the same basic preening gestures as men, including touching the hair, smoothing the clothing, one or both hands on hips, foot and the body pointing towards the man, extended intimate gaze and increasing eye contact. Some women will even adopt the thumbs-in-belt gesture, which even though it's a male assertion gesture that can be used more subtly: usually only 1 thumb is tucked into a belt or protrudes from a handbag or pocket.

Women be more sexually active in the middle of these cycle that is menstrual they are almost certainly to conceive. It's during this time that they're more prone to wear shorter dresses and higher heels, to walk, talk, dance and act more provocatively also to make use of the signals we are going to discuss. Here are some is a listing of the most common courtship gestures and signals employed by women everywhere to show a guy that she could possibly be available.

1. The Head Toss and Hair Flick

This is the first display a woman will use when she's around a person she fancies. Your head is flicked back once again to toss the hair on the shoulders or from the face. Even women with short hair will make use of this gesture. It's a means for a woman subtly to demonstrate that she cares about how precisely she looks to a man. This also lets her expose her armpit that allows the 'sex perfume' known as pheromone to waft across into the target man.

2. Wet lips and Pouting, Mouth open slightly

At puberty, a boy's bone that is facial alters dramatically as testosterone gives him a stronger, protruding jaw-line, larger nose, and much more pronounced forehead – all the essentials for protection into the face during encounters with animals or enemies. Girls' bone structure remains largely unchanged and child-like with additional subcutaneous fat, which makes the feminine adolescent face appear thicker and fuller, specially the lips. Therefore, larger and thicker lips,become a sign of femaleness because of their contrast in dimensions to lips that are male. Some women have collagen injected into their lips to overstate this difference that is sexual thereby make themselves more desirable to men. Pouting simply escalates the display that is lip.

When a lady becomes sexually aroused her lips, breasts and genitals become larger and redder because they fill with blood. The utilization of lipstick is an invention that is egyptian is four thousand years old and it is intended to mimic facially the reddened genitals associated with the sexually aroused female. This explains why is in experiments using photos of women wearing various lipstick colours and men consistently find the bright reds the absolute most attractive and sensual.

3. Self-Touching

Our minds get our anatomical bodies to behave out our desires that are secret, therefore, it is with Self-Touching. Women have dramatically more nerve sensors for experiencing touch than men, making them more responsive to touch sensations. When a woman slowly and sensually strokes her thigh, neck or throat it infers that, if a man plays his cards right, he might manage to touch her during these same ways. During the same time, her self-touch lets her imagine what it may feel like if the man was initiating the touch.

4. The Limp Wrist

Walking or sitting while holding a Limp Wrist is a submission signal used exclusively by women and gay men. A bird feigns a damaged wing to distract prey away from its nest in a similar way. In other words, it is a great attention getter. It's very attractive to men given that it makes them feel as if they are able to dominate. Running a business situations, however, a Limp Wrist seriously detracts from a woman's credibility yet others will are not able to take her seriously. Hence, some men will ask her for probably a date.

5. Fondling a object that is cylindrical cigarettes, a finger, the stem of a wine glass, a dangling earring or any phallic-shaped object is an unconscious indication of what may be in the mind. Taking a ring don and doff the finger could be a representation that is mental of sex. When a woman does these exact things, a person is likely to symbolically make an effort to possess her by fondling her cigarette lighter, car keys or any item that is personal has nearby.

6. Exposed Wrists

An interested woman will gradually expose the smooth, soft underside skin of her wrists towards the potential male partner, and can increase the rate she flashes her wrists as her interest grows. The wrist area has long been considered one of many highly erotic areas of the feminine body since it is one of the more delicate skin areas; its uncertain whether this is certainly a learned behaviour or perhaps is innate, nonetheless, it certainly operates on an unconscious level. The palms may also be usually made visible to the person while she's speaking. Women who smoke cigars find this wrist/palm exposure simple to do while smoking by simply holding the palm up beside the shoulder. The Exposed Wrist and head toss gestures are often mimicked by homosexual males who wish to take on a appearance that is feminine.

7. Sideways Glance Over Raised Should

The Raised Shoulder is self-mimicry of this rounded breasts that are female. With partially drooped eyelids, the lady holds the man's gaze just long enough she quickly looks away for him to notice, then. This course of action produces the experience of peeping when you look at the woman who does it and being peeped at by the man who receives it.

8. Rolling Hips

For childbearing reasons, women have wider hips than men and now have a wider crotch gap between your legs. This means that when a woman walks she has an accentuated roll, which highlights her pelvic region, men can't walk like this, so it becomes a sex difference signal that is powerful. In addition, it explains why few women can be good runners because their wider hips make their legs splay out to along side it if they run, rolling of this hips is one of the subtle courtship that is female that has been utilized for centuries in advertising to sell goods and services. Ladies who see these advertisements have the need to be like the model depicted, which results in an increased awareness of the product being promoted.

9. The Pelvic Tilt

Medical evidence shows that a woman in excellent health and most capable of successfully children that are bearing a waist-to-hips ratio of 70%, that is her waist is 70% the dimensions of her hips, this gives her what's known as an hourglass figure. This is the body ratio that has proved the most dramatic male attention-grabber through out recorded history. Men start to lose interest if the ratio exceeds 80% and for most men, the greater or lesser the ratio the less attentive he will be. He completely loses interest when her ratio reaches 100%, yet still maintains an amount of interest even when it drops below 70%, but 70% still continues to be the perfect ratio for reproductive success. The way a female highlights this ratio is simple – she simply tilts her pelvis when she stands.

10. Handbag in Close Proximity

Most men have not seen the contents of a woman's handbag and studies also show that most men are afraid even to touch her handbag, let open it alone. A woman's handbag is your own item that is treated by her almost as if it is an extension of her body and thus it becomes a strong signal of intimacy when she puts it near to a guy. Particularly, this is attractive, she may slowly fondle and caress her handbag if she finds. She can ask him to pass through the handbag or even is to retrieve something from it. Placing the handbag near him, so he can view it or touch it is a powerful signal she's interested; keeping it far from him indicates emotional distance.

11. The Knee Point

One leg is tucked underneath the other and points to the person she finds the absolute most interesting. This is really a position that is relaxed and also takes the formality out of a discussion and provides the ability for fleeting exposure regarding the thighs. Pointing her knee at the most person that is interesting.

12. The Shoe Fondle

Dangling the shoe on the end regarding the foot also indicates a attitude that is relaxed has the phallic effect of thrusting the foot inside and outside of the shoe. This action unsettles lots of men without them knowing what exactly is happening.

13. The Leg Twine

Most men agree that the Leg Twine is considered the most appealing position that is sitting woman may take. It's a gesture that women consciously use to draw attention to their legs. Albert Scheflen states any particular one leg is pressed firmly from the other to provide the look of high muscular tonus that will be a condition, which the body takes when a person is ready for heightened sexual performance.

Another leg signals used by women include crossing and uncrossing the legs slowly while a watching man and gently stroking the thighs with her hand, indicating a need to be touched.

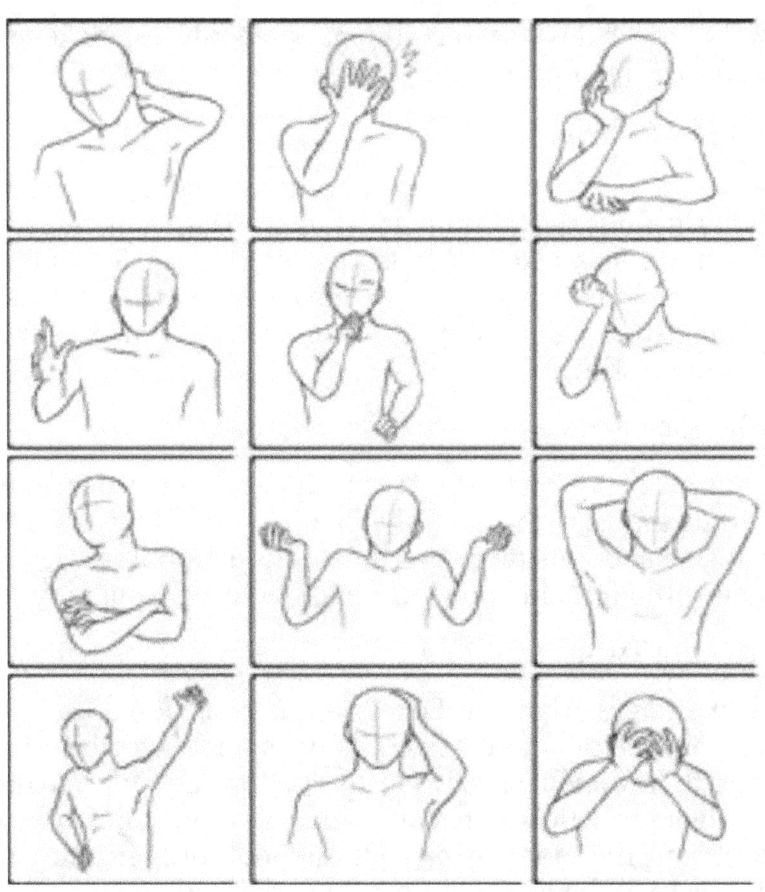

Common Male Dating Signals and Gestures

In The Face

Often when our eyes meet those of an stranger that is attractive our eyebrows raise up then return back down.

This gesture that is split-secondcalled the "eyebrow flash" could be an invitation to start out a conversation.

It is clear that raising his eyebrows in a "surprise" manner, during conversation can be a good signal.

Eye contact can definitely help decode his feelings. A person might hold a women's gaze just slightly more than normal to indicate his interest.

Another male flirting cue is to slightly flare his nostrils, make his face appear wider. His lips may also part slightly.

Male Body Gestures

1. Eyes – Lingering eye contact

- Eyebrow Flash
- Chest & Arms – ILS (Invisible Lats Syndrome)
- Hands – Grooming – Gestures
- Legs – Relaxed, shoulder's width apart
- Feet- Pointed toward you

2. Mannerisms that are manly

> You'll know he is attempting to impress you as he moves into his courtship that is classic stance

> – Head slightly tilted to at least one side – Legs spread about shoulders width apart – Chest out, gut in – Hands at their side, maybe thumbs hooked in belt loops

3. Pretty Boys

> Guys preening themselves is cute — guess that's why it is flirting gesture. Common male grooming signals that are flirting

> Adjusting their collars, sleeves, socks – Smoothing their hair

4. Other Body Gestures Cues and Gestures

> Anything is gesture that makes him "seem" bigger (wide arm gestures, stretching, etc.) Turning his body towards you, feet pointed towards you.

Chapter 9
Analyzing People via Their Verbal Statements

In the event that eyes would be the window to the soul, then words will be the gateway towards the mind, as words represent thoughts. The closest one individual can get to understanding another person's thoughts is to pay attention to the language he/she speaks or writes. Certain words reflect the behavioral characteristics of the individual who spoke or wrote them. I labeled these expressed words, Word Clues. Word Clues increase the probability of predicting the behavioral characteristics of people by analyzing the expressed words they choose once they speak or write. Nonetheless, they alone cannot determine a person's personality traits and they do provide insights into a person's thought process and characteristics that are behavioral. Hypotheses could be developed according to Word Clues after which tested by utilizing more information elicited through the person or corroboration that is third-party.

The brain that is human incredibly efficient. We use only verbs and nouns when we think. Adjectives, adverbs, as well as other components of speech are added during the transformation of thoughts into written or spoken language. The language we add, reflect who our company is and everything we are planning.

The sentence is basic of a topic and a verb, for instance, the simple sentence "I walked" comprises of the pronoun "I" that will be the subject as well as the word "walked" that will be the verb. Any words put into this sentence that is basic modify the caliber of the noun or even the action regarding the verb. These modifications that are deliberate clues towards the personality and behavioral characteristics associated with the speaker or writer.

Word Clues allow observers to develop hypotheses or make educated guesses about the behavioral characteristics of others. As an example, into the sentence "I quickly walked", the expressed word Clue "quickly" infused a sense of urgency. However, it would not provide the reason for the urgency, a person might be "quickly walk" she is late for an appointment or anticipates being late for an appointment. Conscientious people are see themselves as reliable plus don't like to be late for appointments. Individuals who are wish to be on time have a tendency to respect social norms and desire to live as much as the expectations of others. People who have this behavioral characteristic make good employees as they do not wish to disappoint their employers. People "quickly walk" once they are encounter general threats. A broad threat may be possibly occur while walking through a neighborhood that is bad. Approaching bad weather could also present a threat. Walking quickly to prevent a thunderstorm reduces the threat of a lightning strike or getting wet. People might add the term "quickly" for a number of reasons, but there is a reason that is specific to their choice.

Word Clues present a noninvasive technique to effectively read people without their knowledge. The following examples demonstrate how Word Clues provide insights in to the behavioral characteristics of men and women when they speak or write:

1) I won another award.

The Word Clue "another" conveys the idea that the speaker won one or even more awards, which are previous. This person wanted to make sure other individuals knew she win at least one other award, thus, bolstering his or her self-image. This person may need the adulation of others to reinforce his/her self-esteem. Observers could exploit this vulnerability simply by using flattery and other ego-enhancing comments.

2) I worked hard to achieve my goal.

The Word Clue "hard" suggests this person values goals that are hard to achieve. Probably the goal this person achieved is more difficult than the goals she usually attempts. The Word Clue "hard" also shows that this person can defer gratification or holds the fact hard work and dedication produce good results. A job applicant by using these characteristics would probably make a good employee because he or she would probably accept challenges and have the determination to successfully complete those tasks.

3) I patiently sat through the lecture.

The phrase Clue "patiently" presents several hypotheses. Perhaps, this person was tired of the lecture, maybe he or she had to return a telephone call that is important. Possibly he or she is needed to utilize the restroom. No matter what the reason, this person was preoccupied with something other than the information associated with the lecture. Somebody who waits patiently for a rest before he leaves the space is probably a person who adheres to norms that are social etiquette. An individual who receives a telephone call, immediately gets up, and leaves the lecture is somebody who probably does not have rigid social boundaries. People who have social boundaries make good employees because the rules are followed by them and respect authority. Conversely, an individual who does not follow social conventions could possibly be designed for a job that needs thinking that is novel. A person with the predisposition to do something outside social norms would make a better spy than an individual who is predisposed to check out social conventions because spies are routinely asked to violate social norms.

4) I made a decision to purchase that model.

The term Clue "decided" indicates that this person weighed various options prior to the purchase. Perhaps he or she struggled to some degree before making the choice to purchase. This behavior trait implies that this person thinks through things, particularly if the purchase was a minor one. The term "decided" also indicates that this person just isn't likely to be impulsive. An impulsive person would likely say or write, "I just bought that model."The Word Clue "just" is suggests that this person bought the item without giving the purchase much thought.

In line with the expressed word Clue "decided," the reader or listener can form a hypothesis that the speaker or writer is an introvert. Introverts are think before they act on any activity and they carefully weigh each option before rendering a decision. Extroverts tend to be more impulsive. Making use of the verb "decided" does not positively identify this person is as an introvert. However, it does provide a sign she might be an introvert. A personality that is definitive requires a far more comprehensive psychological assessment; nonetheless, an observer can exploit an individual if he knows that person tends toward extroversion or introversion.

Extroverts are get their energy from being along with other people and seek stimulation from their environments. Extroverts often speak spontaneously without thinking and confidently utilize the learning from your errors method. Conversely, introverts expend energy once they engage socially and seek time that is alone recharge their batteries. Introverts seek stimulation from within and seldom speak without thinking. Introverts carefully weigh options before you make decisions. Prior to entering into any sort of business negotiations, knowing whether your opponent tends toward extroversion or introversion can offer a advantage that is strategic. Sales persons should allow their customers that are introverted to think of sales proposals. Introverts can take into the information, mull it over, and then started to a determination. Pressing introverts for impulsive decisions may force them to say "No" since they're not comfortable making immediate decisions. Extroverts, having said that, may be pressured to some extent in order to make immediate decisions because they are more comfortable making impulsive decisions. Rarely people do exhibit entirely extroverted or characteristics that are totally introverted. Personality traits are slide along a continuum. Many individuals are exhibit both extroverted and characteristics that are introverted. Additionally, introverts who will be more comfortable with their surroundings often display behaviors associated with extroversion. Likewise, extroverts can be display introverted characteristics.

5) Used to do the thing that is right.

The Word Clue "right" suggests that this person struggled with a legal, moral, or ethical dilemma and overcame some level of internal or external opposition in order to make a reasonable and merely decision. This trait that is behavioral that this person has sufficient strength of character to help make the right decision even if confronted by opposing views.

Reading people is not difficult. Tune in to whatever they say and let their words do the talking.

Relationship Between Words Behavior and Personality

Personality is a factor that is major how individuals behave and perform in the work environment. For example, "traits which are element of a person's self-concept shall influence how one processes information and predicts future behavior" (Chatman, 1999). By examining a person's personality, human resource managers gain insight into what positions would be the best fit for an individual, or which individual is a significantly better fit for the position the need to be filled. Certain personality traits are good for management positions and other personality traits are better for other positions or careers.

Psychological tests are widely used to measure skills, personality types, and communication styles (Noe, 2010). The tests make it possible to understand an individual's tendencies, needs, types of work preferred, and kind of work the average person is most effective for. Additionally, they help to determine development goals that are best suited for the average person while the needed development to take the employee to higher quantities of skills. For instance, extroverts gain energy through interpersonal relationships where introverts gain energy through personal thoughts and feelings, which determines how a person gets motivated to perform.

In addition, strengths and weaknesses towards decision processes or communication styles can raise or inhibit productivity within the organization. The strengths and weaknesses result are from combinations of personality preferences.

Whatever you say shows who you are

Each and every word a person says shows something about his deep needs and insecurities even if he had different intentions in mind when he said them.

A person might say a joke just to make his friends laugh, but without realizing the words that he used can reveal a lot about his personality to the one who will analyze them.

Conclusion

Body gestures is nonverbal communication that a person communicates, sometimes unconsciously. Through body gestures, it is possible to find out about a person's views and thoughts about different situation, along with meaning of his words. Reading the body gestures could be achieved by the help of observing body movements and understanding about what is their hidden meanings.

Reading body gestures is a skill, which can be easily purchased in courses or through the websites dedicated to this topic. These courses will educate you on simple tips to interpret body movements along with a wide variety of ways of reading body gestures.

An individual with a huge understanding of body language can detect lies and hidden thoughts of those around him along with understanding what a person right in front of him thinks and unconsciously transmits through his body language in an almost telepathic manner.

An individual with body language reading skills can also make use of this knowledge to be familiar with his body that is own language and thereby prevent himself from wrongly using his body gestures and revealing his hidden thoughts through it.

The majority of us do not know the reality that someone's body can transmit a set that is complex. Knowing the signs and symptoms of an body that is individual can help us tell in what frame of mind or condition that individual is, no matter if in words they have a tendency to demonstrate something different. It doesn't matter what you decide to say, the human body signs can betray you into the optical eyes of someone who knows just how to read them. You will ask why this really is useful. Finding how is a person feels makes it possible in improving the communication with him or her. Many people might find it difficult to express in words, so knowing to identify the signs, which are talking the truth about them can be extremely beneficial in situations like this one.

Reading body language is known as non-verbal communication. It really is a technique used quite definitely in today's communication. Around you are feeling whether it is used in a business environment, in personal dating, or even inside the family. It can help you a great deal to find out how the people. Reading body gestures is certainly not difficult at all. You just need to pay focus on the way that the physical body of a person is near to you stands. For instance, the distance someone takes from you can say how comfortable that person is just about you. Closer mean she or he likes you while being means that is distant or she does not as you that much, or feel not too comfortable in your presence. Head position during conversation may also give some aspects away, as it is your head is tilted and combined with a smile. Then your person is either playful or flirty. If the head is pointing down, that individual could be hiding something. Tilted head to the sides can indicate confusion or misunderstanding.

In the event that you notice about your interlocutor is attempting to mimic you along it is trying to repeat some of your gestures, just like seeing yourself in the mirror, meaning he is attempting to produce a connection with you. Arm position is yet another aspect you can have a look at, to see if somebody is transmitting silent messages. Someone is holding the arms crossed can indicate he or she do not desire any social interaction. They have certain reserves or he/she is not happy about his or her character or appearance. Of course, if it is outside that is freezing a person might use this gesture to keep warm. Therefore, you should not misunderstand this sign that is particular. Hands behind the relative back or neck show desire for the discussion and that the person is relaxed. On the other way, keeping the arms in the hips, shows a person that will be impatient and looking forward to something or simply tired. Take into account that a hand held in a position, which is close like a fist, is an indication utilized by angry or irritated people.

This is why body language is a lot like an elaborated book. You probably already consider the gestures that is made today by the people they mean, in relationship to your person around you and what. From now on, you shall manage to see these signs and understand their interpretation, making the communication with others more accessible.

Daniel James Hollins

EMPATH HEALING

A Survival Guide for Highly Sensitive People Can Heal Psychologically and Spiritually. Overcome Negative Mindsets and develop Self-Confidence to Gain Control over Emotions

Introduction

Mystic recuperating has been around for quite a while. The individuals who need some otherworldly recuperating frequently search for a clairvoyant who can rehearse this capacity to mend their soul. There are numerous strategies for mystic and profound recuperating. The primary thought behind mystic mending is that if you are needing recuperating, it is because your soul has been taken to a lower level of awareness. Mystic mending is an approach to lift that degree of knowledge back to typical.

The most well-known strategy of clairvoyant recuperating is "empathic mending." As you presumably know, an empath is a mystic who has empathic instinct and can in this manner experience the sentiments of different people just as they were their own. When an empathic mystic wishes to help somebody whose soul has been harmed or is enduring here and there, an empath can enable them to recuperate and defeat their anguish.

An empathic clairvoyant initially should take advantage of what the other individual is feeling. This can be simple, or troublesome, contingent upon how protected the other individual is. At that point, the empath will almost certainly feel what the other is feeling, and can proceed to "take on," a more significant amount of the enduring of the other individual. The empathic clairvoyant can take a portion of the experiencing the person needing mending, with the goal that that individual has to a lesser degree a heap to shoulder.

This technique for empathic recuperating is viable with any inclination, which makes it a fantastic and versatile capacity.

Chapter one:
Are You An Empath?

I don't get that's meaning to you?

Empathic people are genuinely sensitive. In these evolving times, people who have dependably been sensitive may discover they are much increasingly vulnerable at this point. Furthermore, people who were not so painful may find they are winding up more so.

Affectability is an issue of our occasions. What's more, for the reasons expressed above, I concur. It impacts a wide range of characters, ages, societies. It is particularly common in people who attempt to affect other people constructively.

It is all the more regularly initiated in the circumstances with people who mirror our subliminal sentiments and convictions.

For what reason would it be smart thought for you to think about this? Well as a matter of first importance, when you don't know about it, it can clarify sure wonders occurring in your life that you might not have comprehended before, for example, unexplained emotional episodes, sobbing for no apparent reason or furious about something that may ordinarily simply be an aggravation, expanded exhaustion, sleep deprivation, body throbs and strain, and sickness... additionally could be lightly cheerful..

From a business or vocation point of view, it can affect your capacity to be profitable, interface with others, make a commitment on the planet and have the vitality to bring home the bacon doing it. From an individual point of view, it can affect your capacity to have some good times, share in physical action, your connections, and your prosperity.

What's more, that is only a begin.

What are the signs that you are an empath? (genuinely sensitive)

1. Sincerely sensitive people feel feelings frequently and profoundly. They may feel as though they "wear their emotions on their sleeves; however, not really. Men may feel things; yet, not demonstrate it as much because of social preparing that it isn't alright to do as such.

2. They are acutely mindful of the feelings of people around them.

3. Sensitive people are effectively harmed or vexed. An affront or harsh comment will influence them profoundly.

4. In a similar vein, sensitive people may endeavor to dodge clashes because the negativity affects them to such an extent.

5. Sensitive people are not ready to shake off their feelings effectively. When they are disheartened or

angry with something, they can't simply shift gears and overlook it. (this seems, by all accounts, to be evolving)

6. Sensitive people are enormously influenced by feelings they witness. They feel profoundly for others' torment. They may cry at Hallmark commercials or when others cry or when they associate profoundly with somebody.

7. Sensitive people may experience the ill effects of recurrent depression, anxiety, or another mental issue.

8. On the constructive side, sensitive people are likewise distinctly mindful of and influenced by excellence in artistry, music, and nature. They are the world's most noteworthy craftsmen and craftsmanship appreciators.

9. Sensitive people are inclined to upgrade over-burden. That is, they can't stand huge groups, noisy clamor, or rushed conditions. They feel overpowered and exhausted by an excess of boosts.

10. Sensitive people are brought into the world that way. They were vulnerable youngsters. I think this isn't as valid as it once might have been. As I said previously, people are ending up more painful than they ever were.

11. A compassionate individual, some of the time, feels animosity toward his sensitive nature. Most sensitive people entire heartedly wish they were more complicated and all the tougher. They feel like their affectability is a shortcoming. Like this, some susceptible grown-ups have figured out how to conceal their affectability from others.

What Kind of Empath Are You?

If you are an empath? You know you are touchy, and your most robust spiritual sense is in inclination. For entertainment only, take the test to discover which kind you are.

Hover in your mind or record which applies.

1. You contract an abrupt, repulsive stomach hurt. Consistent personality says it was a terrible lunch or this season's cold virus going around, yet then your pooch goes into the room and vomits on the rug. She looks somewhat green around the edges. (physical or creature empath)

2. While shopping at the adjacent Walmart, you enter the frozen food section and need to blast out into tears. You feel overpowering, profound misery, and depression. (enthusiastic empath or hypersensitivity to inadequately structured boxed foods)

3. While unwinding in the lounge chair, you abruptly hear words originate from your canine, "I need to take a walk now." (creature empath or the aftereffect of smoking such a large number of mushrooms)

4. Sitting in the lawn you feel a rush of happiness come over you and a feeling of harmony, and you incline to smell the flowering shrubbery (nature empath, or the mushrooms are as yet doing their stuff from the day preceding)

5. You feel down and angry when two minutes before you felt tranquil. Your dearest companion at that point calls and says he is feeling down and upset. (enthusiastic empath or you just shopped at a swarmed Walmart)

6. Two days before a noteworthy quake hits another nation you have bad dreams of seismic tremors, nervousness or sentiments of fate (mission empath or observing such a large number of films before bed)

7. You realize that one greenery plant needs more water and to be set in a sunnier window (nature empath or you've perused a lot of books on houseplants)

8. You get secure messages or channelings that will help the world concerning confidence (mission empath or still feel the impacts of the mushrooms)

9. You enter a medical clinic and feel dread, pity, uneasiness. You stroll by one room and feel agony in your side (physical empath or dread of emergency clinics)

If you circumnavigated at least one for nature empath: NATURE EMPATH you're fixed on the Nature Spirits and Fairies. You would exceed expectations at recuperating with Nature.

When you surrounded at least one for passionate empath: EMOTIONAL EMPATH, you're fixed on the feelings of others. You need to take a shot at discovering high devices and far better limits to exploit this blessing.

When you circumnavigated at least one for physical empath: PHYSICAL EMPATH, you're fixed on the physical sicknesses of others. You will need to perceive how to dispose of the emotions and not take it on. You'd make an incredible medical intuitive.

When you orbited at least one for creature empath: ANIMAL EMPATH you're fixed on creatures and can help them extraordinarily when you support this capacity.

When you surrounded at least one for mission empath: MISSION EMPATH you're fixed on the world, and your blessings will be utilized to help the planet on a more noteworthy scale.

Chapter two
Tools For An Empath's Energy Protection

Typical qualities of an Empath and why they need insurance:

Empaths are attracted to recuperating themselves as well as other people. They are generally attracted to mending since they feel that they have so much inside recuperating to do… until that is, they understand that a large portion of the repair required is for other people that they are instinctively 'feeling.'

They are more often than not in a condition of consistent exhaustion. This is a huge issue. Individuals, alongside their energies, are always attacking an Empath's power. An Empath will generally take on something over the top and become depleted all-around rapidly, and it's not effectively restored by rest or rest. It goes much more remote than that and is very debilitating.

Empaths are magnificent audience members. They care about the prosperity of others and end up tuning in to the burdens of individuals they don't know. A great many people discover Empaths so natural to open up to. That is the point at which they begin dumping a wide range of cynicism going in their life. Sometimes, individuals aren't even mindful they are doing this.

By and large, an Empath with deal with the necessities of others even before their own, because they care to such an extent. Since individuals get settled enough around them to open up, they will typically benevolently listen carefully to enable an individual; regardless of whether it's to their very own burden.

Alone time is a need for an Empaths. Many Empaths like to make tracks in the opposite direction from the majority of the feelings and energy that isn't theirs, so they require a genuinely necessary time alone. This is the ideal opportunity for them to return to adjust and distance themselves from all antagonism that isn't theirs.

An Empath can likewise show up as grouchy. Empaths sometimes appear to have significant emotional episodes, and this sometimes is added to the majority of the staggering contemplations and sentiments shelling them regularly. Not exclusively are they barraged with these energies; however, at this point, they have to deal with and make sense of all that stuff coming to their direction.

They are genuinely delicate to viciousness, cold-bloodedness, or any disaster. Most Empaths quit viewing the TV and perusing the papers sooner or later in their lives, as this as well, can be overpowering for an empath.

Out and out knowing is likewise a common Empath characteristic. Empaths sometimes know things that they are sure they were never educated or told. This knowing is altogether different than instinct or a warning.

Being in open spots is frequently overpowering or painful to an empath. Again such a large number of individuals' feelings are in free places that can be grabbed when not in any case attempting to. This is an exciting ride most Empaths will keep away from no matter what.

An Empath can 'feel' genuineness and respectability. They can tell if somebody is being straightforward or not, which is very agitating and sometimes painful in your life. It's particularly agitating when they are managing friends and family.

It is feeling the physical side effects and torments of another. Numerous Empaths will end up building up an affliction that another person has that has nothing to do with them. This is sympathy at its best.

These are only a couple of the traits of an Empath. Once more, being an Empath can be either viewed as a revile or a blessing relying upon the devices you use to secure yourself. There are numerous ways for Empaths to Protect themselves. Keeping away from enormous parties or open places no matter what is one way. There are times when you can't maintain a strategic distance from these things. There are many useful approaches to ensure yourself as an empath.

Precious stones

Rose Quartz is an impressive precious stone for an Empath because its recuperating properties advance unequivocal love and solace. This is particularly useful for an individual that might hold not exactly cherishing energies of something, somebody, or even themselves.

Dark Tourmaline or Hematite are likewise incredible gems for an Empath to enable them to remain grounded. These stones will also assimilate any negative energies.

Malachite is another precious stone that will help assimilate any negative emotions you might have; regardless of whether they are your very own or not!

Labradorite is a precious stone that will help shield your emanation from retaining any issues that are being imparted to you.

Citrine is a precious yellow stone to help light up your state of mind. Another Citrine mending property is that it can likewise help retain terrible energy from your condition.

Another go-to precious stone for me is Amethyst. Notwithstanding the way that it is delightful, it will reinforce your instinct. Increased instinct is brilliant for everybody, except mainly for Empaths to help them genuinely realize that the sentiments they might have are theirs or not.

To wrap things up is Rainbow Fluorite. Rainbow Fluorite might be, as I would like to think, the Mother of all gems for an Empath as it helps all degrees of being! This is a multi-hued precious stone that can enable you to remain grounded to the earth, help clear and parity all Chakras, just as to allow you to continue sensitive to higher measurements.

These are my go-to precious stones to enable me to remain focused, grounded, ensured, and tuned in. Precious stones can and will help recuperate your life!

Contemplation

Contemplation has been utilized for a large number of years as an approach to accomplish a degree of mindfulness that is past the restrictions of the consistently thinking personality. Naturally, it's the act of uniting, the psyche, body, and soul!

Most don't understand that our bodies were intended to act naturally, adjusting to keep up positive wellbeing by just keeping brain, body, and soul in equalization. Envision that it is so natural to be out of parity when the energy of others penetrates your body regularly. It's epic!

At the point when you're out of equalization, your life-power energy doesn't flow an incredible way it should. Being out of parity appears in life as a throbbing painfulness. Furthermore, when you're out of equalization for a considerable length of time, your body starts to make ailment and infection.

Alone time and reflection is an excellent path for an empath to keep themselves adjusted and entirety. This is simply the act of cherishing that most Empaths set at the back of the line when they even placed it in the front of significance by any means!

Empathic Abilities

It is now and then challenging to tell whether someone is an empath, (a mystic who has empathic abilities). The issue is, you don't generally know whether someone has these supernatural forces, or if they are merely touchy, getting individuals. How would you know whether you're incredibly empathic?

Empaths are amazingly touchy to the sentiments of people around them. Regularly, an empath will most likely sense what someone is experiencing, regardless of whether they can't see or hear that individual. Someone with this sort of ability "knows." Many psychics with empathic abilities report experiencing someone else's sentiments just as they were their own. However, this isn't generally the situation.

A clairvoyant with this sort of ability will almost certainly sense the sentiments of others, mainly if those emotions are stable. Regular feelings that an empath will experience incorporate dread, delight, depression, energy, love, and foreboding. The more grounded the believing, the simpler it will be for the empath to detect, comprehend, and feel.

What sets empaths separated from other, "typical" individuals, is that they have a more profound, progressively touchy comprehension for what they are feeling. This instinct originates from inside and is far more noteworthy than what a great many people understand. For instance, a "typical" individual may realize that someone they adore is steamed at easily overlooked details they state or do. In any case, an empath would detect this even without seeing or conversing with that individual, and an empath could sense if that cherished one was feeling sold out, envious, furious, or hurt. This mystic instinct would originate from inside, not from the visual or capable of being heard signs of the physical world.

Empaths can tell when something isn't right, regardless of whether that something hasn't occurred at this point. They are overwhelmed with a profound feeling of foreboding that cautions them that everything isn't as it ought to be. A "typical" individual, then again, would not have the option to tell when something startling or hazardous would occur.

These things all stable extraordinary; however, not every person understands that it can likewise be hard to be an empath. This is because empaths are not ready to "shut off" their abilities at whatever point they need. That is, they can't pick whether to feel something. Instead, they should feel whatever their clairvoyant instinct detects, regardless of whether they would prefer not. This is an enormous weight for empaths, and it is additionally why empathic psychics can become ill from depletion.

Empathic Abilities - What Are They and How to Tell If You Have Them

Empaths are fairly natural creatures, more adept at understanding individuals than "signs" or tarot cards. There are individuals of an empathic nature that have those capacities, yet that is only a little piece of what is an Empath.

Enthusiasm for the empathic individual has just risen lately following crafted by Jad Alexander. An understudy of brain science, Jad started to perceive certain sorts of individuals that had remarkable and raised degrees of affectability. They were natural, having the option to detect things at a level obscure and inaccessible to the average individual. He arrived at the resolution following 30 years of contemplating such sorts, that they were in certainty talented, having the capacity to "know" things naturally, for example, when somebody needed them to call, when somebody was in a lousy position and required assistance, or even how to get someplace while never having been there or following bearings.

He arrived at the resolution that these individuals had one of a kind adjustments to their focal sensory systems (CNS). The collaboration between the CNS and the mind was remarkable to the point that it made an "intuition," one that got messages at a lot further level than "common" people, and unpredictably prepared those messages. Those this wonder has not yet been assessed by science. Many people have put time and assets into researching precisely what is an Empath.

Through these examinations, it has been resolved that those with empathic natures groups specific typical characteristics. The most widely recognized denominator is an uplifted feeling of affectability. Regularly these individuals are marked as over-delicate people; however, maybe ultra-touchy is an increasingly fitting definition. They are incredibly open to scents, clamor, and light, their real organs having a low edge, which enhances how much their faculties respond.

Notwithstanding these high degrees of affectability, Empaths are frequently shelled with a consistent progression of arbitrary, apparently silly considerations and feelings. This is because they often "get" the concerns and sentiments of others, those in their quick region, however regularly of individuals who are miles, if not seas away. This is the mental make-up of what is an Empath, a condition that those uninformed of their blessing battle with. As a result of the immense measures of data, they are accepting, and not understanding its temperament, many become overpowered and befuddled, regularly looking for mental directing, or even medicine.

You may ponder, "What is an Empath instead of a mystic. The basic clarification is; while a clairvoyant "sees," an empathic individual "feels." The hunches and got-sentiments the empathic character encounters are mystic messages. The issue is that these messages are imparted in a kind of clairvoyant language that is both remote and complex. Understanding this language, known as Dreamtongue, is essential to get a handle on precisely what is an Empath ultimately.

Psychic Readings - Understanding the Psychic Empath

A champion among the most well-known kinds of mental capacity is that of the Psychic Empath. Mystic Empaths are people that can detect or feel the feelings of others. They can likewise encounter similar feelings or impressions that another person is facing. Their real gift lies in their one of a kind capacity to concentrate on the vitality or beliefs that are impacting individuals. They likewise have the clairvoyant bent to tune into one's otherworldly aides. Fundamentally, they are dispatchers. Not exclusively would they be able to convey data from the profound domain, they can likewise help by translating ones inward, passionate states.

Somewhat, we are all Empaths. The more in the order we are with our feelings, the simpler it is to tune into the opinions of others. The most common issue that happens, in any case, is the point at which we wind up excessively related to other individuals. Mystic Empaths frequently battle with this. For Psychic Empath, a lot of self-care is required. The gift of the Psychic Empath can be a troublesome one. They continually need to secure themselves by defining proper limits with their subjects. Take, for instance, the person that as of late encountered the passing of a nearby one. The Psychic Empath will face similar distress, pity, and outrage as the person who has quite recently lost their cherished one. The Psychic Empath must build up the suitable abilities to shield themselves from taking this on. They should figure out how to isolate their very own feelings from their subjects.

The Psychic Empath can figure out how to do this through various strategies. The most well-known procedure is through an establishing reflection. This is a kind of intervention where the Empath profoundly, inwardly, and outwardly associates themselves to the earth. It empowers them to ground their body and psyche to the intensity of the planet. This association can keep the Empath in their very own collection and shields them from losing themselves in the domain of feelings.

Another famous system is that of a security contemplation. An insurance contemplation incorporates the detecting or perception of a defensive celestial light. The Empath utilizes this heavenly light as a boundary between their feelings and that of their subjects. Even though regardless they can encounter the opinions of others, they are ensured against "taking on" the feelings of others.

A gifted Empath can give incredible mystic readings. They are especially gifted at interfacing with their subject's aides, blessed messengers, or expired friends and family. If you are encountering an abundance of negative or overpowering feelings, a Psychic Empath can enable you to work through these. They are there to assist you with discovering what might impact your opinions and give you the essential answers for procedure them. They can likewise convey crucial messages from the soul world, regularly giving the understanding to enable you to develop as a person.

Am I an Empath? - Psychic Guide

A clairvoyant with empathic capacities, (likewise called an "empath"), can encounter the feelings and sentiments of others. All things being equal, it is some of the time hard to differentiate between an empathic mystic and somebody who is merely delicate. Here are three inquiries to think about when posing to yourself if you are an empath:

1. Am I more genuinely touchy than other individuals?

> Empaths will, in general, be amazingly touchy in their feelings and emotions. This goes well past what is considered "typical" feeling by non-clairvoyants. Once in awhile simple things like seeing a dead winged creature or the withering of blossom will cause an empath to tear up from enthusiastic reaction.

2. Do I become enthusiastic for no apparent reason?

At the point when an empath encounters the feelings of others, mainly if that individual isn't close-by, it can appear just as the empath is riding an enthusiastic crazy ride for reasons unknown. For instance, while accomplishing something simple like strolling down the road, an empath can encounter the feelings of somebody they don't have the foggiest idea about a couple of squares away. They may not see the individual. Thus it might appear as though their passionate reaction is appearing suddenly.

3. Would I be able to detect how others are feeling, regardless of whether they are concealing reality from every other person?

Empaths are not tricked when individuals are experiencing an enthusiastic test put on a brave face for the remainder of the world. At the point when most "typical" individuals probably won't see and probably won't understand anything wasn't right, an empath is agonizingly mindful of the reality of the circumstance. Empaths can see directly through individuals "putting on a bold face," in a manner of speaking. Their enthusiastic knowledge is a lot higher than that of other individuals.

Emotions and Health

For a long time, conventional medication accepted that your wellbeing involved hereditary qualities, contamination introduction, and way of life. It was a particular uncommon case when emotional experience likewise played a factor in your wellbeing condition. There is currently strong science behind the connection of emotional experience and a large group of diseases and wellbeing conditions, including heart disease, despair, obesity, and perpetual agony. When taking a gander at the body, all in all, emotional experience currently has a significant impact on your general wellbeing. Weakness and stress have been viewed as guilty parties in thwarting your wellbeing.

Without managing their emotional wellbeing, nobody can be truly well. Little advancement can be made relieving a physical condition, regardless of what treatment is utilized, until there is advance at the emotional level.

Uncertain emotional issues add to bombing physical matters. They may be emotional experiences that happened many years prior in your adolescence, covered up and rotting inside the body that turns out sometime down the road as an unfavorable wellbeing condition or disease. Regularly for ladies, menopause is the point at which your body is disclosing to you it is prepared to determine emotional issues and needs mending. Both your emotional and physical wellbeing can be improved together. It tends to be the point at which you can recover your self.

The most clever spot to investigate the emotional foundations of the disease might be the leap forward ACE Study. In the 1990s, more than 17,000 patients of a huge wellbeing plan were joined up with an examination to survey the connection between emotional experience and grown-up wellbeing. The outcomes were shocking, which offered motivation to reexamine the structure of essential consideration in America's medical practice.

Members were solicited whether they had encountered any from eight types of personal maltreatment or useless family conduct before the age of 18, each called an "unfavorable youth experience" (ACE). The more significant part of the patients had one ACE or more. Considerably all the more astounding was the connection to wellbeing results. The individuals who had encountered an ACE were bound to have an unfriendly wellbeing condition or disease as a grown-up. The wellbeing results secured a wide range, including heart disease, fractures, diabetes, obesity, liquor abuse, and that's just the beginning.

In all actuality, all emotional experience influences our wellbeing, regardless of whether positive or negative, and whether it happens before or the present. Negative emotional experiences seem to have additionally enduring wellbeing impacts, maybe because we will, in general disregard managing them.

A few therapists and researchers accept we have five essential emotions: bliss, dread, outrage, distress, and love, with other inclination states being a minor departure from these five. A feeling is a thing that your body does with one of these sentiments.

The Center for Disease Control gauges that 90% of all visits to the specialist are stress-related. There are several medical studies linking stress to a large group of diseases. Stress is personal. Something stressful to one individual isn't really to another because of every individual's emotional history. Our memoir turns into our science, as it were. Individuals create patterns in managing stress. It is critical to know about your habits and to figure out how to control them for your emotional prosperity and your physical wellbeing.

Emotions and Health- Is There A Connection?

Wellbeing is characterized as a condition of physical, mental, and social prosperity and the nonappearance of sickness or other abnormal health. As indicated by certain types of conventional medicine rehearses, an evil state creates because the individual has damaged a course that Nature needs them to pursue. At whatever point, the body's natural cadence is aggravated in some structure, and the body reacts to fix the unsettling influence. The reaction of the body is as indications that cause sickness.

One case of the manifestations showing up because of an unsettling influence is the point at which we have contamination. Fever is a common reaction of the body when any piece of it endures with a disease. As a general rule, the body is attempting to murder the contaminating microbes by raising the body's temperature. From a medical standpoint, fever is a side effect of contamination.

The two realities that you have to think about wellbeing and sickness are identified with our feelings. How the beliefs influence our body and psyche is a not outstanding territory in modern-day medicine. In conventional medical practices everywhere throughout the world, the job of feelings in disease and wellbeing is excellent.

Actuality one-When we experience any negative or awful enthusiastic experience, the body tends to 'assimilate' or 'lock up' the impacts in a gentle manner. The more the individual experiences terrible encounters, the more the body ends up tense or worried. This debilitates the insusceptible framework. The body's capacities to manage any attack by ailment causing life forms is undermined. So when the disease strikes, the medicines and medications influence the body to the extent to how much the body can help them in being dominant. A few people need a higher number of drugs than others in light of this reason.

Certainty two-The more loosened up your body turns into, the better is the resistant framework. The body's mending framework handles the issue without anyone else. One needn't bother with many prescriptions in such a case. The casual body helps in the mending procedure. This is the motivation behind why individuals who practice reflection, yoga, or jujitsu don't endure numerous sicknesses.

Emotional and Health Benefits of Outdoor Exercise

In the present society, an ever-increasing number of individuals are coming to understand the heart-solid advantages and passionate prosperity got from working out. The reality of the situation is that rehearsing not just makes the body look and feel great in blend with a decent dietary program, yet additionally advances pressure discharge, a well-conditioned cardiovascular framework, and the likelihood of fewer maladies or confusions through the span of one's lifetime.

During the mid-year, its simple to consider open-air activities and fun wellness things to take an interest in since warm climate brings such a large number of alternatives. Individuals rush to the parks, shorelines, and bicycle ways for swimming, rollerblading, and biking. Outside exercises are anything but challenging to design throughout the mid-year since everybody is anxious to dispose of the winter blues and get some daylight.

Throughout the mid-year, there are a large number of outdoor exercises to browse with the end goal of both training and fun. For general wellness and cardiovascular continuance, running or running interims through the recreation center is an incredible method to get up every morning and get in a speedy piece of activity as the sun rises. While out with companions or taking the children to the recreation center, playing Frisbee, a round of avoiding the ball, or soccer is sure to keep everybody engaged and make them move at any wellness level.

Any practicing outside throughout the late spring months is probably going to be a tremendous amount of fun, and the vast majority won't understand that fun action is improving their wellness level. Also, as a rule throughout the late spring months, there are a few outside games groups framed that are either for no particular reason, similar to a bar class, or increasingly aggressive ones in which players win prizes and cash. Volleyball clubs, b-ball alliances, and friends softball games are well known open-air practice exercises during the warm season.

What the vast majority neglect to acknowledge, however, is that notwithstanding during the virus winter months, practicing outside doesn't need to stop, and it is still genuinely conceivable. At the point when the snow begins to fall, outside exercise exercises, for the most part, happen at ski resorts or on frigid slopes where wellness sweethearts can take part in skiing- - downhill or cross-country, snowboarding, snowshoeing, or trekking. Any individual who has never gone trekking during the virus winter months is in for a significant astonishment their first time. This exceptional outside exercise includes binding up those boots, putting on a cap and gloves, and conquering the open air components for a mix of running crosswise over blanketed ways, moving up frosty slopes, and investigating the winter climate with a weighted backpack on, consuming right around 1000 calories in an hour session.

For those adrenaline junkies who aren't blackout of heart, a trekking trip is an excellent method to appreciate practicing outside and increment your wellness level, dispensing with the reason that the climate won't allow it. Regardless of whether the exercises are finished during the warm summer season or in the bone-chilling winter climate, practicing outside unquestionably has its place. A few people would contend that practicing outside is progressively best when contrasted with doing conventional cardio on a machine inside or being stuck inside an exercise center throughout the day.

Open-air practicing is exceedingly energized for any individual who might want to have a go at something new to remain fit as a fiddle and challenge themselves since it realizes more to see and do than being restricted to the exhausting indoor machines and same old schedule that the indoor offices can offer.

Chapter Three
Are You Sharing Your Gifts?

We accept that everybody has been given exceptional and unique blessings, and an enormous piece of our voyage is to help and recuperate others by sharing these endowments.

Your abilities and endowments have the potential and the ability to mend and completely change others, however when individuals don't have the foggiest idea about what you and your blessings are accessible if they can't discover you, they can't and won't profit by your endowments.

As a rule, what is preventing us from sharing our endowments, from aiding and recuperating more individuals, is dread. It might be dread about not being adequate, dread about how we'll be seen, dread about requesting cash, the dread of appearing to be egotistical, the fear of "selling," and so on.

As dread comes up, what we have to recall and perceive is that our endowments were given to us by our Source (the Universe, God, the Divine, whatever name you pick). There is nothing amiss with telling individuals how we can support them. We must do as such.

We as a whole can genuinely completely change someone, yet if we don't impart to them that we can, at that point we are retaining and being egotistical with our endowments.

As we grasp and offer our endowments with others, we step onto our Authentic Path. As we enable our customers to pay us for our administrations, we respect and worth our customers by allowing them to offer back to us. In this trade, we likewise appreciate our blessings, our Source, and ourselves.

So how would you begin?

1. Pay consideration regarding your identity being versus who you have to progress toward becoming to epitomize the achievement you need to accomplish. Is it true that you are taking100% duty regarding your activities, your outcomes, and your conditions? If you are as of now typifying the individual, you imagine yourself to be as productive, prosperous, and respecting the unimaginable endowments, you have gotten?

2. Take the following right advance to begin getting out there and quit concealing your light. We don't generally realize what that is, so if you don't have the foggiest idea, discover somebody who can bolster you in making an arrangement. When you have a stability method set up, the way is a lot more straightforward. You can stop the anguish of addressing and questioning and push ahead with certainty and sureness.

3. Connect with others. You do need to do it. However, you don't need to do only it. We're not intended to. Escape your home, interface with others one on one,

and work on discussing what you do. Enable yourself to flub it up. (Brian and I are enormous devotees of the "mulligan" (the "do-over"), so absolutely never feel like what you state about what you do to help individuals can't be changed our change. Get out there and practice, explore. This is the place some of your most prominent lucidity can emerge out of!

Invitation to take action

We welcome you to look at your training, your business, and your life and inquire as to whether you are genuinely sharing your endowments or would they say they are taking cover behind dread?

Your abilities and blessings are intended to be shared, and in sharing them you, not just assistance and mend others, you help and recuperate yourself.

For A Little Lift, Find Your Gift

What a beautiful thing to state, particularly given that such a significant number of people feel came up short on for the work they do. In any case, my customer was talking about having taken advantage of something so critical to be glad in our work and home lives.

When I asked precisely what it was that made him feel so charmed by his activity, he said it was because prevailing at work came simply to him. "I feel like I am doing what I was destined to do."

The Secret Recipe

When we find our endowments and can take advantage of them consistently, we pull in people to us. We interest and draw in our customers, and we make champions for our organizations. So for what reason do all things considered numerous experience difficulty taking advantage of this mystery formula?

Again and again, it begins in adolescence. In kindergarten, everybody is on a level playing field. At that point, an instructor or state-sanctioned test calls attention to that we are excellent in math, however not in English, and are decided for not being great at everything.

The procedure proceeds all through most training frameworks, categorizing us, and very regularly blaming us for not being bosses of everything. Therefore, we discover that simply being great at one or a couple of things isn't worthy.

With an end goal to enhance our feeble regions, we are debilitated from concentrating on what we progress admirably. The outcome is that we dismiss what we exceed expectations at, of what comes effectively and frequently.

As a grown-up, you can reinvent those old messages.

English therapist Francis Galton characterized the term skilled as, "grown-ups who exhibit excellent ability in some zone." actually when we have the mental fortitude and backing to locate those mystical characteristics inside us-the aptitudes, bits of knowledge, and implicit learning that come to us usually the changes in outlook.

You likely have an entirely smart thought of what your blessings are, however, to cement the rundown, attempt this essential exercise.

Ask yourself:

- When you were youthful, what abilities did people disclose to you that you had a blessing or ability for?

- What energizes you, and lights up your face, even though others should seriously think about it "work"?

- What do you do great, however when asked can't clarify how or for what good reason it comes so effectively?

Ask others:

- What do you imagine that I do well that appears to be bizarre or one of a kind?

- What do you feel are my natural abilities, and when do I display them most?

- When you incline toward me for help, would it be that you are looking for?

The reactions to these questions will enable you to plunge further into what it is that makes you tick, just as what others see to be your real blessings. I estimate that it won't take some time before you know precisely what you specialize in.

Presently get the chance to work! What's more, begin down the way to grasping your best self, captivating your customers, and carrying on with a progressively prosperous life.

What Stops You From Giving Your Gifts to Yourself?

Do you think that it's much simpler to convey your most noteworthy blessings to others than it is to get them for yourself? Many change operators don't consider recuperating themselves with a similar effect they have on others, overlooking the savvy saying "Healer, mend thyself!"

There are a few explanations behind this oversight.

In the first place, you may think that it's difficult to respect yourself how you respect others. One of the methods in which we were trained when we were youthful to increase social acknowledgment was simply the bogus quietude of deprecating to make others feel relaxed. It tends to challenge shed such propensities, which are among the most significant obstructions to prevailing as an operator of progress. "Who am I to do these huge things?" These musings shield us from going out on a limb that change producers consistently face and even forestall seeing what may be conceivable.

You are the vehicle of the change that you convey, which requires getting to be unmistakable as a pioneer to bigger and bigger crowds to contact; however, many lives as could be expected under the circumstances. Furthermore, by the idea of your expected set of responsibilities, you don't fit in - supposing that you did serenely fit in, you'd be content with business as usual! However, that hereditary basic to have a place with a clan that guarantees our physical survival drives us to remain little and erroneously modest.

At the other extraordinary, others may wear a bogus expanded personality self to shield a helpless, inadequate inclination self.

Figuring out how to respect oneself incorporates a sound balance of knowing your real limits and impediments at any minute in time, and how your blessings supplement the endowments of others. This regarding likewise calls for significant self-acknowledgment that acknowledges precisely where you are at present, as you grasp the move of alternate extremes inside.

Despite whether you have an affinity for deprecating yourself or misrepresenting your abilities, neither serves when you are talking about your central goal to the individuals who must move without hesitation!

Another critical component of getting your blessings is life balance and self consideration. Life balance praises every one of the decisions and responsibilities that mean the most to you, in bona fide extent. Treating yourself with the account, you give others appreciates the way that you are the hallowed vehicle of your motivation. Pause for a minute at present and lay your left hand tenderly all over. Notice how that feels - have you been giving yourself enough of this sort of loving touch?

This move requires advancing those parts of the self that consistently push and drive you from the attitude of "It's insufficient" or "I'm insufficient." Such a mentality prompts the absence of essence, just as burnout, damage, and sickness.

Instead, begin seeing each one of those parts of your life where it's strikingly clear that you are sufficient.

At last, it becomes conceivable to mend your most profound injuries by giving yourself the equivalent deliberate endowments you offer to other people. At that point, the delight of your total capacity becomes accessible to satisfy the mission you are intended to bring to the world.

Chapter Four
Understanding Energy Star
Rating For Appliances

When you are hoping to turn into a progressively responsible customer and lessening your impacts on nature, you may be interested in which items are more earth benevolent than others. Luckily, some sure seals and marks can piece of information you into the proficiency of particular gadgets and apparatuses. If you are searching for data on understanding vitality star rating for devices, this part can help.

At whatever point you see this seal of endorsement, it implies that the item does not require as much power, water, or different assets, to keep running than other comparative issues. This means you can save money on your power and water charges over the long haul and lessen your natural effect.

To discover items that have this seal of endorsement, you should take a gander at the bundling. Most questions will enlighten you regarding their productivity directly on the crate. In many cases, the rating is signified by a star image with a picture of the Earth. The legislature gives this endorsement.

Items that have this seal should likewise keep going for a long while. They are assessed for their proficiency, yet also to their capacity to last. They are by, and ample of a high caliber and may not have to be supplanted too early.

When you are dubious about a particular thing and its rating, you can discover more by going on the web. Many brands will give data about their thoughts and the measure of vitality that they utilize on the internet. Some shopper magazines will likewise be exceptionally educational about the proficiency of various gadgets.

Whenever you are in the market for another climate control system, washer, dryer, or another machine, you might need to look out for the Energy Star seal of endorsement. This can enable you to settle on an insightful choice and buy a decent, dependable item.

Understanding Energy Healing Techniques

The development of alternative medication has additionally opened the field of quick mending. This specific type of curing enables one to experience recuperating through auric and vigorous fields through the exchange of vitality starting with one individual then onto the next. The comprehension of this philosophy is proceeding to develop, with new organizations being found for those intrigued by protection care and support. Vitality mending procedures that are accessible furnish for differing openings with recuperating an alternative consideration.

When you start scanning for vitality mending procedures, you can move into an assortment of choices from professionals that have investigated the field or that have picked up preparing in alternative treatments. Regular methodologies that are presently perceived globally include Reiki, Chakra recuperating, and bodywork. These are just a couple of the few open doors that are broadly recognized for mending and deterrent consideration. These choices move vitality to your energetic field, which can clear squares and make a more profound feeling of recuperating for your body, brain, and soul.

The first exchange of vitality is just one configuration for vim recuperating methods. You can likewise discover distinctive vivacious recuperating alternatives through different organizations. For example, a few healers will focus on discharging karma or specific kinds of enthusiastic squares in your vitality field. These are noted through youth trauma, generational difficulties, obstructs that you are presently encountering through different situations or from relapses into previous existences or unusual locations. By working these out enthusiastically, you will most likely discharge vitality and move this into an increasingly positive association with your present status.

The alternatives for vitality recuperating methods are promoted with the individual affiliations and history of a professional. For example, many alternative professionals will have extensive experience with bodywork, brain science, Yoga, or other lifeway encounters. These are frequently joined with the strategies in lively recuperating, explicitly to assist the advancement of the systems and to help with the practices that you are utilizing for a mending session. The professionals you are working with may offer alternatives, for example, consolidating breathing, body moves, daily meditation, or mental activities to help with the adjustments in vitality.

Understanding Energy To Get Over An Addiction

The more significant part of us needs addictions since it is an approach to get away. When we are shaky, pushed, exhausted, discouraged, or notwithstanding looking for irregular joy, we utilize our habits to give us that "fix." It is just typical to have them and yet when we need to improve our lives, we ought to dispose of them.

Many of us deny that we have a fixation which isn't great since it can blind spot us from many things. Then again, when we acknowledge and pardon ourselves for having them, we can, in any event, have the decision to continue satisfying them or work on getting over them. Subsequently, when we make issues as a result of them, at any rate, we know where it originates from, and we don't lose ourselves in the haziness of refusal.

We can live much better without our addictions, or possibly figure out how to wind up more grounded as we figure out how to get over them. Habits offer desires to surrender to them, and we can figure out how to either control our inclinations or go further than that and let them go.

Controlling urges will work; however, there will dependably be a fight regardless of whether the inclinations, in the end, get more fragile. Or on the other hand, we can take in where they originate from and dispose of them. Along these lines, we don't need to manage the fight, and we can be free!

A large portion of the controlling is done through rationale and reason, yet then the desires can endeavor to utilize that against us to surrender. Perhaps we adhere to this arrangement since we would prefer not to get into the harder work. We don't need to look for assistance; we can do that without anyone's help just from being increasingly mindful and understanding their examples of presence.

Addictions start when we pick a minor propensity that we as of now appreciate however then take it to the following level.

It can begin from being a getaway instrument that gives delight and can develop into a simple method to look for joy. From a higher point of view, a habit gives us vitality that joins with adrenalin, and this inclination in itself can likewise be addictive. At that point, our psyches or cerebrums get molded to appreciate this vitality.

The issue with this joy and vitality looking for propensity is that we lose ourselves to it, our psyches go into a lower level of awareness. We lose our very own capacity; we give our ability away to the fixation. Also, the more we surrender to dependence, the more it will fortify itself after some time. The more we have it, the more our personalities are molded to want them, along these lines, the harder it is to break free of them. Not to stress, there is no good reason for feeling awful when we gave in for a long time because as long as we deal with conquering them, we are improving ourselves and positive change regardless is an extraordinary thing.

The ideal approach to get over a fixation is to step by step discharge the vitality and adrenalin that accompany the desires. This way to take full breaths and feel the energy that downers up from the attractions and discharge it. We need to contact the vitality in our bodies and see the adrenalin that it makes in our psyches. As it were, we are standing up to the urges when they occur, and when we can appropriately discharge the vitality, the calls will debilitate until we get to the source.

Completely getting over enslavement is going in the turn around bearing of its creation. That is the reason a few inclinations might be simpler to stand up to than others; it relies upon the molding of their nature. If we ultimately need to get over them, we need found a superior method to manage weakness, stress, weariness, and wretchedness. Additionally, we have to discover better helpful approaches to look for vitality or delight. However, this will come as we chip away at our addictions and increase bits of knowledge.

The best thing about chipping away at a habit is that we can figure out how to recoup portions of ourselves that got lost to them. We additionally get familiar with ourselves, which is significant. It takes more work than merely controlling the inclinations. However, the entire procedure is fulfilling. It is a voyage in itself towards individual flexibility. Once in a while, we can't accomplish the things we genuinely need in life because our addictions keep us down and influence our karma.

Understanding Energy Monitoring

A standout amongst the enormous worries about vitality checking is its long haul applications. Concerned people will say that they wish they could lease a vitality screen, discover their progressions and return it. Others will utilize their observing framework, see a few reserve funds, and after that, quit checking their use by and large. To legitimize this perfect, they state that the most significant investment funds can be discovered immediately and that once they have found their utilization propensities, they don't have to screen their framework continually. Things being what they are, the inquiry progresses toward becoming, what can be picked up by continuously observing your vitality utilization?

Vitality observing can be utilized in a few unique designs. It tends to be used to supplant a vitality review, as it were, it very well may be used to bring up regions that should be made progressively proficient, for example, lighting, channels, HVAC frameworks, and different things. Utilizing this framework you will see a ton of reserve funds immediately, in any case, much the same as with vitality reviews, and you should direct another consideration in the end since gear does not generally remain the equivalent. Your hardware and building are always showing signs of change, something exceptional one minute may separate the following. A little preview won't give you enough data to know whether the progressions you made are sufficient or will last after some time. Consistently checking your framework demonstrates you if you have to roll out further improvements or if your sequences were successful.

Structures and offices are a ton like people. They contain various working parts that all need to cooperate for the entire framework to work effectively. If you choose to start eating less, you will buy a scale and gauge yourself routinely to ensure you are getting thinner to ensure that your eating regimen is compelling. When you quit weighing yourself, how would you realize your eating routine is successful, how would you know you are getting in shape? Without a scale, you will have no chance to get of knowing whether your eating regimen is fruitful, and in a ton of cases, your weight will either remain the equivalent or even increment! If you gauge yourself a month to month, there is no real way to determine what caused the fluctuations. Vitality observing is synonymous with the scale. When you intend to cut your vitality utilization, you need to get your office a range to persistently gauge the outcomes, to ensure that your vitality diet is fruitful and viable.

Looking at results from your month to month vitality bills won't reveal to you what changed. It could be something as straightforward as the climate or a noteworthy issue. Ongoing vitality observing enables you to see your office changing after some time. It allows you to alter your framework and make changes before the problem makes it to your bill. Your month to month vitality bill gives a little depiction, yet it isn't sufficient to fundamentally oversee and control your vitality utilization.

Chapter Five
Highly Sensitive Person
Through Lifespan

As people venture in the difficulties of life, it will fundamentally change them from various requests as they grow up trim them to be a superior individual with their numerous encounters throughout everyday life.

The empathetic individual will be liable to various worries just as troubles joined by it. They can modify with so many concern as they are figuring out how to adapt to them.

In the phase of early stages and adolescence, it will take a hard time controlling because high affectability is available from birth. Without staying alert with the tyke's condition, the guardians treat their babies and youngsters as to be profoundly requesting individual without perceiving their genuine need. As they grow up, the kid will set up their psyches that they are hard to deal with and that their folks don't need them any longer.

Susceptible youngsters may require creating capacities and deal with those aptitudes to inspire themselves. This thought will be useful to evade them from being very animated with occasions. They can utilize shaping capacities, for example, drawing.

At the point when an individual reaches teenage life, it would be increasingly agreeable for them to direct their concentration toward companions instead of the family they grow up. Susceptible teenagers will pick up security with their social companions and build up their public activity alongside them. In this stage, it would be more on learning the open business in their general public they are in as opposed to uncovering issues at home. They get themselves outrageous enough conquering issues when they are with their companions and quietly chuckling around and hosting a gathering throughout the night. Friends are likewise useful with susceptible people since they can pick up certainty inside themselves. It is a result of companion impact that they can demonstrate what they resemble volunteering themselves to associations together with companions.

At the time of mid-thirties, a compassionate individual will be more spotlight on the errand that they should be done in their general public just as their job they have to create. They should be more prepared for what's going on in the network they are living. By this age of their life, the individual will find out about their useful capacities that are profoundly critical to their work just as related passionate abilities in minding with themselves as well as other people particularly relatives and companions. They are presently fit in managing obligations throughout everyday life.

With this stage, profoundly sensitive individual needs to demonstrate to themselves that they can find out about the requests of the network they are living just as to be increasingly gainful as an individual from a system.

At the point when an individual reaches the period of the 60s, it will require such dominance of what they are doing and have the option to adapt up additional to the burdens brought by such a significant number of encounters and conditions defeat through their life. For them, it would be increasingly about of acing their considerations inside themselves just like their needs.

The Highly Sensitive Person Disorder

Exceedingly Sensitive Individuals as a general rule make incredible detectives, forecasters, and specialists as their enthusiasm for data, information, and exasperating questions push them more profound into the territory of comprehension. Regularly in scrounge around of themselves, they can get a handle on that everything fit all things considered, yet miss the mark to acknowledge how. Some can see Their characteristics as a hermitic individual who is hesitant to develop social skill outside of a couple of innocuous settings. As a result of their comprehension to numerous things and their ability to take in more aspect than other individuals, Highly Sensitive Individuals frequently feel strange or alone.

What's more, generally, they are distant from everyone else. Their reality is one that pressure confinement, yet their oblivious wishes outside progression and to have the option to fit in the general public. Like the marginal character, the profoundly sensitive person's attitudes propose the must for solid self-safeguarding confinements as they also search for their very own pith throughout everyday life.

Regardless of whether they are profoundly sensitive, it is fundamental to appreciate that the character they hide is those which go well with their best distinction. Information to comprehend that they dislike every other person is what is generally significant. As a vital aspect of their limit structure, they possess the need for energy for advancement, examination, and compensation of the data of each event that happens in their lives. They need to acknowledge how every occasion supply to their adventure, how it fits with the vast living being of things and they attempt to discover to fathom the essence that few of that data has for their life at a progressively intuitive level. They additionally need to connect with the clarification of why their sentiments get squeezed to a colossal and how these sentiments fit into the disdain captured.

Exceptionally Sensitive Individuals are quickly over-animated with the various environment. Too many requesting or brief time constriction courses can add to their defeat. Every now and again, however, these are the general population who care for the sincere and oppose the hardest so as not to hurt others by saying no. They regularly debilitate themselves by including themselves in numerous unnecessary activities instead of giving away their longing or need to settle home and slacken up. They think that it's confused to verbalize communication as they fear to say no will leave them in an untouchable position. In the center, they require communication for affection since they fear hurt.

5 Myths About Highly Sensitive People

A highly sensitive individual is somebody who will, in general, be receptive to their environment. They are frequently intuitive and empathic, have a sharp creative mind and may feel very overpowered by clamor, turmoil, and groups. They can experience difficulty fitting in and have been seen as "excessively timid" or "excessively sensitive."

It is evaluated that around 20% of the populace is highly sensitive. The term is ending up progressively understood, mainly since Elaine Aaron distributed her books 'The Highly Sensitive Person' and 'The Highly Sensitive Child.'

Numerous individuals item to the term 'highly sensitive' since it is regularly thought of just like an awful thing. Some incline toward names like highly adjusted or highly mindful, since those terms don't convey the negative implication of being 'excessively sensitive.'

It might be difficult to appreciate or identify with highly sensitive individuals. I feel that is for the most part since we don't generally get ourselves. I positively didn't for a large portion of my life. Since we were viewed as being not the same as every other person when we were growing up, other individuals, especially our folks and family, didn't have the foggiest idea how to identify with us. A highly sensitive individual frequently makes a decent attempt to fit in yet can't do as such. Thus they presume that there must be a significant issue with them. We're regularly told things like "no doubt about it;" "get over it;" "you're adolescent, grow up;" and, my undisputed top choice "don't be so idiotic." As if when we state that we are awkward in specific circumstances or would prefer not to do certain things, we're troublesome.

If you are highly sensitive or know somebody who is, these tips may enable you to have a superior comprehension about what it implies:

We're not fragile. Being responsive means that we are more fixed on the earth and to the general population around us. We get on things that most others don't. We see things. It doesn't imply that we will self-destruct when you are immediate and legitimate with us (in truth we incline toward it since then we know where we remain with you).

There's nothing amiss with us. We are not broken. We needn't bother with fixing. We are simply extraordinary. We don't frequently appreciate very similar things that numerous others enjoy - and this isn't merely in our minds, it's a real thing. We feel physical manifestations that are awkward because of stuff like commotion, fluorescent lighting, smoke, scents, substance smells, swarms, violent situations, etc.

We are not unsociable, nor show improvement over every other person. The individuals who are highly sensitive and furthermore thoughtful people can react to over-incitement by pulling back and winding up calm. We may decrease to go along with you at a bar or an occasion where there are heaps of individuals, not because we're unsociable, but since we realize we wouldn't appreciate it, and we would endure a short time later. We know that it can take us days to recuperate from such over-incitement.

Not all highly sensitive individuals are self observers and the other way around. Some individuals are outgoing but then additionally highly sensitive. The thing that matters is that a contemplative HSP will in general pull back when encountering over-incitement, while a friendly individual may lash out and become forceful or irate. Albeit once more, this relies upon the individual, not all outgoing HSP's will demonstration like this.

It's anything but difficult to believe that HSP's strength does not flourish in leadership positions. The inverse is valid. They can thrive (even though they may not generally need to). HSP's make incredible leaders since they can be more tuned in to different colleagues have a more extensive point of view. They additionally will, in general, get on things that others may miss -, for example, feelings, non-verbal communication, outward appearances - because they are so highly mindful.

There's no uncertainty about it; being highly sensitive can be troublesome. Those troubles are extraordinarily diminished, and your sensitivities can be transformed into extraordinary qualities once you comprehend entirely and possess your identity. It's anything but difficult to think there must be a significant issue with you when you are not equivalent to most of the other individuals. Being diverse isn't an issue; it's a blessing. Realize your identity and when testing circumstances come up, help other people to get it. Try not to anticipate that they should naturally know; you should support them - and realize how to defend yourself.

A Survival Guide for Empaths and Highly Sensitive Persons

Empaths are extraordinary individuals, and face different day by day challenges. You interface with the vitality of others sharing your space, and furthermore your condition (through energy engraves). This can be overpowering on occasion, and to pick up control and deal with your very own vitality, a couple of apparatuses can be essential. Here are a few hints and strategies that have demonstrated to be significant resources for the empath's tool kit.

Figure out how to withdraw from the vitality of others. How would you achieve this? You should initially know your very own life. The attention to what is yours versus another individual is vital to this progression. I recommend perusing Yvonne Perry's book, Whose Stuff Is This? This is an incredible reference book to start finding out about vitality the board. Trouble and unwinding space is another need. It very well may be your man cavern, your perusing nook, or patio swing. It merely should be where you can go to have a break and be far from the vitality of others so that you may focus and energize yourself.

Positive confirmations are, likewise useful. A positive assertion is a short sentence or two that supports positive idea designs and can re-train your cerebrum. A model, let me get what is in my best and most astounding high as of now, is both raising your vivacious signature and open-finished. For what reason is open-finished something to be thankful for? It doesn't characterize, which can here and there spot breaking points or desires, giving an unintended outcome. What's going on with everything is the best and most elevated high is superior to anything you have envisioned? When you leave it open-finished, it can stream ideal to you. I appreciated Outrageous Openness by Tosha Silver, which completed an excellent occupation of separating this and giving more knowledge into how this functions.

Protecting is another apparatus you can utilize when you are merely beginning. This includes bringing in a high vibrational fiery field to ensure you. You can bring in Angels and see them remaining by you in your inner consciousness, or envisioning a white light encasing you. Another strategy is to see yourself in a protective layer made of mirrors which send vitality appropriate back to its source. A created empath will almost certainly enable life to course through without retaining any. This takes certainty and ability. You can build up this with training. The information any vitality that streams towards you is brief, similar to a breeze. It can flow directly through you. You can feel it, realize it doesn't have a place with you, and enable it to go through without engrossing any of it.

Great fiery cleanliness is an unquestionable requirement for any empath. It begins with an essential comprehension of chakras and after that, a basic perception of purifying them. A few people see the chakra wheels of shading and envision them turning with brilliant solid shading, and any dim spots of cynicism are expelled. Doing this in the shower can be very successful as any antagonism goes directly down the channel with the filthy shower water! You can likewise envision white light coming in through your crown chakra, sustaining and renewing the chakras.

Contemplation and focusing are additionally significant resources for your empathic tool compartment. Reflection for 10-20 day by day will bring substantial change. Focusing includes returning to self. Empaths interface with others, and it resembles a fiery handshake. Your vitality goes out to meet and welcome others, and focusing brings you over into your body altogether. This enables you to line up with soul/source vitality and venture out of a sense of self. Care is incredible for focusing. Attempt to live at the time, and whatever feeling comes up to recognize express, and after that discharge it.

Stones and essential oils can likewise be useful. Contingent upon how you are wired, you may incline toward one more than the other. Keep in mind you are an individual, your appearance of empathic capacity and empathic experience might be like another person's, anyway. You are a one of a kind perfect articulation. That implies you will vibe unequivocally and have a fondness with certain things and not others. That is your magnificence and why the world needs you!

Pardoning others and excusing self is a standout amongst the most incredible assets you have. It will clear your vitality and raise your vibrational rate. Keep in mind absolution is for your prosperity the other individual doesn't require "to excuse you" for advantage. It tends to be a test to do this; anyway, it is fundamental for your development and advancement. Nobody has strolled this world and not hurt, deliberately or unexpectedly, another being. It is a piece of the human experience. So like the petition says... excuse others and pardon yourself.

The root chakra associates us to the earth. Know about this and utilizing representation ground into the surface. See (using your inner consciousness) a line interfacing you to the planet. You would then be able to use it to send negative vitality into the earth where it is retained and to draw up sustaining life from the focal point of the planet. Doing this will build your vitality stream.

Others supportive systems incorporate tuning in to music or nature sounds. Investing time in nature and with your pets is an incredible method to unwind, clear your vitality, and focus yourself. Exercise projects will bolster a decent lively stream. Yoga is excellent since it consolidates breathing with represents that support arrangement and stream of vitality.

Keep your condition clear of pessimism. Raise those vibes! The Native Americans' have been smirching with extraordinary outcomes for a considerable length of time. Consuming sage while expressing an aim is an incredible strategy for clearing vitality. In your office zone, you can utilize a spritzer bottle with water and salt, or make a fragrance based treatment spritzer. When you use essential oils recall that oil and water don't blend so, you'll need to include some witch hazel or liquor to the sea and oils. Some rain, ¼ cup of witch hazel and 7-10 drops of oil. Diary the appreciation! Completion, the day by composing a rundown of things you are thankful for in a diary and afterward expressing a goal or attestation, keeps the positive vitality streaming.

Chapter Six
Addictions: Are Addictions A Bad Thing?

With regards to current societal issues, the word enslavement is frequently mentioned. What's more, for the most part, spoken about, with regards to what individuals are dependent on.

These are regularly: medications, liquor, and betting, for example. Furthermore, because of the introduction that these addictions have gotten throughout the years, they have turned into the images of enslavement.

This has prompted changing degrees of shame being joined to them. In any case, even though one can wind up dependent on these things; there are likewise numerous different things that one can end up dependent on.

But then a few addictions are more socially worthy than others. This implies there will be addictions that are disliked and others that are ignored. So dependent on this viewpoint, one individual would then be able to feel embarrassed for what they are dependent on, and another can think that what they do is satisfactory and excellent, even though it might likewise be a compulsion.

High contrast?

It would then be anything but difficult to reach the determination that addictions are a terrible thing and should be maintained a strategic distance from no matter what. Also, this is because of the affiliations that have been confirmed to addictions.

Through looking a little more profound, it winds up apparent that it isn't just liquor or medications that one can end up dependent on; one can end up dependent on nearly anything. This can identify with pretty much all things everywhere.

Presently, here and there a fixation can be incredibly ruinous and assume control over one's life. What're more, different occasions it very well may be something profitable yet still is inside one's control.

Development Or Destruction?

Being dependent on medications, liquor, or betting is unavoidably going to have hindering impacts, and these can influence ones physical, enthusiastic, and psychological wellness, just as one's accounts.

It can likewise prompt one winding up inconceivably capable in a specific everyday issue. To pick up a degree of authority in pretty much any daily item, it takes proceeded with training.

What's more, to wind up dependent on consummating one's specialty, whatever that might be, is an incredible method to make this a reality. It is not necessarily the case that since one displays added substance attributes that it needs to assume control over their life.

What one was dependent on at one phase in their life may have had an advantageous reason, and as time has transformed, it never again had an idea. What's more, here, one changed their concentration to something different.

Worthy Addictions

So while a few things are socially referred to as addictions and are named as terrible; there are numerous other addictions that individuals can have that can be similarly as dangerous. Also, these can be things that are held in high regard by society.

Here one might be dependent on: volunteering, helping/satisfying others, and working. Even though these likely could be viewed as honorable things to do; they can likewise wind up crazy and dangerous.

What's The Purpose?

As addictions can be both helpful and damaging, contingent upon components, for example, what one ends up dependent on and for to what extent; one might say that addictions are mainly part of the human experience.

They are mainly part of the advanced world, and every single one of us is dependent on something. This possibly be something that is classed as high, terrible or even unbiased

It is anything but difficult to accuse the regular outside things, for example, medications or liquor, yet these addictions and any others so far as that is concerned are simply outcomes. What they lead to is the interior guideline.

Guideline

To be human is to have feelings. Presently, a few people know about them, and a few people are not, however, in any case, they are there. Also, what one does when feelings emerge will frequently rely upon how enthusiastic keen they are.

The sense of self-personality is about control, and a fixation permits the inner self-personality to control one's feelings. It turns into a custom for one to direct their emotions. What's more, this can occur so frequently and rapidly that one isn't even mindful of their feelings.

So as this is one way that the sense of self-personality capacities, it isn't quite a bit of a shock to see that people are for the most part addicts necessarily. This could be a compulsion that is painful, or it could be one that is very damaging. Also, the sort of addictions that one has will rely upon various things.

Possible Causes

Ones grown-up life and youth can have a significant impact on one's addictions. What ones companions and parental figures did, as an approach to managing their internal procedures, would all be able to be replicated. Just as the choices that society offers for guideline.

It may be the case that through encountering a youth where one didn't get empathic consideration, one didn't build up the capacity to control themselves. Empathic attention would be the point at which one had a parental figure that for the most part: approved, reflected, and tuned into their needs and feelings.

Through doing this, one would then have the option to disguise along these lines of being. What's more, therefore, step by step, build up the capacity to manage their very own feelings or to look for others to aid this procedure.

If this sort of early consideration did not occur, at that point, it is impossible that one will at that point have the option to manage their feelings. That is except if they look for the help of an advisor, companion or healer in later life to attempt to address this.

And afterward, looking to outside sources to direct ones inward procedures will be a natural outcome.

Mindfulness

The general perspectives that we are given; however, the media are regularly one-sided and unhelpful. Also, seldom get to the core of something. I would state that one of the reasons why addictions have turned out to be such an issue in the cutting edge world is because of passionate constraint.

Passionate insight is regularly a particular case and not the standard in the western world. Also, this is step by step, beginning to change because individuals become progressively mindful.

Drug Addictions That Occur After An Injury

Most people can relate to the experiencing that may happen a type of damage at some time in our lives. A few cases might be more regrettable than that of others. However, most appear to make them comprehend what it resembles to bring about extreme torment and the recuperation procedure everything involves. The individuals who have not can see themselves as the minority, and fortunate few.

In recouping from broken bones, sprained lower legs, tendinitis, or notwithstanding something as genuine as a staggering fender bender; we are frequently given a reliable supply of agony prescriptions by our doctors, to facilitate the anguish. In taking these prescription drugs securely and according to our specialist's suggestions, we may recuperate fine and dandy. Although, there are cases in which an individual may wind up dependent on the sentiment of a lesser torment, or a casual condition of the body. With this, there might be an opportunity for chronic drug use after causing damage.

How would I know whether my cherished one is getting to be dependent on their agony drugs or potentially prescription medications?

It is frequently the situation that a person who is getting to be dependent on agony medications or prescription medications will over-overstate their torment level. They will quickly request the agony pills as opposed to finding different manners by which to limit their torment. These ways may include: straightening out themselves in bed, correcting their harmed body part, slackening a swathe, and so on. At the point when this is the situation, tragically you might serve pills to a friend or family member who is getting to be dependent on their prescription.

Another sign that your companion or relative might wind up dependent is the point at which your cherished one is by all accounts recuperating wholly and reliably, however, are as yet falling into the propensity for going after the prescription medications. You may test your hypothesis by removing the prescription from the patient's bedside, with the goal that they should ask each time they need their pills. This is a decent manner by which to screen their medication use, and maybe, misuse.

One more indication of conceivable compulsion is if the measurement keeps on running out before the refill is expected; or before another container of the prescription is vital. Screen your companion or relative's pill admission every day. When the pills are rapidly vanishing, there might be an issue close by.

Prescription medicine must be taken with consideration and isn't endorsed to be a reliable method to keep away from the current issue - damage. At the point when an individual is harmed, a specific measure of torment ought to be standard. The drugs are there to facilitate that torment, not numb the patient.

When you or someone you care for is experiencing a potential dependence on prescription or torment drugs, it is frequently best to talk straightforwardly with the experts. A medication and liquor rehabilitation focus in your general vicinity may have the responses to questions you have been contemplating. Rehabilitation projects are all over, and experts inside those focuses and plans are prepared and willing to be of administration.

Overcoming Addiction: Asking for Help

Regardless of whether you are somebody who has been in and out of treatment programs, 12 stage gatherings and treatment or this is your first time approaching your family and companions for assistance, and there are approaches to request help that are significantly more viable than others. Unmistakably if your family had put several thousand in various treatment programs possibilities to be down and out when you came back to substance use, at that point moving toward them once again is sure to be an overwhelming prospect. Numerous families, life partners, and companions have a limit; for example, a measure of adoration and cash they are eager to contribute before they lose trust totally and are reluctant to add any more. When your family is close or has achieved that limit, at that point, you have a challenging situation to deal with, and I suggest perusing this part cautiously.

As you settle on this choice, you might need to approach somebody you trust; a companion or relative, be straightforward with them and told them you are genuinely thinking about rolling out this improvement, and you may require their assistance and backing. Significantly, you are not requesting anything from them, or notwithstanding anticipating anything of them. Keep in mind; you may have said this multiple occasions previously, so they might be suspicious. When the situation the primary path for them to see you are not kidding is for you to catch up your announcement with activity. It might sound trite, yet if liquor is an issue for you, cut back altogether on your drinking or quit totally. If you believe you need expert assistance, start exploring projects or specialists. Look for a program or specialist whose way of thinking isn't that of furnishing you with an instant reason for future disappointment, for example, the individuals who analyze, name, and cure individuals. Look for a program or specialist who is sure that you can conquer your issues; and whose mission is to assist you with learning from quite a while ago, defeat your problems and fabricate a future loaded up with progress.

When you are looking for monetary help from companions, relatives, your manager, or others, the most significant recommendation I can give you is to stay humble and anticipate nothing. Keep in mind, those nearest to you have likely been harmed over and again by your activities. Maybe you have moved toward them for assistance before, to utilize their support to keep doing what you needed to do. Possibly you have made requests on them and controlled them; or have lied, stolen from them or physically harmed them; or perhaps you have been far off or unfeeling. It is critical to start to sympathize with them and comprehend their distrust. What's more, it is likewise essential to understand whether they are eager to support you, you have numerous choices, and you can change your life, paying little mind to their activities.

The minute I advise somebody who has been to treatment or been presented to 12 stage projects that they can change paying little mind to their outer conditions, I gain proficiency with the full brunt of their suspicion. Most are persuaded they have a severe disease called compulsion that renders them frail to change. This conviction, while incorrect as there is no such disease, is their concern. Examples of idea and conduct can form into propensities, and propensities create dependent on redundancy and recurrence of the design and behavior. If you have a cigarette with some espresso each morning, your brain and body become acclimated with this custom, and transforming it appears to be unthinkable - yet it just seems that route because of propensity. Nobody would contend that individuals can and do quit smoking and additionally quit drinking espresso. In like manner, individuals who put the majority of their vitality into getting high on heroin all day every day feel as though they can't stop, yet numerous individuals do, everywhere throughout the world, every day.

It is their conviction that they can't that keeps them buried in the conduct.

In this way, there it is, you can stop! You can choose, 'I'm finished with this; I would prefer not to be this individual any longer. It's the ideal opportunity for me to roll out an improvement.' If you have been utilizing liquor or potentially benzodiazepines exorbitantly and routinely, I firmly prescribe setting off to a nearby detox emergency clinic for a medicinal test, as a sanity check. However, numerous individuals can and do a detox from most substances all alone.

Remember that by the day's end, your substance use has nothing at all to do with your conditions, occasions, or other individuals. Your substance use is a decision you make sense that is the thing that you need to do. Completely changing you, defeating your issues and building the existence you genuinely need may not be simple but rather it is workable for those eager to make a dedication and finish on it.

Your loved ones owe you nothing. However, chances are they would like to see you cheerful and active. If they start to trust you are earnest in your endeavors, I can nearly ensure they will move paradise and earth to support you.

Detox From Alcohol and the Therapist

Medication and alcohol detox is the way toward halting drinking and the resulting withdrawal impacts. It is these withdrawal impacts from alcohol that make Alcoholic rehab a troublesome and some of the time horrendous experience for the alcoholic. Alcohol recovery is another critical advance which happens after the alcohol detox is done. In both of these cases, the alcohol detox advisor will assume an outstanding job. The adequacy of a portion of these alcohol detox advisors will be vastly improved than a part of the others. A superior comprehension for the patient and his issues is one of the territories where great advisor's flourish. Backing and sympathy are different components of proper treatment. Another indication of a decent specialist is to have the option to keep the patient concentrated on his or her objectives; this is basic in the long haul treatment, additionally, in having the opportunity to use outside organizations to profit the patient.

We are stuck in somewhat of a trench right now with the supply of competent specialists being extremely short. This has a ton to do with the absence of cash supply. Awful Alcoholic detox treatment and terrible advisors are distinguished by not tuning in to and accusing the patient they can likewise be blamed for being controlling and nosy. They can similarly be blamed for being far off mentally, and they tend to stay away from issues that they find disagreeable, regularly being just keen on themselves.

Where a few advisors tumble down is in not having the option to deal with loud patients or the individuals who turn up for their treatment sessions in an inebriated state. Additionally here and there alcoholics won't turn up for planned sessions. Shockingly a few alcoholics and substance abusers will experience the lives with the steady risk of emergency approaching over them. Lamentably a ton of the time alcoholics and medication abusers will fall foul of the law and should manage the equity framework. To concede that they have an issue is continually going to be hard for an alcoholic. Any alcoholic or medication abuser in the Western world ought to have the option to anticipate the best of treatment, help, and participation. The administration will set aside cash for the citizen in the long haul by relieving the issues of alcohol abusers and other substance abusers. They likewise have an ethical obligation to support these individuals.

Chapter Seven
Why the World Needs Empaths, and How Empaths Can Survive the World

Medication and liquor detox is the way toward ceasing drinking and the ensuing withdrawal impacts. It is these withdrawal impacts from liquor that make Alcoholic detox a troublesome and now and again awful experience for the heavy drinker. Liquor recovery is another significant advance which happens after the liquor detox is done. In both of these cases, the liquor detox advisor will assume an outstanding job. The adequacy of a portion of these liquor detox specialists will be vastly improved than a part of the others. A superior comprehension for the patient and his issues is one of the territories where great specialist's flourish. Backing and compassion are different components of proper treatment. Another indication of a decent specialist is to have the option to keep the patient concentrated on his or her objectives; this is basic in the long haul treatment, likewise, in having the opportunity to use outside offices to profit the patient.

We are stuck in somewhat of a groove right now with the supply of good advisors being extremely short. This has a lot to do with the absence of cash supply. Awful Alcoholic detox treatment and terrible advisors are distinguished by not tuning in to and accusing the patient they can likewise be blamed for being controlling and nosy. They can also be blamed for being inaccessible mentally, and they tend to maintain a strategic distance from issues that they find undesirable, frequently being just inspired by themselves.

Where a few advisors tumble down is in not having the option to deal with loud patients or the individuals who turn up for their treatment sessions in an inebriated state. Additionally, in some cases, heavy drinkers won't turn up for planned sessions. Lamentably a few heavy drinkers and substance abusers will experience the lives with the consistent danger of emergency approaching over them. Shockingly a great deal of the time heavy drinkers and medication abusers will fall foul of the law and should manage the equity framework. To concede that they have an issue is continually going to be hard for a drunkard. Any heavy drinker or medication abuser in the Western world ought to have the option to anticipate the best of treatment, help, and participation. The administration will set aside cash for the citizen in the long haul by restoring the issues of liquor abusers and other substance abusers. In any case, they additionally have an ethical obligation to support these individuals.

How to Have a Satisfying Love Life

Check the approaches to have an extraordinary love life. Such a significant number of and most are relevant, yet for me, one emerges. Correspondence. You usually need sentiment, good sex, fun, travel, diversion and giggling and how about we do not overlook pardoning. Talking to one another, good talking is at the core of an incredible love life. Correspondence ranks number one,

To acclimate, talk, connect, kid around, chitchat, or more all talk from the heart just as from your mind. Sure some casual conversation is OK. However, it's the private discussions when you contact feelings and even cry together that unite couples. Sharing painful recollections and realizing you have an empathic and adoring audience tie the power of profound devotion.

The correspondence comes in numerous pretenses. You needn't bother with them all. When you are a sensitive feely sort of individual, and you met somebody or have somebody in your life who wants to contact and also feel you're now on top of things. Associating through touch is a victor for most.

Contacting incorporates physical contacting, stroking, embraces, kissing, clasping hands, strolling affectionately intertwined and brushing against one another at odd minutes and out of the blue.

Correspondence likewise means getting into the thick of sentiments and realize when to test into yourselves and uncover what should be known to determine issues and set another course. Evaluating strife and contentions and doing everything to discover goals is continuously positive and frequently develops relationships. The outrage that is uncertain will in general wait and gradually develops until even little disputes can begin a fire.

Furthermore, remember that correspondence suggests not avoiding yourself. You have to listen near what your accomplice says. Notwithstanding when you don't at first concur with the remarks, appraisal, or assessment that might be a piece of a contention.

Correspondence likewise includes uncommon endowments, astounding each other with a card or ballad or blossoms. These demonstrations are demonstrations of mail.

The damages and snapshots of euphoria, times of misery, and times of uplifted feelings altogether partake in good correspondence. There is a mixing of spirits and a sense of harmony that accompanies quiet and dynamic communication.

Correspondence is comprehensive, and for darlings, it is likewise selective.

In a word, correspondence is a full, composite, close, and adoring communication between two individuals. It contacts the core of affection and the embodiment of what an incredible love relationship is about. The outcome is a beautiful love relationship that will dependably rise above hardships and time of struggle and individual troubles of each accomplice.

Why Disguising As "Empathic," "Loving" and "Caring" Doesn't Lead You to an Intimate Relationship

There are the individuals who "dedicate" themselves so aimlessly to their accomplices that such a commitment verges on penance. Maeve Binchy, a well-appreciated Irish creator, has a short anecdote about a lady who began to look all starry eyed at, cut off her investigations to enable her accomplice to sort out his scholarly gatherings and helped him in altering his educational plan vitae. All went "fine and dandy" between them until she got pregnant - and he left her...

Are individuals so credulous? Does it bode well to forfeit yourself to such an outright degree? Does love daze you and makes you bleary-eyed? Try not to individuals comprehend that intimate connections should be standard, give and take, and that if this isn't the situation, the relationship will finish up downslope? Try not to individuals comprehend that putting resources into themselves while in a relation (and not just in their accomplice) implies contributing, in the meantime, in the relationship?

What drives individuals to be there 100% for their partner(s)?

What drives individuals to "love to such an extent"? To act as though they are absolutely "empathic" towards their accomplice?

I state "as though" since this is neither a genuine sympathy nor a valid one. What they attempt to do with their "sympathy" is persuade their accomplice they are there 100% - all together for their accomplice to adore them, value their "compassion," have a favorable opinion of them.

It might be said, appearing much "sympathy" is control: you don't carry on that path since you are without a doubt so empathic; you act that route to get something "consequently."

What drives you to carry on that way are your very own issues, and needs, which control you and cause you to act in manners which you think will present to you whatever affection, consideration, thankfulness, and acknowledgment you endeavor to get. Understanding that these practices helped you in the past to accomplish only that, you keep utilizing them on numerous occasions, in this way controlling others on multiple times. What's more, goodness! This works supernatural occurrences!

Now and again you may carry on that route to escape depression: you have to encircle yourself with individuals ("accomplices" now and again) to not be distant from everyone else; to feel you merit something. To achieve this objective, you have "created" yourself as an "empathic," all-seeing, all-ears individual; somebody others want to be with (since they get from this individual - you! - all the "adoration" and "care" they need!).

This "move" among you and them makes you feel better: hello, you have figured out how to control them to adore and value you, and, progressively significant of all, to need your organization! Doesn't it make you feel better? Doesn't it make you think shrewd?

At that point, how comes that, gradually, however, most likely, they takea bit of leeway of you, requesting that you advance them cash (which they never payback); to take care of their feline when they travel; to enable them to fix their PC when it quits working?

You do these readily. You believe you are being cherished and acknowledged...

Have you understood that your accomplices take a bit of leeway of your "compassion" and "love"?

Have you anytime pondered that they have come to understand your controlling methods for conduct and have figured out how to take the favorable position of you - without you realizing that they have "found" your false legitimacy and "compassion"?

Not. It may be unreasonably hard for you to concede that they have understood that you are not merely the individual you present to be. Furthermore, more than that - it may be unreasonably hard for you to concede - to yourself - that you haven't been straightforward with them (with your dear companions/accomplices!). What's more, over everything, it may be hard for you to admit to yourself that your practices are driven by requirements and sentiments of sorrow and uselessness which are in the foundations of who you are!

In most probability, you will continue acting how you do. In most chance, you won't take an opportunity to end up mindful of what rouses you to carry on how you do. In most probability you have achieved a point in your life that you let yourself know - "let me simply continue doing what I have done as such far; let me simply appreciate the little companionships I have made up until now, without seeking after better ones or a genuinely decent relationship."

Without a doubt, it is simpler to keep the present state of affairs as opposed to attempting to transform somehow. What's more, you comfort yourself by advising to yourself that at any rate, with the individuals who are around you, your forlornness isn't really awful; and the craving for a genuine closeness can be supplanted - as it has been as of not long ago - with different sorts of securities among you and others.

Empaths - Who Do You Go to in Times of Need?

The sentiments of others can without much of a stretch influence empaths. It's a word related peril when you can feel what other individuals think. Regardless of whether you realize how to deal with your Empath abilities, there are times when the general population around you will influence you...This is particularly valid in hardship, where you are increasingly powerless to splash up another person sentiments unwittingly.

This raises a significant issue for Empaths: who will you invested energy with when you feel miserable?

For instance, when you are having issues at work, discussing it with somebody who is ALSO miserable is bound to exacerbate things since you'll be adding their troubled sentiments to your despondent emotions! What a snowball effect...Pretty soon you'll feel like a weight cooker prepared to detonate!

If instead, you ate with somebody cheerful at work, you're "pulling yourself up" by absorbing their sentiments of happiness. As Empaths, you don't need to *talk* to them, since you can feel their feelings straightforwardly. Simply being in their essence and giving them a chance to encompass you with positive emotions will have an inspiring impact on you.

In like manner, when *you* feel stable, you can inspire others by communicating your sentiments of joy by being around them! Keep in mind that everybody has the original hardware necessary to do peruse other individuals' feelings. Empaths happen to be progressively touchy to feelings and ideally, ready to examine others all the more deliberately.

This is additionally a noteworthy motivation behind why Empaths invest a great deal of energy independent from anyone else. They usually don't care for group or gatherings. They more often than not favor one on one discussions where it's significantly simpler to keep track of who's feeling what. Sadly, such vast numbers of Empaths figure they do this since something isn't right with them. That they *should* be out there in enormous gatherings of individuals that they have "issues" and can't have a typical existence. That isn't TRUE!

Spending time without anyone else's input when you feel powerless is a GREAT IDEA! It makes things so a lot less stressful, enabling you to truly concentrate on how *you* think as opposed to dealing with what's yours and what's theirs. It's, as a rule, the sharpest thing you can do.

So if it's not too much trouble as individual support to me, don't thrash on yourself since you invest a great deal of energy alone. That doesn't mean you're broken. That doesn't mean you can't make companions. It means you're savvy enough to recognize what you need.

The Love In Being Empathically Hypersensitive

HAVE YOU at any point thought the stuff to connect for help? The vast majority who are debilitated or lamenting or forlorn will possibly join when they genuinely feel overpowered.

At the point when life gets a lot for us - at that point, we connect. For the most part, at precisely that point.

At the point when the situation is reversed, when we are the one's torment, we all of a sudden comprehend the immense gorge socially - individuals have no clue how awful it needs to get before we open up. Along these lines, it pursues that we have no clue what others are containing from inside themselves before they at long last open up. We have a chance to give others the open door for undercover investigation of their spirits.

It must be God's will for us to perceive the individual before us: the individual who has his or her battle - a reiteration of distress, a 'treasure' of tumult covered under a sea of torment, or merely a universe of disappointment.

Is there a superior kind of extreme touchiness than being empathic - being absolutely in order as any person can be with another?

This is the God-roused calling of the individual with a peaceful heart. The peacefully hearted have a method for recognizing the incoming tide and remainder of solidarity of an individual in their middle - it's just because they are intrigued. They can detect that all isn't well inside the individuals who are pulled back, latently forceful, concise, or watched. They need other liberated of excessive weight.

Having that feeling that all isn't well in someone else is dissatisfaction of closeness to the peacefully hearted individual. They are OK with triviality for the wellbeing of its own, yet not when insignificance must be the standard due to dread in this other individual for helplessness and divulgence; they need to help - without needing to cause torment (reviewing that their empathic extreme touchiness is about the other individual).

Being empathically extremely touchy isn't so much a blessing as it is the empathy of God inside us for someone else. It is taking God actually - to adore another similarly as we wish to be cherished. It's tied in with lifting the need of the individual before us so they would feel securely close to us, imperative to us, on the voyage of life.

Chapter Eight
Divorcing the Narcissist - 4 Strategies to Protect Yourself

Separation is never charming or straightforward, even under genial conditions. It is genuinely hard to relinquish a perfect, and roll out considerable improvements in life, for example, in living courses of action, accounts, way of life, access to youngsters, work, and closeness. Shockingly, there are occasions where the procedure turns out to be significantly increasingly troublesome and having an accomplice who is a narcissist position high on the rundown of confusing variables. It is likely the part is going on because of some damaging and confounding conduct by the narcissist mate, and the separation itself, particularly when it is deciphered in an antagonistic manner, turns into a stage for surprisingly more terrible maltreatment. Here are four procedures to take to enable you to shield yourself from a prospective ex who unquestionably does not have your best advantages on a fundamental level:

1. Discover great lawful portrayal. This is a vital piece. When you have resources, property, or youngsters, it is imperative to ensure all viewpoints are taken care of and settled suitably. Accept your narcissist accomplice won't pay extraordinary mind to you in any capacity whatsoever, paying little respect to what might be said verbally. Discover a lawyer you feel is certifiable and who comprehends the elements of a possibly "high clash" accomplice - explicitly a narcissist. Attempt to get a lawyer who knows about this issue. Preferably, the attorney will be knowledgeable about how to defuse unpredictable circumstances and settle cases - but on the other hand, is educated about going to court against a narcissist.

2. Make financial arrangements. Get a Visa in your very own name, while your acknowledge is as yet consolidated for your spouse's. Open a financial balance in your name and put some crisis assets in it. Even though court arranges generally prohibit blocking access to joint assets, it is in every case better to make sure you have some entrance to some cash of your own. Cause duplicates of each financial record you to have - incorporate tax returns, W-2's, paystubs, mileage plan articulations, worker repayment/account explanations, protection arrangements, advance data, bank proclamations, property examinations, financial records, and so on. Your lawyer can give you a total rundown of what the person in question needs to survey your business picture thoroughly.

3. Report everything and anything your accomplice does. Take downtime, dates, and occasions as though you were a journalist. When you have kids and are worried about your mate's parental wellness, this is especially significant. Note each immoral, unethical, illicit, and conceivably or harming act that your mate submits. Request a child-rearing time assessment when you are

stressed for the wellbeing of your kids, and it looks as if guardianship will be contested.

4. Shut out the controls and sincerely injurious strategies of your mate. Your narcissist life partner will most likely do all the individual in question can to undermine you, challenge your believability, make you feel dumb or insane, and cause you to question your very own discernment. Try not to take part in close to home talk. When you should have contact by any means as if you should talk in regards to youngsters, stick to the current point and pull back from the discussion if it strays from the subject. It is frequently useful as of now to have a guide and believed loved ones close within reach so they can help "deprogram" you from the expressions of your narcissist companion.

When are you keen on tending to the test of separation from an all-encompassing outlook, evaluating the physical, enthusiastic, viable, and relationship parts?

How to Free Yourself From a Narcissist's Abuse in 3 Steps

Building up your own life is the best way to carry on with a full life, and narcissists by their very nature can't enable you to carry on with your very own life. They need you to live in their reality, drenching up their issues and terrible emotions. You serve them, live for them, and do the things they need on their principles and terms.

The issue is, if you've been included with a narcissist, you'll have various hindrances to look than casualties of different kinds of maltreatment. Psychological mistreatment is not the same as physical. The harm it incurs is extraordinary, thus treating the scars from that injury will be unique.

How is it extraordinary? Well, you're more customized and adapted to individual behavior and ongoing exercises by the narcissist when you're sincerely mishandled. So it's not merely your response to manhandle you'll be changing in your routine, yet your whole contorted perspective they've customized into you.

So the initial step is expelling their sole effect on you and getting different impacts from more beneficial individuals.

Getting New Input from a Healthy Environment

This is significant. The majority of a narcissist's propelled traps and strategies, regardless of what they are, tumble to the wayside in case you're getting the contribution from other individuals. They depend exclusively on disconnecting you and being your solitary impact.

You have to discover and associate with individuals who have comparable interests to you, and those you don't also. Contribution from all bearings and all sides, insofar as it's sure and steady, is welcome and helpful in these circumstances.

Reconnecting with individuals you put some distance between due to the narcissist is another choice. That is, individuals the narcissist didn't care for, was undermined by thus didn't endorse of and didn't enable you to associate with them to your benefit, by making you feel terrible for a partner with them.

This has a couple of fascinating features to it. For a specific something, you'll have lost contact with individuals you loved and thought about given the narcissist.

For something else, you'll have lost contact with individuals you thought you preferred because the narcissist power-related you with them... you should like them, so you did. Then again, you'll discover that a few (if not most) of the general population you never preferred in any case.

Getting once more into contact with them causes you to pick up something: not exclusively did dislike them. However, they were only vessels to facilitate the narcissist's maltreatment. So never again realizing them ends up being a surprisingly positive development, yet in any event, now you comprehend what your emotions are.

Also, last are the general population you at present know and through recuperation learn you don't care for them and they aren't beneficial for you. You exceed them through your recovery.

Setting up Your Schedule, Irrespective of Others

This is significant for two reasons. To begin with, it's normal for us to build up our very own timetables dependent on our character characteristics, way of life decisions, and individual inclinations (and work commitments). Settling on our own choices is essential to being a capable grown-up who pays on reliable choices for themselves.

Using sound judgment for yourself is essential for using sound judgment for other people; like supporting your family or being a decent companion.

Second, and maybe more critically, is that narcissists make it their labor of love to get your day by day calendar to spin around theirs, in both individual and expert lives. Any way they can control what you do whenever they wish is a success for them.

This implies you will feel slanted penance your own needs to address others' issues, instead of structure your life around gathering your individual needs.

I'm not recommending that you ought to be childish before all else, yet that the significant subsequent stage for you is distinguishing what you have to accomplish for yourself to be upbeat and profitable. Ask yourself what fulfills you, not what makes you agreeable from making another person glad.

That implies doing things based around your life and individual decisions, not theirs, by having your very own calendar with your occasions you live by.

Presently, a timetable isn't content. That doesn't mean you need to plan the majority of your time in hour-by-hour squares, however at whatever point you're accomplishing something, realize that for what reason you're doing it, not to sidestep misuse or feel better from the injury if it's a break or a guilty pleasure.

Continuously realize what you're doing and for what reason you're doing it.

Working through It independent from anyone else and With Others

This last one sounds like a cop-out. However, it isn't. You have to comprehend your maltreatment, anyway excruciating, and not flee from it. Ideally, you'd likewise work through it with an expert.

For what reason is this progression last? Since is anything but a stage; it's a continuous procedure you should ingrain through propensity. Recuperating is work in practical sessions, not a fixation on the consequences of your maltreatment without recognizing the abuse itself.

By recognizing it, you can disengage the issues it makes throughout your life. By following them back to the source, you can isolate the maltreatment and resolve it as opposed to being an injured individual to it by enjoying broken behavior.

I'm making such a major ordeal out of this one minor point because most mishandled individuals just castoff and "proceed onward" or "get over it." They do as such at their very own hazard and cost.

You don't merely "proceed onward" from psychological mistreatment, you either recognize and work through it or ingest it and have it seep into every other part of your life. It transforms you for the more awful when you don't stand up to it, once in a while until the end of time.

Okay rather stand up to it now and the majority of the torment it causes you, or stay away from it and pay that obligation over your lifetime with intrigue?

Perceiving the full range and extent of the damage done to you and its impact on your life is the best way to recuperate, from now into the long haul. If you don't, you deceive yourself through broken behavior as well as those nearest to you also.

I'm likewise going to pressure that you see an expert as open yourself to individuals who are reliable and secure in your own life. Both are priceless apparatuses; it's not only either. At the point when the utilized couple, they're shockingly better and serve to complement and enhance one another.

For instance, centering your resentment from the maltreatment by fuming without really going up against the underlying driver would enjoy your abuse and wasting your time because your indignation from being manhandled and nobody ensuring you.

It begins a descending cycle where it proceeds and feeds itself from the blustering and directing sentiments onto the off-base things, instead of an upward cycle where you can recognize the maltreatment and deal with it.

What happens when you don't adapt is that minor things begin to wear on your nerves and trouble you, yet you don't recognize that you're aggravated the majority of the time since you're angry about the maltreatment, besides everything else.

This has to do with you, not them. There are a lot of things the narcissists can and ought to be accused of, yet your response isn't one of them. You pick how you react and respond to their behavior.

Working through it means assuming liability for your empowering them just as not enabling their awful behavior to make you feel like a decent individual. You were deceived and controlled into supporting them to stick around; presently, you can stop.

How to Divorce a Narcissist

Being hitched to a narcissist is by a long shot the most genuinely depleting background you can suffer in your life. Managing the psychological mistreatment expedited by such an individual can make you feel like you're the one with the issue. You most likely feel controlled and controlled nonstop, and it's incomprehensible for you the different the lies from reality since they persuade themselves regarding a fact that does not exist. Have you anytime had a discourse with your narcissistic spouse and toward the finish of the debate, felt like there must be some problem with you since he is so persuaded he is correct? You could state the grass is green. You at that point disclose to yourself he can't be pressing because it's so distant from the truth it must be a joke, to acknowledge the indeed implied what he said.

I was startled with the idea of how to separate from a narcissist spouse; however, it was significantly scarier to consider remaining with this individual. How might you be with somebody so detached with reality sincerely and rationally, somebody who does not think about how you feel or how others around you feel, somebody so egotistical he trusts himself to be superior to other people and somebody so proud he makes you and everyone around you feel like filth. You likely feel embarrassed every time he addresses your loved ones, and not as a result of what he was stating, but since of how he was saying it.

You Must Have A Plan

Give me a chance to caution you at present. If you need to realize how to separate from a narcissist, particularly one with cash, you should be arranged and have a course of action. Never let your better half recognize that you need to get separated or that you're contemplating it. A genuine narcissist accepts he is exempt from the laws that apply to everyone else and feels like the principles don't concern him. He will show you out of the house and accuse you, channel the financial balances, drop the Visas, decline to see the children and tell the court your estranging his kid, endeavor to have you captured and make up every single falsehood he can about you.

Here is somewhat a mystery

Your Narcissistic spouse will accuse every one of his defects on you. In the event that he is a heavy drinker, eats fast nourishment for every meal, doesn't remain solid, dozes in throughout the day, parties throughout the night, pawns the children off at his mothers and whatever else you realize he fouls up, he is going to state you do each one of those things yourself. It makes it difficult to guard yourself, and as opposed to being on offense during the separation you're on protection the entire time attempting to refute every one of his falsehoods. The genuine kicker is because your significant other is a narcissist, he will accept his untruths are valid, which makes him battle like the devil for kid guardianship to shield the youngsters from your conduct, and he will take the necessary steps to guarantee the separation turns out to support him.

The narcissist hates to lose and will never concede rout, and because they are so focused and vainglorious, they will deplete their financial balances in attorney's expenses and flawed morals to get the result they need. Secure yourself and pursue my proposals on the best way to separate from a narcissist without losing your children, your cash, and above all, your mental soundness. You're in for a wild ride, however, trust me, it's superior to staying around because solitary you will get injured over the long haul if you remain.

Chapter Nine
Are Your Children Empaths? Teach Them How To Manage Their Emotional Intelligence

We are out and out brought into the world with the capacity to detect feelings in others. It's is a fundamental survival aptitude for people and creatures. This capacity usually dies down in youth as we figure out how to concentrate more on verbal prompts than enthusiastic ones.

Empaths, then again, have an elevated affectability to other individuals' feelings that continues creating after some time. As different children quit getting enthusiastic signals, Empath children become entirely overpowered by the sheer amount of passionate data that they get in social settings.

Since most guardians don't have the foggiest idea when they are Empaths, they don't perceive the signs in their children. It likewise forestalls them for adequately showing their children how to oversee passionate flood. For a more inside and out dialog on assets for grown-up Empaths, you can peruse my articles on this theme here.

Passionate Intelligence is characterized as "the capacity, limit, or ability to see, evaluate, and deal with the feelings of one's self, of others, and gatherings" (Salovey and Mayer, 1990). When you show your children how to deal with their Empath abilities, you are building up their Emotional Intelligence.

Three key ideas should be tended to oversee passionate data adequately.

1. **Strengthening:** Do you control your Empath aptitudes, or do they control you (revile or favoring?)

2. **Centeredness:** Can you generally hear your interior self most importantly (raise over the disorder)

3. **Stream:** Does passionate data come in AND out openly (do you have an outlet?)

Is your kid an Empath?

Children have an alternate method for taking care of their Empath capacities. Their scope of the accessible reaction is littler, so they usually pick peaceful (as an approach to quiet down the enthusiastic disarray they feel) or carrying on (as an approach to be more intense than the passionate clamor).

Remember that children figure out how to deal with their Empath capacities by watching you handle yours. In case you're an Empath yet don't have the foggiest idea how to deal with it, get help for yourself first!

These are practices I have seen in Empath children who don't have the foggiest idea of how to deal with their capacities:

Gets unusually peaceful (regularly observed as modesty) around groups yet approves of the close family or littler gatherings. Your tyke is attempting to feel enabled and focused by pulling back from the world.

Gets physically or verbally wild around individuals, however, is smooth at home. Your tyke is attempting to discover an outlet to the mind-boggling stream of approaching feelings.

Opposes hitting the hay or awakens regularly. Your youngster is attempting to remain focused while encompassed by the enthusiastic movement of grown-ups.

Gets every illness accessible (cold, influenza, ear diseases, and so forth.). Your youngster is attempting to feel enabled in closing down undesirable enthusiastic action. Being wiped out is regularly the primary way a youngster can use to pull back from social circumstances.

This portrays about 85% of children. I accept that most children do experience the ill effects of a botch of their Empath abilities. I likewise take that increasingly more Empath children are brought into the world every day. So 85% is anything but an astonishing number to me.

The primary concern is: would you be able to enable your kid to have a more joyful life by utilizing Empath instruments? When it helps, at that point, you're progressing nicely!

Empathic Babies, Children, and Teens

Compassion is the thing that makes other individuals matter to us and reminds us to recognize the general population around us as we comprehend and share their sentiments. Sympathy exists in early mother-baby holding. Indeed, even before birth, a child in the belly is delicate to the mother's feelings, regardless of whether positive, unbiased, or negative. When conceived, a child demonstrates receptivity to the two guardians' outrage, pressure, and melancholy, just as their minding, responsiveness, and love. You've most likely seen how they mirror your outward appearances, grinning because of your grin. They likewise may cry when they hear another infant cry. This kind of reaction is a stage in the improvement of sympathy and the capacity to share the sentiments of someone else.

Children assimilate the psychological and passionate vitality of the general population around them. They don't channel anything; they get. As a youngster age, this empathic propensity may increment and gain out of power. A few kids get the feelings, vitality, or contemplations of others to the extent that it winds up overpowering and intrudes on the improvement of their social and enthusiastic life. Since these kids don't have a clue how to define individual limits (or that they have to), they don't understand when they are in someone else's psychological or enthusiastic space, considerably less how obtrusive this can be to that individual. It can likewise bring down the tyke's vibrational level.

An empath is touchy to what is clear just as concealed things, for example, phantoms and the contemplations, feelings, and sicknesses they sense around them. Empaths may get hunches, see mental pictures, hear voices, or have a warning that provisions hidden data about individuals and circumstances. They may likewise get a physical sensation in their body that tells them where someone else is harassed or enduring.

You may have known about Indigo Children or Crystal Kids who have instinctive endowments that shock or even surprise grown-ups. These empathic kids effectively get on the emotions and considerations of adults and others as they unwittingly venture into human and soul vitality fields to accumulate data and comprehend things around them. Seeing with their otherworldly eyes, feeling with their profound faculties, hearing with their abstract ears, they may give data about a previous existence, recount occasions before they occur, see apparitions, or know something about someone else or circumstance that nobody else does. Today, upwards of one out of four kids have this capacity and are fixed on the higher recurrence steadily.

Being an empath is incredibly depleting for a grown-up. A kid who is over-burden with the vitality of others may have on-going diseases, show burdensome scenes, lash out in resentment, cry without reason, or attempt to "fix" things between grown-ups who contend or don't get along well. A tyke or high schooler who sees or hears in the soul domain may carry on because the individual in question feels overpowered and does not realize how to express what the person is encountering. The issue is aggravated when grown-ups won't tune in, attempt to quiet the tyke, or decline to accept the kid's report of mysterious occurrences.

We do our natural youngsters an extraordinary bad form when we refute their encounters and inherent capacities. Now and again, the "quieting" parent additionally has some paranormal endowments in a task that the individual in question isn't open to discussing perhaps they were shushed by their folks and are just impersonating the child-rearing good example they were given. As guardians, instructors, and advocates, we have to show kids how to utilize this empathic blessing appropriately, yet numerous grown-ups don't trust their instinct substantially less perceive their kids' otherworldly capacities. Empathic kids need somebody they can converse with, and they need data on the best way to keep their quality clear, to open and close their natural capacities freely, and set lively limits. However, where do grown-ups go to figure out how to support these empathic kids and adolescents?

The more you read and concentrate on this subject, the better you will most likely answer your youngsters' inquiries and help them deal with their inherent blessings.

Raising Sensitive Children

Do you have a touchy tyke?

You know, a kid who takes all that you or others state to heart; a tyke who has a thin skin and stresses excessively, especially about things out of their control.

Touchy kids stress over what others consider them. They frequently sense risk a long time before others, and they see the results of practices a long time before their friends.

Is this affectability nature or sustain? I speculate the previous is the guilty party. It has been evaluated that 15 percent of kids are brought into the world with a progressively touchy demeanor. That is a disposition that makes them especially mindful of their environment and of any progressions that may happen.

Delicate kids resemble mind-set analysts with their reception apparatuses up, attempting to distinguish modest changes in the dispositions of everyone around them. Somehow or another, this is solid as emotionally intelligent individuals are fixed on the practices and sentiments of others. Touchy kids, for the most part, have high emotional intelligence quotients.

However, regularly delicate kids frequently read a lot into what others state or do.

Once in, guardians will say something without speculation, or a companion will disregard them for an entire day for no other explanation than they were narcissistic. Touchy kids acknowledge these issue. They take the missteps of others and transform them into something they are most certainly not. They see basic bungle and consider it to be an individual slight or something evil. Delicate kids can overthink and read a lot into straightforward circumstances. That is the reason tricky kids can end up on edge, timid, or both. They can be challenging to live with.

When you have a touchy youngster, you have to see and acknowledge both their sides. The side we frequently observe is the timid, restrained, frightful worrier. The flip side is that delicate kids, for the most part, have caring hearts; are compassionate, natural, and more often than not have an innovative streak. These are superb credits to have.

As the world kids occupy at school is similar to a wilderness, fine spirits can leave themselves open to being harmed by their companions.

The ongoing investigation into the territory of youngsters' affectability and uneasiness by Professor Barrett from the

University of Queensland uncovered that 40% of touchy kids experience some genuine tension.

The key to the 60% of kids who DON'T encounter uneasiness are sure 'defensive' factors. The highest priority on this rundown is child-rearing style. Delicate kids profit by having a hopeful, resilient parent who supports them yet doesn't enable them to pay attention to themselves as well. It additionally helps if guardians can urge their youngster to risk socially and praise their social triumphs, regardless of how minor.

The one-two punch for kids of affectability and negative or critical guardians isn't perfect. Kids need a parent who gets over the message that there are some terrible occasions and things, yet we can figure out how to adapt, and the world is commonly an extraordinary spot.

It is excellent if guardians are steady; stunningly better if a parent is resilient, so the delicate tyke perceives how to adapt to a portion of life's damages, dismissals, and dissatisfactions. Indeed, sensitive kids are more reluctant to create uneasiness if, in any event, one parent is of the 'tough,' constructive, even convivial character.

At the point when delicate kids are brought up somewhat with legitimate comprehension and support, they are well-put to grow up to be upbeat, sound, surprisingly balanced, and imaginative grown-ups.

How to Raise Your Children - 3 Great Tips

In this new age, a time of innovation and data you see many guardians looking for ways on the most proficient method to bring up their kids; we see a ton of books and a lot of magazines discussing the subject. We can likewise discover a great deal of this data through the Internet, that is the reason I have the ideal equation for you, on the most proficient method to bring up your kids.

You got the opportunity to be cautious where you get this data from, because there is a decent and terrible data out there, particularly when you go to the Internet searching for answers, you need to utilize your correct judgment and presence of mind.

The primary 80% is on demonstrate to your youngsters that you adore them the most:

There will be a lot of times when you are worn out from consistently regular, or you simply had a stressful day at work and didn't feel like playing with your kids or taking them to the recreation center, here is and counsel, regardless of whether you don't have a craving for saying the amount you cherish them, simply state it, push your self a tad and disclose to them that you adore them the most, here is the reason.

When you practice this strategy, you are not merely strengthening the way that you adore them, and yet you are building their fearlessness, and furthermore, you became acquainted with that the littlest minutes can have the most significant effect on your kid's life.

Second is 15% on showing your kid:

You presumably ask your self 15% isn't sufficient, however your youngsters will adapt better and quicker in the event that you blend educating with fun, by making diversions that will show your kids a few abilities, such as spelling, numbers or math amusements, in the event that you play each day with them like this, they are having a ton of fun and learning in the meantime. Additionally, they will gain from you; if you set a genuine model and invest quality energy with them, by applying these tips, you are putting your kids in the right track of learning.

The keep going 5% is in order:

You have to set guidelines, and let your youngsters know whether they break them there will be outcomes, have your kids rehash them back to you, so you are 100% sure that they comprehend what this standard is.

You most likely consider 5% discipline in this equation isn't sufficient; the genuine is this. Since at this point you are very much limited with your youngsters and have a decent correspondence, it won't take a great deal of order to have them to tune in and comply with your principles, since they are so used to be cheerful more often than not, than when you disclose to them that you are baffled for what they did, and there will be outcomes since they defied your norms, they won't appreciate this terrible inclination and by you not being content with them, due to what they did wasn't right, they will be heartbroken, positively and hear you out next time. Kids are cheerful commonly, yet also, delicate and aren't anything but difficult to remove their joy.

Chapter Ten
7 Roles of Emotional Intelligence and Teamwork

An ever-increasing number of associations understand that hard skills testing, and character evaluations are simply not slicing it as devices to use in choosing new contracts. As associations understand the significance of social skills like the capacity to work together and work with a group, they are currently searching for those "emotional knowledge" characteristics in new hopefuls as well as in existing staff too. Emotional knowledge in group building is a flat out must benefit from any gathering of individuals, and here are seven reasons why.

1. Mindfulness

It is outstandingly hard to comprehend the feelings and inspirations of others if you don't have any acquaintance with yourself first. People with high emotional insight can rapidly recognize their emotions, which is the initial phase in having the option to control or oversee them. Mindfulness is the central structure square of emotional insight.

2. Restraint

Having the option to perceive your feeling is a specific something yet having the opportunity to control those feelings, especially in upsetting conditions is very another, The individual with a created EI comprehends why they sense that they do which offers them a chance to inspect the feeling sanely and control it.

3. Natural motivational tendencies

Inspiration is key to group energy, and each part assumes a job in giving that inspiration. Created EI shows itself as an inspirational frame of mind, steadiness, and a characteristic help for other people. In short, it is irresistible, and others will pursue the lead.

4. Sympathy

The individual with high emotional insight can comprehend the feelings in another and identify with them. They contain individuals of varying backgrounds and the effect that various societies have on primary leadership forms. Understanding these distinctions enables the individual to acknowledge assorted variety and not have it fill in as a hindrance to cooperating viably.

5. Profoundly created social skills

Essential to colleagues is a high feeling of social skills. Having the option to determine clashes in a commonly acceptable manner is critical to the general accomplishment of the group. Very much created social skills can unequivocally add to joint effort and participation, which like this will drive profitability.

6. Social relationship

At the point when a group is made, it will make a situation of social reliance, and that can be something to be thankful for or terrible relying upon how it is overseen. When the group leader clarifies that the gathering will concentrate on group objectives and requires the contribution of all colleagues to be useful, the outcome is a more prominent exertion to team up. If the group is set up as contenders, i.e., "the first to sell 100 gadgets get a significant reward's then you have a group that comprises of people with individual objectives.

7. EI and collaboration

Positive and compelling relationships between colleagues have been exhibited to be a better emotional setting that drive results. Individuals who offer a bond both expertly and by and by will work more diligently to make progress for those for the gathering than a group where those relationships have not been created. Creating emotional insight through activities and preparing can extraordinarily improve the chances of robust group execution.

If you are a group director, you truly set the pace. When you need the most out of your group, work to establish a situation that builds up the relationships, not tears them down through challenge.

Chapter Eleven
Perception and Spirituality

We do recognize an arrangement of philosophical and religious ideas or even way of thinking of life; however, in living reality when particular states of psyche and heart are satisfied, we will, in general, see it.

We wish to understand the incomparable truth through otherworldliness; however, we should interpret our profound thoughts into profound life to achieve change in states of our brain and heart.

We should be resolved to know this incomparable reality and give the necessary conditions slowly for this reason.

Quest for scholarly information, without really getting transform us and interpreting this hypothetical learning into accurate observation and genuine encounter is so significant.

It may be a vain exercise to know quite a bit of this preeminent and individual learning; however, not live it and experience it.

We should contemplate and scatter the certainties of otherworldly life; however, it calls for genuine commitment in the acknowledgment of the reality of the otherworldliness or perfect knowledge.

Sanctuaries, Churches or any religious establishment may offer you the stage to look for awesome certainties, yet it would be good for nothing if we understand the truth and are not in contact with deepest substances of life.

The spread of thoughts concerning the substances and standards of profound life will consequently set up the ground for the slow development of the otherworldly standpoint and the acknowledgment of otherworldly facts. So a well-coordinated and far-reaching exertion ought to be made to delve somewhere down in the more profound realms of experience and support.

Advancement in the life of soul brings about obtaining a dynamically more profound impression of otherworldly truth and their demeanor in the life of the individual, however it is essential to recall that this articulation is put together, as it were, with respect to recognition and witticism on the conscious guideline of one's life as per an unmistakable and inflexible set of principles.

The life of the soul is a characteristic articulation of what we see legitimately or sense naturally and not visually impaired after what others request that we do.

It isn't something where you pursue the sacred writings, regulations, ceremonies, or the books of shrewdness without plainly seeing or naturally detecting otherworldliness.

It has along these lines the nature of freshness, inherent quality, and ease, which quickly pulls in us and quietly influences our life and viewpoint.

A person who faculties instinctively that all life is one will act towards others with genuine sentiments of compassion and delicacy and help them under all conditions usually and efficiently.

Here we talk about compassion as well.

Envision this as a scholarly perfect without compassion, and, best case scenario it will accommodate the external code of conduct which needs warmth and ability to move trust in other individuals.

Consequently, we understand that genuine learning or otherworldliness worried to the preeminent truth - divines knowledge doesn't involve scholarly appreciation however of profound discernment.

This implies these facts never again stay intriguing or notwithstanding motivating thoughts yet substances of direct encounters.

Reality consequently is reflected in its actual structure in the field of our cognizance and not just as a shadow on the screen of our psyche.

The otherworldly experience we consider here is an exceptional encounter; however, the very embodiment for self-acknowledgment is to comprehend its temperament and figure out how to recognize it from pure scholarly cognizance.

When we are to bring this profound internal change of cognizance, we need to logically hone or refine our discerning workforce so we can see further centrality with regards to our psyche without changing the idea of that content.

It is this honing or refining process which did to as far as possible empowers us to see ultimate reality that infests and contains the showed universe yet stay obscure for the absence of recognition.

Since your cerebrum - insight is the workforce or intensity of discernment, the fact of the matter is seen distinctly by bit by bit honing the power of recognition.

It involves moderate development when you become increasingly touchy, and the psyche turns out to be progressively unadulterated.

Creating Extraordinary Results

Never think or state I don't have a clue or I can't!

How would you make exceptional outcomes!

You realize that your world is brought about by your reasoning - that is no mystery! Our contemplations become things! I'm not disclosing to you anything new yet such a large number of regardless we get got up to speed with the considerations of need and constraint.

We live in a bounteous universe where there is no lack of anything. Check out you, and you will see there is sufficient food, water, cash, garments, lodging, love, and satisfaction to go around. For what reason do a few of us have so much and others have pretty much nothing. To change any condition in your life, you should wind up mindful of how you are utilizing your brain.

You may not know how you are reacting to occasions. I don't get my meaning? When you are on edge when considering remaining before a gathering to give an introduction to your assessment of your experience is just your observation. It's not reality. It's what you figure you will feel. It's dread taking a few to get back some composure of your creative mind and envisioning the most exceedingly terrible.

Ask yourself:

What do I see is so hazardous? We're such animals of propensity. Much the same as Pavlov's canine, we rehash designs.

Here is our main thing:

- Make suppositions
- Self-scrutinize
- Stress over being flawless
- Disaster

- Thinking in 'shoulds' and feeling remorseful

- Supposing you are preferable or more terrible over another person

Remarkably, this is the thing that goes on in the human personality, again and again. We incorporate examples that turn with mind maps and our cerebrums pursue that way, rapidly and effectively, ever diverted from our inner truth. These maps strengthen our destructive observation, and the fact ends up slanted. You could rehearse progressively exact reasoning. Hello, there's a thought - correct thinking - not Winterizing!

You are distant from everyone else the one in particular that can administer your psyche. It is up to you which considerations you center around and what the world would resemble for you!

At whatever point you ask yourself an inquiry, you are tweaking your brain to look for the appropriate response. Esther Hicks dependably states, 'Ask you and will Receive.' Your research will center your psyche, and when you change your mindfulness, you will change what you know. When you re-outline the inquiry, your understanding will improve. When you change your sentiments, you doubtlessly will change your activities. This is the intensity of addressing and monitoring your considerations.

So how might you change your reasoning?

Have a go at altering your musings through representation; attestations; acting the part you need to feel; set an expectation for what you need; be completely legitimate with yourself, feed your mind reality and don't fall back for the default position that cuts you down and takes you further from your high.

To make insistences, record what somebody who adores you would state about you or a circumstance. Or on the other hand, if that is too hard even to consider bringing forward, find what you would say to somebody you adore — an accomplice, a youngster, or, best case scenario a companion, kin. Envision them in a similar personality space or circumstance you wind up in. What kind of words would you say? How might you help them imagine a more exceptional picture, a progressively illuminated, bolder vision of themselves?

You can do that for you. You can bring that adoration, and minding and profound inclination to your very own suppositions and reactions about yourself. Record them as insistence. Peruse them and re-read them. Be gigantically kind and card to yourself. What will occur? You'll change, you'll mellow your heart, and you'll pillar that generosity and finding out, and you'll get it back, and it will duplicate. Delightfully and effectively. Presently you suppose how you were intended to think, feel about yourself how you were designed to - adoring and kind.

Chapter Twelve
Learn More About Altruism
and Empathy in Children

Albeit a few children are here and there forceful toward each other, they are additionally positive proof practices in their cooperation's and are even equipped for benevolent conduct. Benevolence is a part of ethical behavior that includes a worry for the welfare of others. The unselfish manner is characterized as a voluntary and deliberate activity that advantages another and isn't propelled by any longing to acquire outside remunerations. Three years old who sees another youngster cry and heads toward offering him a toy to play with is proving unselfish conduct.

Such demonstrations of graciousness toward others require compassion, the capacity to feel someone else's feelings vicariously. They uncover that even though the ability to relate with age, even a few years old children are equipped for separating between such feelings as cheerful, tragic, and frantic. Likewise, the children know about and can react to other individuals' emotions.

The causes of sympathy are vague. Psychoanalysts propose that compassion creates with regards to the mother-baby relationship as the parent passes on her dispositions to the kid be her manner of speaking, outward appearances, and contact. Social learning scholars, on the other hand, the battle that compassion is obtained through molding. The upsetting emotions that went with one's challenging past encounters are evoked by cries of misery from someone else. For instance, a youngster who cuts her finger feels torment and screams. At some other point, when she sees another tyke cut himself, examining blood and the other tyke's cries bring out in her the sentiment of trouble she had encountered at a previous time.

Even though they differ on the starting points of sympathy, specialists note that how children react to other's trouble changes with age. These discoveries rose up out of the research of American researchers who watched children in lab and naturalistic settings to perceive how they responded when their moms hurt her elbow and demonstrate her trouble. They found that the response by babies was passionate excitement, for example, crying or disturbance. Bit by bit, this conduct reduced, and by age two, a portion of the children moved toward the mother, endeavoring to help or reassure her. They carried articles to the mother, they made recommendations about shouldn't something be said about she could do, they verbalized their compassion. Not exclusively did these youthful children endeavor to help their mom when at least one of their endeavors fizzled. This proposes they saw the mother's pain as an issue to be understood. These and different perceptions of genius social practices demonstrate that babies and youthful children are not just assistance looking for animals, they likewise "unreservedly offer their very own consideration, friendship, compassion, help, and assets to other people."

Expectation this valuable data will assist you with understanding the conduct of the charitable child. There are numerous models which will control you. If you presume anything, contact your specialist right away. Look for assistance when it is essential. You are going to require it.

Conclusion

Do you ever feel overpowered by feelings at cafés, motion pictures, parties, or in groups? Does your state of mind ever change when you are around sure individuals? Do you ever feel an abrupt vitality channel when around somebody? Do you ever think the physical side effects of everyone around you? If you can answer yes to any of these inquiries, you might be a clairvoyant empath.

A clairvoyant empath is an individual who is particularly touchy to vitality and its related vibrations. All contemplations and sentiments produce vibrating dynamism, and we all discharge these into the group continually. We as a whole influence all, even in complete disengagement. Most likely, you've known about the butterfly impact, where a butterfly moving its fragile wings in Africa impacts the vitality wherever else. Similar holds valid for our considerations, words, expectations, and deeds. Everything made inactive space or through idea has a vivacious charge that winds up accessible to all. An empath unknowingly decodes others' vitality and acclimatizes it as though it were natural.

Since powerful feelings are the most vigorously charged, a mystic empath frequently grabs and acclimatizes these. This isn't an issue if the empath is one who has a consistent positive frame of mind and a consistently upbeat and cheerful attitude. Such an individual will end up happy around other people who offer that proclivity, and no damage is finished.

Compassion regularly ends up tricky, in any case, for one who has encountered much affliction and battle throughout everyday life. Such an individual will, in general, get exceptionally adversely charged feelings or even physical side effects of people around them. They understand, similar to a magnet, the sentiments of others that mirror their own; and they will every now and again feel over-burden.

Clairvoyant compassion is a blessing, not a revile; however, many would oppose this idea. Vitality healers, restorative intuitive, and otherworldly advisors regularly have this aptitude and use it in their day by day work. These people can frequently discharge the pessimistic energies from themselves and those they serve. At all, sympathy gives the expert a premise from which to coordinate the customer's recuperating procedure.

www.ingramcontent.com/pod-product-compliance
Lightning Source LLC
Chambersburg PA
CBHW061747250726
48657CB00001B/38